Protecting New Jersey's Environment

Protecting New Jersey's Environment

From Cancer Alley to the New Garden State

THOMAS BELTON

RIVERGATE BOOKS

An Imprint of Rutgers University Press

NEW BRUNSWICK, NEW JERSEY, AND LONDON

Library of Congress Cataloging-in-Publication Data

Belton, Thomas J.
    Protecting New Jersey's environment : from cancer alley to the new garden state /
Thomas Belton.
        p. cm.
    Includes bibliographical references and index.
    ISBN 978–0–8135–4887–6 (pbk. : alk. paper)
    1. New Jersey—Environmental conditions.   2. Environmental protection—
New Jersey.   3. Environmental health—New Jersey.   4. Environmental quality—
New Jersey.   5. Environmental policy—New Jersey.   I. Title.
    GE155.N5.B45   2010
    363.7009749—dc22   2010017319

A British Cataloging-in-Publication record for this book is available from the British
Library.

Visit our Web site: http://rutgerspress.rutgers.edu

Manufactured in the United States of America

For my wife, Bernadette Duncan,
who shared my journey and believed in a dreamer

Contents

Figures

Preface and Acknowledgments

New Jersey is a state of national significance both in terms of its industrial, economic, and transportation infrastructure, as well as its rich traditions of agricultural resources, land preservation, and fisheries management. The Garden State is one of the smallest states in America but has the highest population density. It also encompasses a wide range of natural resources extending from its ocean beaches to the high Appalachian ridge. It is this dichotomy that creates unique challenges for environmental managers. This book will show how disparate physical and social sciences have been blended by necessity into one science of the environment, how public policy is married to legislation and litigation, and how headlines and public debates can speak to issues that transcend the region.

I decided to write this book because of what I see missing in the environmental literature—the stories and faces of those thousands of professionals who tirelessly work to protect the environment at the elemental level of daily crisis management. They include emergency responders, scientists, policy analysts, and even neighborhood activists who fight the negative impacts of unregulated sprawl or industrial growth. My hope is that this book will present my career experiences as surrogates for theirs, describing a chosen way of life and at the same time showing what may be at stake for public health and natural resources in America. More important, I hope this book will reveal why the crowded little state of New Jersey became a critical ecological landscape in the growth of environmental protection.

I would like to acknowledge the *New York Times* for generously allowing me to reprint the introduction to this book, which previously appeared in its entirety in that newspaper. I would also like to acknowledge the New Jersey Pinelands Commission's Science Office, which supplied me with many of its photographs; the Patrick Center for Environmental Research at the Academy of Natural Sciences in Philadelphia; and the many professors at Rutgers

University and other New Jersey state and local colleges whose research I have participated in over my career. I would also like to acknowledge all the governors and legislators I have worked for, as well as their environmental commissioners, whose unwavering support for environmental protection has made New Jersey a leader in scientific-based policy and decision making. But the greatest kudos go to the thousands of unsung civil servants that I have worked with over the years, whose unflagging devotion to keeping the state green and its citizenry healthy is testimony to their public service. Finally, I would like to thank Doreen Valentine from Rutgers University Press, whose support helped turn my thoughts into coherent words.

DISCLAIMER

It should be noted that the statements and opinions in this book are those of the author and in no way reflect the official policy of any municipal, state, or federal governments.

Introduction

It was 1971. The United States had just invaded Laos to shut down the Ho Chi Minh Trail, George Harrison had organized a benefit concert for starving Bangladesh—and I had just graduated from St. Peter's College in Jersey City with a degree in classical languages. "Wonderful training for an archbishop or a college don," my dad said sarcastically. But I was destined to be neither. Instead, I took what came my way: work as a telephone lineman for Bell Telephone.

It was my first day on the job, and I walked quickly through the Ironbound section of Newark, cruising over rusted railroad sidings and along the Passaic River, past abandoned factories with busted windows that welcomed pigeons whirligigging in the early morning sunshine. Brown-bag lunch in hand, I was off to pole school, where I would learn to strap gafters on my legs and shimmy up a telephone pole like a demented monkey. From atop my perch, I worked heavy tools for ratcheting cables across backyards, ate my lunch on the fly while dangling like a macaque, and scanned the soiled landscapes of Newark like a hawk.

Years later, when I returned to Newark as an environmentalist, visions from my days as a telephone lineman would come back like a distorted dream, helping me locate abandoned oil tanks and toxic waste piles behind seemingly innocuous buildings. But on that first day on my telephone pole in the Ironbound, I had no clue as to my impending transition from classicist into environmental scientist. That metamorphosis was a long way off, although the seeds for transformation were already germinating.

I first thought about the link between environment and disease when my brother Joe learned that he had leukemia. Joe wondered if he had gotten it from an extreme case of sun poisoning at the Jersey shore. It was not until years later—after Joe's death and my return to college for a second degree in marine biology—that I learned that ultraviolet radiation does not cause leukemia. It can cause deadly melanoma or skin cancer, especially for us fair-skinned Celts who are more inclined to the foggy shores of the misty isles than the steamy cities of hothouse America. Leukemia, though, can come from exposure to common chemicals such as benzene (formerly used in dry cleaning) and ionizing radiation, which was common from atmospheric fallout and atom bomb testing before 1963.

Growing up in Jersey City in the 1950s, Joe and I played with our older brother, Jack, in one wasted moonscape after another: scrap yards where giant magnets lifted junked cars and dropped them into crushers; abandoned factories with walls pitted from chlorine gas; and, of course, the empty lots where we made our ball fields, many impregnated with carcinogens. I still remember a game we called Kong's Island that began at an old railway cut where freight trains rode slowly along a canyon blasted through granitic rock and overgrown with weeds as big as trees. The rail beds were immersed in boggy green water that we waded through before climbing the gray cliffs, our clothes covered with slime, as we pretended to be Army Rangers assaulting Pointe du Hoc at Normandy. There we would wait for some boxcars to roll by so we could jump aboard for a ride to the Hudson River, where the contents of open storm drains, sewers, and mystery pipes with steaming yellow cataracts were being absorbed into the universal solvent of New York Bay.

The river was where my dad, Red, would take us to "recreate" on a hot summer's day. To Red, recreating meant hanging out with his police buddies at the Liberty Yacht Club, a 24/7 saloon on a barge in a dilapidated marina behind Ellis Island, while my brothers and I explored the finger piers that jutted out a half mile into the swirling river current. We'd jump in and pull ourselves along the pilings, avoiding the crabs that nipped at our toes, all the while obeying Dad's admonition: "Don't open your mouths, boys! And definitely don't swallow that black water!"

Black water was everywhere around the Liberty Yacht Club because of the nearby coal-unloading towers—monstrous devices some six stories tall, which clamped on to loaded coal cars, inverted them, and dumped a black avalanche of bitumen into the open lips of waiting barges. For some reason, tasty blue crabs in the harbor liked to converge and feed underneath these towers; so Dad sometimes would borrow a rowboat from one of his nautical buddies and row us toward the thundering dust cloud, where we would scrape crabs off the pilings with ten-foot-long netted poles. Unfortunately, the coal dust was so fine it permeated every crease in our knuckles and eye-folds, until we all looked like raccoon-eyed miners.

To clean up before we went home to Mom, Dad would row us away from the coal piers and into the pulsing current of the Hudson. There he would set the oars down and we would jump in and swim, following the drifting boat to Bedloes Island and the Statue of Liberty. We would tie up our crab-filled boat and crawl ashore like drowned rats, our bare backs still striped with soot, as Dad led us up to the snack bar in the statue's base, past all the fine tourists in their holiday clothes, playfully tipping an imaginary hat as he said "Halloo!" and "Good day!"

Once at the counter, Dad would slap down a fistful of money to buy us all lemonades and hot dogs, then lean back and admire the view from beneath the protective shadow of Lady Liberty's gown. I remember one day, looking up at big Red, the space between his smiling teeth still black with soot, and him saying: "It doesn't get any better'n this, now does it, Tom?"

It was only much later that I thought about the dirty water—perhaps the day Dad lay dying of lymphoma and asked as I sat beside his bed: "Why is this happening? I'm still a young man." I could not answer that question, but I had this crazy idea that if the doctors would cut him open, they would probably find some of that Hudson River coal dust floating around inside. Now, after years as an environmentalist—helping to close pesticide factories in the Ironbound and shut down coal piers to make way for Liberty State Park—I think about Joe and Dad and their unanswered questions.

I have come to realize that living in a city presents many risks and that it may not be a single person or thing that kills you, but the weight of a hundred coincidences. And as I move about New York Harbor in my work boat, netting fish for analysis, taking water samples, or scouting out mystery pipes and midnight dumpers, I am sometimes seized by the vivid memory of that warm summer night in 1962. It comes unbidden, often spurred by some random reminder, like the scent of sweet honeysuckle across open water. I see my dad's face once again, smiling as he rows my brothers and me home from Liberty Island in the darkening twilight. And when that happens, I look up at the gibbous moon peeking out from behind the New York skyline, shout "Halloo!," and tip an imaginary hat to its lunar grin.

It has been more than twenty-five years since I bid farewell to my father and brother, and I now have a lifetime of experience under my wings. Not surprisingly, I have met people with similar career-initiating stories as mine, although often attuned to other issues. For environmentalism has many faces and varying features based on where you live or what is relevant to your personal landscape. If you are from the Jersey shore, it might be oil spills on the beaches or dune loss from sea level rise. If you live high in the Kittatinny Mountains, it

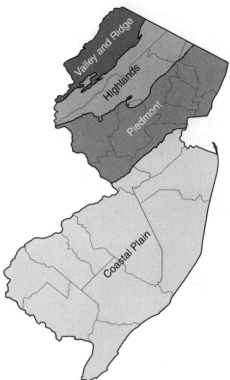

Figure 1. New Jersey's four
physiographic provinces.
(Source: New Jersey
Geological Survey.)

County boundaries for reference only.

might be algae-choked lakes, deforestation, or mercury-contaminated fish that
gets your attention. Nevertheless, wherever you live, I have learned that
environmentalism is best understood through the lens of case histories and
transpiring events rather than dry newspaper accounts or essays on legislation
and political infighting.

These stories can be framed in a unique way by separating New Jersey environmentally along geologic and ecological dimensions. For example, looking at
a topographic map, which depicts the landscape in relief (elevations to show
hills and valleys); we can see four large geological provinces. Moving from
north to south, these include the rugged Valley and Ridge (V&R) geophysical
province in the upper northwestern corner; the water-rich Highlands province
stretching just below the V&R as an oblique band across the northern counties;
then the Piedmont, or rolling foothills, below that. In the southern half of the
state is the Coastal Plain, including the fire-blasted forests and acidic waters of
the Pinelands Preserve.

Environmentalism also embraces a number of unifying themes, including science, public policy, enforcement, community action, and justice/equity issues—all of which affect people and events. In the following chapters, I will blend these themes with issues keyed to geophysical provinces and with portraits of environmentalists. These professionals have effected change and protection of the public good, often in the face of opposition by disparate corporate and political forces. In their portraits, I hope to convey the struggle for scientific solutions in the public arena of environmental protection.

CHAPTER 1

The War on Cancer

Cancer the disease, like *Cancer irroratus*, the rock crab, seems to scuttle sideways whenever our biomedical or environmental research closes in on a proximal understanding of its causes. For with a crustacean's sense of armored evasion, the biochemical secrets of human cancer slip silently deeper into the burrow of its nucleus whenever observed, eluding our understanding of what turns on and off the genetic machinery of carcinogenesis. Similarly, the role that toxic chemicals play in causing cancer, especially in our food, water, and air supplies, was poorly understood until recently. Until the early 1950s, reports of cancer linked to environmental causes were mostly anecdotal and primarily driven by extrapolations from industrial hygienists studying factory workers. Yet by the late 1960s, medical professionals in the U.S. Department of Health, Education, and Welfare saw a potential epidemic on the horizon for increased cancer mortality, so they raised the alarm in Washington, D.C.

President Richard Nixon responded to this call to arms in his 1971 State of the Union Address by declaring "War on Cancer!" He said: "The time has come in America when the same kind of concerted effort that split the atom and took man to the moon should be turned toward conquering this dread disease."[1] Subsequently, he signed into law the National Cancer Act, which allocated millions of dollars to the National Cancer Institute (NCI) and the National Institute of Environmental Health Sciences (NIEHS). This money expanded their missions to investigate the role of cancer-causing agents in the environment as well as the interactions between chemical contaminants and genetics in the development of cancer.

Thus, as I walked out of college in 1971, great social upheavals were fermenting all around me—the war on cancer, the Vietnam antiwar movement, and the birth of the environmental regulatory establishment with the creation of the U.S. Environmental Protection Agency (USEPA). Coincidently, the New Jersey Department of Environmental Protection (NJDEP) was created that year. To some extent, I sensed these changes as I helped my brother cope with his cancer treatments and drove my truck around Jersey City installing telephones. For if you live in a factory town, you develop a second sense about pollution and how it affects the people that live under its pall.

For example, my dad once asked me to help him on a moonlighting job. Red was always on the lookout for these after-work opportunities, since the salary of a city detective was barely enough to keep a family of seven afloat. Dad and his buddies came up with a perfect scheme to make some extra cash that was right out of a Joseph Wambaugh novel like *The Choirboys*, but without all the boozing and mayhem. Six off-duty cops moonlighted for a taxicab company in the South Bronx, collecting beat-up cabs to drive across the Hudson River to Newark, New Jersey. There the old taxis boarded a train to Chicago under the spiderweb girders of the Pulaski Skyway. In Chicago, the battered vehicles got new carburetors or motors, had the dents beaten out and a glossy coat of paint applied, then were passed off to some midwestern town, just as an old nag would be set to pasture in a less stressful environment.

One night someone could not make it, so Dad asked me if I would like to make a few extra bucks. It was around midnight when we got to the Bronx, my dad's friends ragging me all the way over on my driving abilities, telling me to run lights and ignore the stop signs. Of course I would get a moving violation if pulled over by the New York City cops, especially in a car so conspicuous as my dad's 1957 canary yellow Chevy. Once we arrived, though, it was all business. Each man selected a cab and drove like a screaming banshee back to Jersey with me in hot pursuit. My job was to follow this ramshackle convoy in case one of the cabs broke down on Route 1.

I remember marveling as we delivered those dilapidated pieces of automotive junk to the railyard at how they could be resurrected—that something as barely functional as a beat-up New York City taxicab could find new life in Sioux City, Iowa, or Medicine Bow, Wyoming, and that broken machines could be reused. Yet it was that late night ride along Route 1 in Jersey City that was so startling. For without the distractions of daytime traffic, I observed the crumpled warehouses and the hulking factories that flowed past my green dashboard lights. They stood out like apocalyptic ruins beneath the red neon lights of Newark Airport, which illuminated the darkness like a great bloodstain. It awoke in me a sense of environmental dread.

Cancer Alley

Coastal Route 1 was the first interstate highway in the United States, extending from Maine to Florida, and it predated the New Jersey Turnpike, which was built after World War II. In New Jersey, Route 1 runs in a straight line from Philadelphia to New York City, a bloated industrial snake filled with pharmaceutical companies, car manufacturers, pesticide formulators, and the largest concentration of landfills, hazardous waste sites, and people in the United States. This segment of New Jersey roadway was infamously labeled "Cancer Alley" in 1973 by journalists after the National Cancer Institute released a map showing high incidences of cancer clustered along its length.[2]

This map was called a "cancer atlas," which portrayed organ-specific death rates from cancer (i.e., brain, lung, leukemia) on both a state and a county basis. The limited goal of the atlas was to demonstrate that geographical patterns might be useful in developing and testing causative hypotheses on cancer mortality (e.g., identifying occupational and/or environmental factors). The cancer atlas depicted cancer mortalities as clusters of red dots on a map of the United States. NCI hoped that analysis of the environment would link patterns of mortality with suspected localized risk factors such as occupations, ethnic enclaves, and predispositions. A subsequent statistical evaluation of the data underlying the atlas revealed striking differences in the geographic patterns of cancer mortality. This included a cluster of specific cancers in the northeastern United States, especially in New Jersey.[3]

For example, lung cancer rates were highest in the northern New Jersey counties around New York City for both males and females. However, high colon and rectal cancer rates in this same area were limited to males. This suggested an occupational determinant, because few women worked outside of the home in the 1950 and 1960s. In contrast, Salem County, in the southern part of New Jersey, had the highest bladder cancer rate (for males) in both the state and nationally. This was considered significant by the researchers because at that time almost one-fourth of the workforce in Salem County was employed in the chemical industry.

Unfortunately, this analysis allowed only a cursory view of cancer mortalities and possible environmental or lifestyle factors. The data were too coarse to develop any detailed statistical relationships without further investigation. It was only in follow-up studies funded by state health and environmental departments that the details started to emerge. For example, Michael Greenberg of Rutgers University, using more state-specific data, showed higher incidences for childhood leukemia, young adult Hodgkin's disease, and lymphoma on a Philadelphia-to-New York City transect (the Route 1 corridor). However, he declined to refer to it as cancer alley.[4] He subsequently debunked the use of this pejorative term in a fascinating paper that pointed out the dangers of using cancer atlases without careful follow-up. He argued that you need more detailed epidemiological and statistical evaluations to come to any definitive conclusions about clusters and causes.[5] He cautioned that to infer the cause and distribution of cancers using only a map was akin to "cartohypnosis," a discredited method that assumes that a trim, precise, and clean-cut map in itself guarantees scientific authenticity. Greenberg felt that the more appropriate use of a cancer atlas was as a screening device to formulate more detailed epidemiological and environmental hypotheses for investigation. The National Cancer Institute subsequently agreed with him, cautioning against purely graphical analyses without taking into consideration confounding lifestyle variables such as smoking and diet, workplace exposures, and the mobility of populations.[6]

Yet the panic after the release of the NCI cancer atlas and the depiction of New Jersey as cancer alley had political repercussions, which empowered New Jersey's Governor Brendan Byrne in 1976 to establish a Cabinet Committee on Cancer Control.[7] This committee was tasked with the prevention, study, and control of cancer. In support of this committee, the New Jersey Department of Environmental Protection was specifically directed to develop a program to determine the presence of carcinogens in the environment by analyzing air, water, and waste materials. It was also ordered to inventory the production and transport of toxic substances, to monitor the environmental conditions at areas determined to have either known (or the potential for) high cancer incidences. And finally it was directed to establish standards to control emissions of carcinogenic substances into the environment. The Program on Environmental Cancer and Toxic Substances (PECTS) was created to coordinate these activities. PECTS evolved into many names over the years under numerous governors and NJDEP commissioners, including the Office of Cancer and Toxic Substances Research (when I was first employed as a research scientist), the Office of Science and Research, and lastly the Division of Science Research and Technology (now known simply as Science and Research).

It was during the time that Nixon declared war on cancer and New Jersey started to seek environmental causes that my brother Joe was diagnosed and started to lose his battle with the disease. I watched helplessly as he slowly succumbed to leukemia under the debilitating effects of experimental chemotherapy that daily sapped his strength. After he died I decided to change careers and pursue a path in medicine with the jejune notion that I might be able to cure cancer. I returned to college and took pre-med courses at the University of Pennsylvania, volunteered at the Children's Hospital of Philadelphia, and worked as a nursing assistant for the Veterans Administration. My desire to go into medicine was fueled both by my impotence at understanding why Joe had died so young and why cancer struck so disproportionately in my hometown. Everyone I knew in Jersey City seemed to have someone near to him or her dying of cancer, and to my limited experience at the time, this pointed toward some environmental agent at work.

My quest led me to unanticipated places. Having a few holes in my academic schedule, I took a limnology course at the Philadelphia Academy of Natural Sciences and ichthyology at the American Museum of Natural History in New York City. In the back rooms of these museums my passion to become a physician was sidelined by my growing interest in marine biology and ecology. From these disciplines, I learned that the environment around us holds both pitfalls and promises of largesse. I realized that the city was a habitat, New Jersey my biome, and both were filled with animals and people, as well as materials that flowed around me in an ever-deepening soup of air and waterborne molecules. I saw much more was at stake in the connections between the health of the environment and my own health. It was not only about curing cancer, it was about preventing it in the first place. Our relationship to the environment was key. Thus, after a few more years of graduate school and scientific retraining, I started work in the Program on Environmental Cancer and Toxic Substances (Science and Research) in NJDEP, where my intellectual curiosity was set free to wage my own personal war on cancer, not one person at a time, but through the air sheds and watersheds potentially affecting us all.

Science and Research, with all the hubris and attitude of the X-Men, was given the deceptively simple task of discovering the link between cancer and the environment, rooting it out like a bad tooth, and then coming up with a cheap cure. I was one of the scientists chosen to join this environmental SWAT team. We were young, feisty, and full of ourselves. I was the marine biologist of the group, which also included an analytical chemist, a botanist, an epidemiologist, a microbiologist, and a fisheries biologist. Not one of us had been trained as an environmental scientist in college because such an academic major did not yet exist. We simply improvised and made it up as we went along.

Science and Research matured in its mission in the 1980s, when state environmental agencies took on a stronger scientific and management role. Under the Reagan administration, the federal budget was severely reduced, and deregulation caused the USEPA to demonstratively reduce its role in the oversight of natural resources and pollution control. Under Governor Thomas Kean's leadership, however (a Republican but pro-environment policymaker), New Jersey developed a "polluter pays" philosophy (where the polluting party pays for the damage done to the natural environment) and a strict "command and control," enforcement-driven management approach to environmental protection (using detailed regulations to prevent environmental problems by specifying how a company will manage its facilities).[8] This resulted in some of the most powerful environmental laws and statutes in the country, which were subsequently mimicked by other states and eventually by the USEPA and other federal agencies. These innovative laws include the Spill Compensation and Control Act, the Major Hazardous Waste Facilities Siting Act, the Worker and Community Right to Know Law, the Environmental Cleanup and Responsibility Act, and the Toxic Catastrophe Prevention Act.[9]

One of the first tasks that Science and Research undertook to support its mission was to develop strong relationships with state universities as a means to evaluate more region-specific cancer mortality and incidence rates than those delivered in the federal cancer atlas. Judith Louis from Science and Research worked with Michael Greenberg of Rutgers to analyze more localized cancer registry data developed by the New Jersey Department of Health. They calculated geostatistical spatial distributions of cancer mortality in New Jersey and the factors associated with any increased risk of cancer mortality in the New York City–New Jersey–Philadelphia metropolitan region. The study confirmed that this region did indeed have excessively high childhood leukemia, young adult Hodgkin's disease, and lymphoma cancer mortality rates compared with the United States as a whole.[10]

For me this finding was chilling, since the study period overlapped exactly the timeline of my brother Joe's birth and diagnosis with leukemia. My initial response to this finding was a sense of "I knew it!" It seemed that our family was not alone in its battle with cancer in those years but only one among thousands clustered in the industrial states across America. Yet the years of my training as a scientist warned me not to jump to conclusions based on mere statistical associations.

The NCI defines cancer as "the uncontrolled growth and spread of abnormal cells anywhere in the body" and cautions that cancer is not just one disease but also a catchall term for more than one hundred different but related diseases. The process by which a normal cell transforms into a cancer cell is called carcinogenesis, which involves a series of changes within the cell that usually occurs over many years. There are thousands of carcinogens, however, that can cause cancer. A carcinogen can be a chemical, a virus, hormones, or ionizing radiation. Carcinogens produce cancer by changing the information that a body's cell receives from its DNA, disrupting its ability to differentiate into a normal functional cell. Most carcinogens have been identified through laboratory exposure studies to animals (e.g., rats, mice, monkeys), but others are known through human exposures over time. These include cancer in cigarette smokers and leukemia in people breathing benzene in the workplace (e.g., dry cleaners used benzene in the past). In addition, ten years or more can go by between the exposure to a carcinogen and a medical diagnosis of cancer. This makes it difficult to pinpoint any possible environmental cause of that specific cancer.

Therefore, the cancer atlas was only the first salvo in the war on cancer. Other more detailed studies were needed that would combine precise data collection and research into the availability of carcinogens in the environment with documented impacts on humans. Only then could we test correlations between carcinogen sources and human populations. That was the original mission of Science and Research when it was formed: to track down the causative agents of cancer in the environment and to develop (through the New Jersey Cancer Registry) significant correlations. We were aided in this endeavor by information supplied by the U.S. National Institute of Environmental Health Sciences and its National Toxicology Program (NTP). The NTP is tasked with coordinating toxicology studies among federal agencies and for identifying substances that might cause cancer. NTP publishes a biannual "Report on Carcinogens" to Congress, which identifies the most current information on substances that cause, or are suspected of causing, cancer. The most current report lists 246 substances with supportable scientific evidence for carcinogenicity.[11] These include ultraviolet radiation (e.g., sun and tanning beds), viruses (e.g., human papilliomavirus), ionizing radiation (e.g., radon), pesticides (e.g., DDT), solvents (e.g., paint, dry cleaning), benzene (e.g., gasoline and tobacco smoke), fibers (e.g., asbestos, exposure to which accounts for the largest percentage of occupational cancers), dioxins (e.g., paper manufacturing and smelting), polycyclic aromatic hydrocarbons (e.g., burning fossil fuels), and heavy metals (e.g., arsenic, beryllium, cadmium, chromium, lead, and nickel).

Yet these NTP results were based primarily on lab studies. In the 1970s and early 1980s there was little data on the ambient (outside) concentrations of toxic chemicals in the air, waters, or soils of the state. Nor was there a good understanding of what kinds and amounts of toxic chemicals were used or disposed of by industry. To that end, Science and Research devised a three-part research strategy that included epidemiological investigations, sampling of ambient air and water for known toxicants, and the development of a survey to poll industries on the types of chemicals they released into the environment. No one had studied this issue so broadly and comprehensively before. The epidemiological evidence was summarized by Michael Greenberg using extant health department vital statistics to establish cancer trends at the state level. The sampling effort was more time-consuming and place-based as we initiated ambient monitoring for toxic chemicals in the rivers, groundwaters, and air of the state, especially surrounding industrial corridors. This dataset resulted in a 1981 report coauthored by Thomas Burke, the director of Science and Research, and Greenberg.[12] Their analysis estimated population exposures to toxic substances based on groundwater results, which confirmed the presence of known carcinogens in more than 95 percent of the wells tested. These concentrations were relatively low, yet no one knew at that time what ambient levels might trigger organ-specific cancers. The analytical results fell into three broad categories: pesticides, light chlorinated hydrocarbons, and heavy metals. Gross pesticide contamination in groundwater tended to occur in agricultural and forest areas, whereas light chlorinated hydrocarbon pollution was in urban areas. Toxic substances in the air also showed low levels of contamination, with ubiquitous organic chemicals in urban areas, two groups of specialized organic chemicals near industrial sites, and high lead levels near major highways.

The third initiative was called the Industrial Survey and was managed by Edward Stevenson, a tough-skinned, former enforcement inspector for NJDEP who had walked most of the major industrial sites in New Jersey and knew pretty much where all the illegal discharges were located or the drums buried. The primary goals of the survey were to poll industries and develop inventories of what chemicals were in common usage. An important secondary goal was to document uncontrolled and unregulated releases of toxic pollution related to industrial activity. The survey, in collaboration with the Department of Labor and Industry, developed a questionnaire to poll fifteen thousand factories on what kinds of chemicals they used and what wastes were emitted. When the industrial survey report was delivered to the state legislature in 1986, it was a groundbreaking environmental policy document because for the first time we understood the types and quantities of toxic substances used by manufacturing industries, and we now had a sense as well of the fate and transport of those substances if released into the environment.[13]

The Industrial Survey supplied justification for lawmakers to draft critical legislation for monitoring these chemicals and to inform the public about what toxic materials were used in their neighborhoods. These included the New Jersey Safe Drinking Water Act, Community Right to Know Act, and the New Jersey Worker and Community Right to Know Act. The Worker and Community Right to Know Act was used as a model by the U.S. Congress in its formulation of USEPA's Toxics Reduction Inventory (TRI) to keep track of emissions from industrial facilities and to safeguard surrounding communities. So by acting locally New Jersey facilitated many federal environmental programs that are still in existence today. Recognizing the importance of defensible science in the formulation of public policy, Governor Thomas Kean signed an executive order in 1986 establishing the Office of Environmental Health Assessment (OEHA) within Science and Research. It was tasked with developing quantitative "risk assessment" methodologies for developing environmental health standards in New Jersey, which soon became the primary method for quantifying actionable levels for environmental enforcement in the country.

All of these executive and legislative policy actions in New Jersey were the result of research carried out by executive mandate yet unencumbered by overbearing political interference. The fact that Science and Research was outside the divisions within NJDEP that issue waste permits allowed us impartiality. Our singular mission was to develop technically defensible science in support of the operating divisions within NJDEP. This removal allowed us stay clear of the adversarial and litigious aspects of environmental regulation. Yet the outcomes of these studies were not ivory-tower ramblings read only in esoteric journals; this was pragmatic and applied research meant to answer specific regulatory questions and supply tools for management. The creation of the Science and Research program at NJDEP showed that with enough scientific independence, a research group could rise above political criticism, making it more difficult to tag a departmental decision as a bureaucratic or partisan maneuver.

However, because of Science and Research's analytical studies of air, soils, and water; the Industrial Survey's findings; and in response to "command and control" laws passed by the legislature, the New Jersey public became more aware of the environmental threats around them. They began to make informed and independent associations between what they saw as "cancer clusters" in their neighborhoods, especially childhood cancers, and the proximity of factories, landfills, and abandoned hazardous waste sites. After the release of the first NCI cancer atlas, the requests for cancer-cluster investigations became more common across the country, but not as much as they did in New Jersey, where NJDEP aggressively sought out orphaned hazardous waste sites and poorly operating factories, identifying the culprits of pollution and environmental destruction.

Cancer Clusters

My father, like most cops, had a quirky sense of humor. Once when I came home with a petite girlfriend in high school, he looked up and asked, deadpan: "Did you ever think about suing the city for building the sidewalk so close to your ass, honey?" Moreover, he was an equal opportunity comic. My sister's boyfriends got the Red Belton routine as well. He once went out to a car parked in front of our house in his boxer shorts, knocked on the steamy driver's side window, and asked my sister Pat's boyfriend for his driver's license and if he had ever been arrested.

Yet what came with this sense of humor was the common touch of the street cop, the ability to talk to all kinds of people in stressful situations and to bring calm to the moment so that he could then ask questions and determine what had transpired at a crime scene. I later realized that my own outlook in life, and in communications as a public official, came inherently from listening to my dad, although I was never one for wisecracks like Red's. For in environmental monitoring and risk communication, we professionals may be only one step removed from the cop at a crime scene. We are both forensic experts looking for clues and both charged with relaying to the public the news of risks and dangers. In many instances it's anything goes—not just reporters, but average people stepping up to a microphone at a public meeting, TV cameras recording your response as citizens ask deeply hurtful questions about why they had been forsaken, lumping us in with the industrial miscreants who had caused the environmental damage in the first place—in short, attacking the messenger for the message!

Yet to be good at communicating environmental risk it is necessary to meet the bitterness and the invective with silent approbation, a knowing acceptance of the outrage, letting the endangered individuals vent as we nod affirmatively and listen. Then at an appropriate moment, we tell the department's story about what has happened, what we are planning to do about it, and, most important, what they need to do. And in most of these situations, it's my father's voice whispering in my ear: "Keep it simple, Tom!" Therefore, I keep my responses measured and to the point, try to find that common touch without condescension, respecting the intelligence of my listeners in a stressful situation.

There were many people good at this in NJDEP but an equal number who were terrible. The latter group could turn a concerned crowd of soccer moms into a screaming mob by their inattention to outrage. And I found that one of the worst scenarios for dealing with distraught citizens was public meetings related to cancer-cluster investigations. In most instances these were held in local school auditoriums, and the fear and impotence bubbling just below the surface was like a volcano about to explode. Having gone through this fear myself with my brother's diagnosis of leukemia, I could relate to their hysteria. Yet as a scientist, I had to remain somewhat aloof and not raise false hopes or unattainable expectations. The person that I found best at dealing with these types of crowd situations was Thomas Burke.

Burke was the director of Science and Research in the early 1980s when I first joined NJDEP. As an epidemiologist Burke succeeded in bringing toxicology, public health, and environmental characterization tools together at a time when environmental risk assessment was in its infancy. His career epitomizes the phases that environmentalists go through in developing on-the-ground experiences that help inform public policy. Burke is currently a professor at the Johns Hopkins Bloomberg School of Public Health, Department of Health

Figure 2. Thomas Burke (*left*) and myself, Thomas Belton (*right*), at a public meeting in New Jersey. (Source: Thomas Belton.)

Policy and Management, with joint appointments in the Department of Environmental Health Sciences and the School of Medicine Department of Oncology. He is also the director of the Johns Hopkins Risk Sciences and Public Policy Institute. He chairs the National Academy of Sciences Committee on Improving Risk Analysis, and in 2006 he was named a Fellow of the Society for Risk Analysis.

Yet I knew Tom Burke from much earlier in my life, on Randolph Avenue in Jersey City where his family lived around the corner from mine. The Burkes and the Beltons both went to Saint Patrick's grammar school. We all saved our pennies for Cokes at Brummers ice cream parlor with the red leather seats, the smoky grey mirrors, and the killer jukebox that played Motown and rock and roll. We all ate at the same delicatessens, danced at the same dances, and walked past the same factories that burned coal and spit out toxic fumes.

Tom and I lived on the Junction, a civic square where five streets intersected, including Communipaw Avenue, which was built on the remains of an old Lenni Lenape trail that crossed another Indian trail that led north to south along the ridge of the Palisades escarpment. The Junction's five corners were a noisy sprawl of stores, saloons, bakeries, and ice cream parlors. Tom's uncle owned Burke's Corner Saloon, right across from a Veterans of Foreign Wars clubhouse. The old rusted cannon on the lawn of the VFW Hall pointed right into the window of Burke's, where my dad used to sit me with a Coke and a free sandwich as he and his friends kibitzed. From my vantage point on the high bar stool I could see news kiosks, shoe shine stands, and barber shops. There was even a hand laundry where old Irish washerwomen gossiped night and day, and variety stores filled with clothes, toys, and school supplies.

I lived in the Arlington Gardens housing project, set aside for World War II veterans. In my house there were two veterans. My dad had been a staff sergeant in the Army Air Corps and ran a motor pool while my mother, Ethel Dewees, enlisted and worked as an airplane mechanic in the WACs. Arlington Gardens comprised more than ninety apartments with close to four hundred kids running around through clusters of moms hanging wash, girls skipping rope, boys playing box ball, or just kids chasing kids for the fun of it. The project loomed on a hill overlooking the downtown neighborhood of Lafayette, where my father grew up. He considered moving up the hill from the mosquito-infested wetlands upward mobility because from our window in Arlington Gardens we could see New York Harbor and the Statue of Liberty.

Tom Burke was in my brother Joe's class at Saint Patrick's grammar school, a tall lanky kid, easy to laugh or make a joke. He grew up to be a tall, easygoing scientist. Tom and I followed a parallel path for years, though we did not know it at the time. He followed me at Saint Peter's Preparatory School for boys, a Jesuit high school, and later Saint Peter's College, but we majored in different subjects. I studied Latin and Greek poetry while Tom studied biology and eventually went to the University of Texas at Austin. There he received a master's degree in public health. Meanwhile, I got out of college with an unmarketable degree in classics and worked as a telephone installer, a primary school teacher, and a social worker before finally returning to college in Philadelphia, where my girlfriend and soon-to-be-wife, Bernadette Duncan, was studying law at the University of Pennsylvania.

In 1978, Tom called me in Philadelphia when he decided to take a leave of absence from NJDEP, where he was working, and pursue his PhD in epidemiology at the University of Pennsylvania. He needed an apartment while attending the school and wondered if we knew of a place. Fortunately, an apartment was vacant right downstairs in our West Philadelphia row house, so he moved right in. Shortly thereafter I finished my master's degree in biological oceanography, and Tom informed me that Science and Research was looking to hire a marine biologist. I traveled up to Trenton and met Robert Tucker, who interviewed me for the position and surprisingly hired me. I had beaten the marine biologist's curse, because it was said anecdotally that only one in four marine biologists could find work in that profession, the rest either driving cabs or working as techs in biomedical labs.

Tom subsequently finished his studies at Penn and returned to Science and Research as Dr. Burke, its new director. This made life much more interesting for me, as I now had a fellow compatriot from Jersey City to hang around with, someone who could talk as fast as I could and make good-natured wisecracks that rolled effortlessly off the tongue. But more important, as factory town kids, we had both grown up in the valley of the drums, where lax environmental protection left a more personal taint. Tom Burke and I were now in a position to do something about that. Using the epidemiological methodologies he learned at Penn, Tom found new ways to measure the impacts of industrial practices on public health. One of the first projects he investigated was a cancer cluster.

The National Cancer Institute defines a cancer cluster as the occurrence of a greater than expected number of cancer cases within a group of people, a geographic area, or a period of time.[14] One of the best-known cancer clusters proven to be related to a specific environmental factor was mesothelioma, a rare cancer of the lining of the chest and abdomen, which researchers traced to industrial asbestos exposure. NCI also points out that a cancer cluster is more likely to be a true cluster (rather than a coincidence) if it satisfies one of the following situations: there are a large number of cases of one type of cancer rather than several different types; it is a rare type of cancer; or there is an increased number of cases of a certain type of cancer in an age group that is not usually affected by that type of cancer. However, in many instances a variety of cofactors can create the appearance of a cancer cluster where nothing unusual is occurring, so that most reports of suspected cancer clusters are not shown to be true clusters. In some cases reported clusters do not include enough cases for epidemiologists to arrive at any conclusions, or sometimes there is a statistical shortcoming (e.g., when a greater than expected number of cancer cases cannot be demonstrated), or in some instances a true excess of cases exists, but health officials cannot find an explanation for it.

Cancer-cluster investigations were a totally new beast to public health and environmental investigators in the late 1970s and early 1980s. But they became more commonplace with each newspaper article or television exposé on a hazardous waste site found beneath a building or toxic exposures found in the neighborhood school. In contrast to industrial hygiene investigations, which are confined to the workplace and exposure-populations of young adults and middle-age workers, cancer clusters usually encompassed neighborhoods with playgrounds and backyards, and factories both near and far whose emissions might be a causative agent in the investigation. The entire community may be at risk but especially the young children, whose sensitive developmental age makes them much more susceptible to toxic and carcinogenic exposures.

For example, there are a large number of potential contaminants in ambient air and water, many coming from diverse sources such as nearby factory pipes, automobile emissions, lawn pesticides, sewer emanations, and even paint and household goods stored in garages and basements. Many of these chemicals are released at low concentrations (e.g., parts per trillion per liter of air), at chronic exposures (i.e., steady, day and night concentrations as opposed to an eight-hour workday exposure), or reciprocally in pulses punctuated by dispersion and random exposures (e.g., related to weather events like wind and rain washout). This makes cancer-cluster assessments difficult to perform, especially in the 1970s and 1980s when regulators lacked basic toxicology and environmental fate information on many of these ambient contaminants.

The Rutherford, New Jersey, Cancer-Cluster Investigation

One of Burke's first studies as an epidemiologist for Science and Research was to develop a new paradigm for environmental investigations and methods to evaluate cancer clusters. In March 1978, the New Jersey Department of Health apprised local school and health officials in Rutherford of an apparent cluster of childhood cancers at the Pierrepont Elementary School. Rutherford sits on a bucolic ridge above the Hackensack Meadowlands with a wonderful view of the New York City skyscrapers in the distance. It is a town of approximately twenty thousand people and about five miles west of Jersey City. My cousin Anne had moved to Rutherford a short time before the announcement of the cancer cluster, ironically, to get out of the city and away from the crime and pollution. Her children attended the Pierrepont Elementary School where leukemia, the same disease that claimed my brother, was rampant.

Seven-, eight-, and nine-year-olds were diagnosed with childhood leukemia and Hodgkin's disease cancer, both known to have conclusive environmental links with two potent carcinogens, benzene and ionizing radiation. Shortly after the Department of Health confirmed the cancer cluster, Tom Burke was asked to manage a two-phase investigation into the environmental conditions unique to the municipality.[15] In the first phase, a profile of potential carcinogen sources was developed (industries, contaminated air and water) that might explain the cluster. In the second phase, monitoring was performed on the surrounding air, water, and soils, as well as measurements of ionizing and non-ionizing radiation. Radiation was a concern because east of Rutherford and not far from the school there was an enormous complex of radio and television transmitter towers. Burke knew from toxicology studies that radiation had produced an increase in the incidence of leukemia in mice; therefore, NJDEP conducted a monitoring program of radio frequency and microwave levels in Rutherford.

Environmental monitoring found no elevated levels of ionizing radiation or any benzene in drinking water. However, benzene was detected in air samples and soils but at low concentrations. This was not unexpected, since it was used in a lot of industries surrounding Rutherford and is also present in gasoline. There were also no industrial facilities within the community itself, although there were forty-two plants involved in chemical manufacturing within three miles of the town, as well as several landfills. The dilemma for Burke's investigation was the absence of toxicology relating the levels of benzene detected in the air to accurate community exposures. We had no idea what kind of dosages the children were exposed to and only limited conjectures on how the air transport related to the industries three miles away.

In essence, we knew benzene was in the air and soil, but could not unambiguously identify the levels we had measured as a threshold to cause the cancers in the cluster. So unfortunately, based on the environmental science and public health tools available at the time, no clear statistically significant associations were found between carcinogens and the cancer incidences in Rutherford. In fact, the study raised many more questions than it answered and subsequently propelled Science and Research into performing statewide comprehensive monitoring studies over the next ten years for contaminants in air, water, and soils. The objective of these studies was to determine background levels of suspected cancer-causing chemicals in the environment, in addition to evaluating the health risks associated with low-level exposures to these carcinogens. Yet the most valuable outcome from the Rutherford investigation was the development of a standardized method for future evaluations. And indeed, the next cluster investigation in Dover Township, New Jersey, did find significant correlations between chemical exposures and the incidence of cancer.

The Dover Township (Toms River), New Jersey, Cancer Cluster Investigation

Dover Township is a sleepy coastal community surrounded by deep forests and drained by the dark red cedar waters of the Toms River. Yet in spite of its isolation, this historic community has seen its share of history and trauma. Chartered in 1767 by the colonial legislature as one of New Jersey's original 104 towns, it stood for only fifteen years before its destruction by the British during the Revolutionary War. Dover Township was the port-of-call for a flotilla of privateers that plundered British and Tory ships along the Atlantic coast. In March 1782, a group of British soldiers and colonial loyalists attacked the town's fortified blockhouse on the river, routed the local militia, and captured its leader, Captain Joshua Huddy. Huddy was subsequently hanged as a pirate by the British in their nearby fort at Sandy Hook. The red coats also destroyed the salt works in Dover that supplied colonial militias from Philadelphia to New York City. The raid was a small conflagration typical of the largely unchronicled guerrilla warfare that raged at the edge of major battles during six years of war. Nevertheless, the battle flamed tempers abroad so late in the hostilities and delayed the war's closure until 1783 when Ambassador Benjamin Franklin signed the peace accord in Paris.

For the next two hundred years, Dover Township remained a small, back-woods community in the heart of the undeveloped part of the state. In 2006, it legally changed its name to the Township of Toms River, recognizing the urbanization that had occurred surrounding the forgotten blockhouse where Captain Huddy was dragged off to be hanged. Today the township sprawls across forty-one square miles with ninety thousand residents, most of who live in densely populated towns amid the sprawling woodlands but with some scat-tered industries among the trees.

In the mid 1990s, township officials alerted the New Jersey Department of Health and Senior Services (NJDHSS) to the possibility of a childhood cancer cluster in their municipality. Following the public health procedures developed in the Rutherford cancer-cluster investigation and the groundwater fate stud-ies to identify sources, the health officials announced that the incidence of childhood cancer in Dover Township appeared significantly higher than expected for the period from 1979 through 1991.[16] Specifically, childhood leukemia was above the expected rate, while brain and central nervous system cancers were twelve times higher than expected. The leukemia cluster was only in females.

Science and Research helped the Hazardous Waste Program in NJDEP to perform an exposure pathway investigation, looking for potential sources of carcinogens in the local environment. This analysis indicated that past releases of toxic chemicals from two nearby Superfund sites, Ciba-Geigy/Toms River Chemical Company and Reich Farm/Union Carbide, might be the sources of the groundwater contamination that affected Dover Township's water supply wells.[17] Ciba-Geigy is the largest chemical company in Switzerland. In Dover Township the Ciba-Geigy (Toms River Chemical) plant manufactured dyes and epoxy resins. Solid and liquid wastes from the manufacturing processes were disposed of in twenty areas on the site's sprawling property, including landfills, open-air drum dumps, and unlined lagoons, which caused wide-spread soil and groundwater contamination. It is estimated that from 1952 to 1990 Ciba-Geigy buried approximately seventy thousand drums of hazardous waste onsite and pumped millions of gallons of liquid wastes per year through a pipeline that led to the Atlantic Ocean beside a popular bathing beach. In 1980, NJDEP ordered Ciba-Geigy to monitor groundwater and begin drum removal at the plant. But by 1983, owing to poor responses from the manufacturer, DEP asked the federal USEPA to take over and put the site on its Superfund list. It was not until 1989, however, that the USEPA investigation was completed and the agency ordered Ciba-Geigy to begin cleaning up the site and the groundwater.

In another section of Dover, the owners of Reich Farm leased part of their property in 1971 to an independent waste hauler who dumped almost five thousand drums collected from the Union Carbide Corporation. In addition to the buried drums, the waste hauler also poured liquid wastes into open trenches, thereby contaminating the groundwater. Union Carbide Corporation is a specialty chemical and polymers company whose products are used to manufacture a broad spectrum of products including paints and coatings, packaging, wire and cable, household products, personal care items, pharmaceuticals, automotive goods, textiles, agricultural products, and oil and gas. In 1920, Union Carbide developed an economical way to make ethylene from natural gas, one of several key chemical innovations that gave rise to the modern petrochemical industry. In August 1999, Dow Chemical Company purchased Union Carbide for $11.6 billion. From 1972 to 1974, however, Union Carbide was busy in Dover Township removing drums, draining the trench wastes, and digging up contaminated soil. Unfortunately, the groundwater beneath Reich Farm served as the main source of drinking water for Dover Township.

In 1974, the Dover Township Board of Health closed more than one hundred private drinking wells near the Reich Farm site after finding contamination with a unique chemical called styrene acrylonitrile trimer, which was made only by Union Carbide. The board ordered that the nearby homes be connected to an alternative water supply, but even this other source came under some suspicion, as 30 percent of the township's public water supply was downgradient from the toxic plume. By the mid-1990s, locals were concerned that the Toms River Water Company (now United Water Toms River) had not adequately treated the water to make it safe. What added to the people's concern was their belief that local childhood cancers seemed high. This was brought to their attention by a pediatric nurse who worked at Children's Hospital of Philadelphia and who observed an inordinate number of children from Dover treated for cancer. She speculated to the visiting parents that an environmental cause might be elevating the pediatric cancer rates in Toms River. The parents brought this to the attention of the New Jersey Health Department, which subsequently performed a preliminary epidemiologic survey in 1996. The study showed that between 1979 and 1995, ninety children in the township were diagnosed with cancer. This was twenty-three more than would be expected in the population, meaning that the children had developed leukemia and brain and central nervous system cancers at higher than the national rate. However, the researchers added that there was no cause for alarm. Based on existing data about cancer rates, the Health Department felt a comprehensive cluster investigation would not be economical or useful, because the numbers of childhood cancers were "not statistically meaningful."

There was a public outcry over this finding, since many of the affected parents had already made up their minds about the likelihood of the Superfund sites supplying an environmental explanation for the tragedy that had afflicted their children. Subsequently, more than a thousand people attended a meeting in March 1996 demanding answers. Linda Gillick, the mother of a cancer victim and spokesperson for a citizen's committee organized to address the issue, said: "In my heart and in my mind, I have no question. Now, it's up to the scientists to use logic and common sense to get at the truth."[18]

At the end of the meeting, the New Jersey Departments of Health and Environment agreed to look more closely at the two Superfund sites as possible sources of carcinogens into the local environment and developed a cancer investigation Public Health Response Plan.[19] Not willing to wait for some long, involved site investigation to be completed, the township residents also contacted their congressmen and sought a more detailed epidemiological investigation. Linda Gillick even traveled to Washington, D.C., to testify and to defend a special line-item allotment of $1 million for the Toms River study in one of Congress's annual appropriations bills. Ultimately, Congress passed the allotment and the study was undertaken as a joint effort between state officials and the federal Agency for Toxic Substances and Disease Registry. The study, which took more than five years to complete, concluded: "No single risk factor evaluated appears to be solely responsible for the overall elevation of childhood cancer incidence in Dover Township."[20] The study found that most of the childhood cancer cases in the area have no explanation; the only supportable environmental link was that between prenatal exposure to contaminated drinking water and pediatric leukemia in girls. An association was also found between prenatal exposure to the air from the Ciba-Geigy plant and leukemia in female children diagnosed prior to five years of age. The children in Dover Township were being diagnosed with cancer at a rate over 34 percent higher than the national average.

In January 2002, Union Carbide, Ciba Specialty Chemicals, and United Water Toms River, without acknowledging liability, agreed to a multimillion-dollar settlement with sixty-nine families whose children were diagnosed with cancer.[21] Other families declined the settlement and are pursuing a class-action suit. At the time, Linda Gillick, as spokesperson for the families, said: "The numbers do not reflect, in any way, what the families and the children went through." The money is surely no consolation to the fifteen families whose children have died nor to the new cases of childhood cancer being diagnosed each year. In 2005, NJDEP presented Linda Gillick with the state's prestigious Women's Environmental Leadership Award in recognition of her work as chairperson of Citizens Action Committee for Childhood Cancer Cluster in Dover Township. The mission of this committee is to provide the public with timely and honest information about investigations into the increased rate of childhood cancers and to ensure that government agencies serve the public interest. Gillick is also the founder and executive director of Oceans of Love, a support group for children with cancer.

The Debate on Environmental Cancer

One might imagine from these highly publicized investigations that cancer-cluster studies are a valuable and frequent tool in the public health and environmental professional's arsenal for ferreting out vectors of chemical contamination, health effects, and possible corporate or criminal malfeasance. Yet cancer-cluster investigations have been disparaged as time ill-spent, if not wasteful, considering the many other demanding things a health official must do. A study in the *American Journal of Public Health* surveyed state health departments around the country and found that most cluster investigations showed no associations between the types of cancers reported or the suspected hazards.[22]

And there have been more forceful criticisms of the value derived from cancer-cluster investigation. Atul Gawande, a professor at the Harvard School of Public Health published an essay in the *New Yorker* magazine titled "The Cancer Cluster Myth." He called cancer clusters an alarmist and hysterical reaction by the public in response to widespread media attention and the availability of too much information on hazardous waste sites and cancer registries. Gawande insisted in the article that clusters rarely turn out to have an environmental cause and referenced the National Cancer Institute's own findings that "many cancer clusters, if they do exist, may occur by chance alone yet people have a tendency to see patterns in random events, or to isolate a cluster from context."[23]

In a rejoinder to this *New Yorker* article, Richard Clapp, a professor at Boston University's School of Public Health and director of the Massachusetts Cancer Registry from 1980 to 1989, argued against Gawande's conclusion that clusters are just statistical artifacts with no real cause and are a big waste of personnel and resources.[24] Clapp stated that the Dover Township, New Jersey, cancer cluster resulted from real chemical exposures and that the statistically significant excess of leukemia in young girls could not be ignored. Clapp concluded that public health practitioners need to be vigilant and respond to citizen's concerns whenever there is a suspicious exposure that might have a cause.

This exchange of views between environmental and health practitioners is emblematic of the confusion that the general public feels as it listens to professional disagreements that routinely occur in any declared state of emergency. The technical message translated through television and newspapers, or poorly planned public meetings, can get caught up in poorly defined or misappropriated facts. This can confuse the public instead of informing them. Communities going through a cancer-cluster scare respond emotionally and with poor forethought. The role of a government scientist in such a situation is to balance fear with concern and to use good listening skills with a calm and measured response. In fact, because of the ambiguities often encountered in cancer-cluster investigations, many states have developed cancer-cluster protocols, including a meeting with community members to educate them about the issues. Only then, with more details in hand and using a phased approach, do they set out on an exploration for environmental toxins as a potential source of the seeming cluster of cancers.[25]

WHO IS WINNING THE WAR ON CANCER?

The night before my brother died, I visited him in the hospital in New York City. I remember he was too weak to sit up, so I pulled a chair to his hospital bed and sat quietly beside him. His hair had fallen out from the latest round of chemotherapy, and his face was pale, almost porcelain, although his blue eyes were quick but scared. He said he had been passing blood and the pain had gotten worse. I raised my hand with spread fingers as he raised and placed his against mine. His fingers were thin and longer than mine, a pianist's fingers, but he had never played, never had the time to do anything since he had turned seventeen except fight the cancer that ate his flesh, his body a battleground of modern biochemistry.

I felt stupid and inadequate. What the hell can you say to your little brother who's wracked with pain and so weak he can barely wiggle his fingers against your own? "When I took yoga," I told him, "my teacher said if I focused on my breathing and went inside the breath, I could make the world go away."

"Does that work?" Joe asked.

"I don't know," I said, feeling foolish for suggesting it. "For a bit, I guess."

And he smiled at the time and we went on to some more small talk. He told me his roommate, an elderly Russian, was studying Kirlian photography, a form of electrophotography that depicted an aura around people. His roommate was convinced the aura was a picture of the soul, and he handed me a copy of the book with incredible images of fingertips and blue halos around them. The cover Kirlian photograph was a bright blue luminescent handprint from the former Beatle, George Harrison's, latest solo album, *Living in the Material World.* Joe and his roommate were really animated about this subject, both of them so close to death yet wondering about the unseen soul with great passion.

I left them shortly thereafter as visiting hours ended with the book still in my hand as a present from the kindly Russian gentleman. I did not realize then, but it was the last conversation I would ever have with my brother. The next night Joe died of a cerebral hemorrhage, the chemotherapy eventually wearing his system down to the point that his body collapsed before the cancer could kill him. Not believing he was dead when I heard the news, I went to Sloan Kettering hospital on the upper east side of New York with my fiancée, Bernadette Duncan, and made a scene. I wanted to see his body before I would admit he was really dead. They would not comply. With so much anger welling up inside me, Bernadette and I left and wandered across town into the frozen winter paths of Central Park and out onto the emptiness of the Great Lawn. Her hand in mine was the only thing that kept me from drifting away into the darkness of despair. I felt her warmth in my heart and Joe's cold and insubstantial hand on my shoulder, his incorporeal spirit hovering above me under the monstrous noise of that indifferent city.

A month later, after the funeral and alone in our shared bedroom, I found the book on Kirlian photography in my backpack and read it avidly. The Kirlian effect, I read, was a pulsed electrical field that created an electrophotonic glow.[26] Kirlian photography and the "soul auras" were later debunked by serious studies that showed the halo effects in the electrophotography were only moisture on the photographic plates. However, this simple conjunction of events—my last conversation with Joe and finding that book—sent my intellectual curiosity spinning in search of scientific explanations for life and death. Of course the aura of Kirlian photography was not based on physics but rather on paranormal psychology. Yet it provided me with a new perspective in ways I had not thought of before. I had not known there were fields of electricity attached to the body. What other wonderful things might I learn that could help me endure the world without my brother in it? I read more popular science books and became intrigued. My untrained mind was not aware of the scientific method or the mathematical means to separate out unsubstantiated assumptions from true hypotheses. My mind was still filled with all the emotional cloaks that a poet and a classicist used to adorn his intellect. I had not yet found that bridge between serious scientific inquiry and the unknown physical and biochemical forces that rule our lives. Yet I was eager to learn and set out to study science as if my brother Joe had willed me to it.

Six years later, I was a scientist in the New Jersey Department of Environmental Protection. We felt ourselves newly recruited soldiers in the war on cancer, our mission to reconnoiter the hidden trails through the factory stink and the foul effluents leaking into the river from mystery pipes. Now you may think that sounds pretty grandiose and a bit melodramatic, but that was the essence of how we felt as young, eager environmental scientists. We were the heady professionals just out of graduate school with a license to test hypotheses about exposures and the risks associated with the towns we lived in.

Of course there was a social and an economic context to what we were doing. The big signs along the highway announced the power of our adversaries: the industrial giants that manufactured automobiles, distilled alcohol, and made gasoline, pesticides, and plastics. They were all well-heeled industries that employed scientists and lawyers with pedigrees as good as ours. But that was part of the thrill! The sense of power was overwhelming as we walked into corporate boardrooms with the inestimable mass of the New Jersey state government behind us; the lawyers in the attorney general's office, the physicians and epidemiologists in the Health Department, the geologists, ornithologists, and even herpetologists. All these experts were available to support us as we found our tempered voices in corporate boardrooms across New Jersey.

However, my original idealistic zeal to find an environmental cause for my brother's death proved unrealistic. After the first few years of working as an environmental professional, I recognized that the issues were much too complex for a "one factory, one molecule, one cancer" model. There were too many sources and too little information on the toxicology to understand it. I learned that cancer alley did not really exist but that cancer clusters do, although it's hard to pin down the causes. I also discovered that many corporations will fight tooth and nail to limit their liability under an environmental complaint, regardless of the facts and whether it is the morally right thing to take responsibility.

I found that cancer risks from environmental contamination are as real and as deadly as first surmised in the 1970s when President Nixon declared war on cancer and Governor Byrne of New Jersey declared the first state of emergency and created the Science and Research program within NJDEP. Many environmental laws have been passed since then, many risk-based standards promulgated and approved. Many carcinogen sources were identified by the Industrial Survey, and emissions were reduced. The hazardous waste disposal business was totally restructured to prevent unopposed toxic releases from operating industries. Citizens and politicians were sensitized to the need for more stringent environmental protection, and the overall environment in New Jersey improved. But more important, a new generation of environmental scientists was born, trained, and set loose to protect the public.

Recently the National Cancer Institute released a report in the journal *Cancer*, summarizing the nation's progress toward reducing major cancers.[27] It reported a reduction in the death rates from the four most common cancers (prostate, breast, lung, and colorectal) and an overall decline in cancer incidence since the early 1990s. This it attributed to American lifestyle changes, such as reduced cigarette smoking and better diet. The report also credited significant reductions in public exposure to carcinogens in the workplace and ambient environment as cofactors in these declines, as well as the effects of more stringent environmental regulations. The institute also noted that the largest ongoing source of carcinogens affecting public health is in food, specifically seafood contaminated with industrial chemicals like polychlorinated biphenyls (PCBs) and dioxin.

This finding was of no surprise to me, since my first research project at NJDEP was to catch fish both on the high seas and in small ponds throughout the state and analyze their edible flesh for carcinogens like PCBs. This fish work would bring me both notoriety and fleeting fame but most of all a sense of worth that I had finally done something of value to reduce exposures to carcinogens in New Jersey. In some small part, I had won a skirmish in the war on cancer and satisfied the mandate laid down by Governor Brendan Byrne's 1976 executive order to establish standards to control emissions of carcinogenic substances into the environment.

CHAPTER 2

Poisoned Fish

THE FISHING CREW

When you are on the Atlantic Ocean in a nineteen-foot powerboat, the world compresses into a very tight universe. Three men are about the most we can fit in our workboat. No one sits as we drive out into the fishing grounds, since the pounding momentum of the boat as we hurl over the waves would most likely warp our spines if we braced them against anything solid. Keith Lockwood invariably pilots us out by compass to some shoaling area where the fish congregate. Bruce Ruppel and I hold on to the console, alternately bracing then flexing our knees against each rising wave as we breach. No one speaks as we make our way seaward because the wind and spray make speech impossible, especially over the driving pistons and churning propellers that keep us up on plane and skimming across the blue-green water.

Typically, when we motored offshore we would notice others making their way out, big party boats filled with day-fishermen hanging off the railings, speedboats heading to all points of the compass, a few tugboats pulling barges as the pilots waved at us from the flying bridges some thirty feet above our heads. Then there were the wallowing ore carriers, the festive white cruise ships, and even a few garbage scows steaming out to burn the city trash and dump the ashes into the ocean. The sea off New Jersey in summer is like Times Square at rush hour. A bit wider and less noisy but filled with the same kind of chaotic traffic whose rules of the road are understandable only to the captains and pilots that work its waters. The inshore channels are even called roads. These are routinely dredged deeper and marked on nautical navigation charts, the deepened trenches running past hazardous reefs, treacherous rocks, and sunken wrecks that are highlighted in red. The largest roadway into the Atlantic just outside of New York City is Ambrose Channel, which drops precipitously from the inshore estuary into a mile-deep canyon at the edge of the continental shelf. Into Ambrose Channel come supertankers filled with crude oil from the

Middle East for landfall at the refineries in Elizabeth or else boxy auto-carriers from Japan that look like wobbly Lego Block houses afloat. Fast racing boats called "cigarettes" plow past us like angry wasps, leaving old tubs in their wakes whose pilots in ragged Yankee caps curse and shake their fists, yet continue to push their thirty-year old-wooden vessels to the limit. And of course, there are the Coast Guard cutters with their distinctive red stripes across the bows, policing the traffic and keeping everyone civil and reassured.

As fisheries biologists we do not always go out in the halcyon days of August to get our samples. Frequently, we go abroad in the early days of spring or the shortened days of fall and winter to catch fish as they migrate along the Atlantic coastline. One memorable field day took place in April 1984 when we planned on catching female blue crabs, *Callinectes sapidus*, before they awoke from their winter torpor buried in the bottom mud. There were two others that day, Bruce Ruppel, who had learned to fish by the Great Falls on the Passaic River in New Jersey beside its thumping mills, and Keith Lockwood, our pilot. Keith was the only true bayman and blue water fisherman among us, a boy raised "down the Jersey shore" when it was only sedge islands and cedar swamps, wandering the back bays like Huck Finn or some colonial trapper from the seventeenth century. Then there was me, the Jersey City kid who had earned his sea legs crabbing off the pilings in New York Harbor and swam from the railroad piers that cribbed the city like braces on busted teeth.

Figure 3. PCB Project field crew (*left to right*): Thomas Belton, Keith Lockwood, and Bruce Ruppel. (Source: Thomas Belton.)

Bruce was built square with a physique topped by muscular shoulders and bottomed out by legs that braced against the rolling sea as we motored into the rising sun. Balding even as a young man, he kept a camouflage hunter's cap firmly planted on his peeling head lest it turn as bright as a maraschino cherry. His lively blue eyes scanned the horizon overarched by bushy eyebrows above a face suffused with a florid complexion that he had inherited from his dad, an Air Force bombardier who flew out of England during World War II, and who had regaled him with stories about bailing out over the English Channel from aircraft pierced through by starburst shells, the plane too crippled to make it home.

Keith, who worked the wheel, was Bruce's opposite in everything except his love for the ocean. He was thin and tall, topped by red hair that flowed from beneath a strange green long-billed watch cap that he often wore. It made him look a bit like a photograph I had once seen of a young Ernest Hemingway fishing for marlin off Cuba in the 1920s. The hat made Keith look a little deranged, like a tall duck, as he conned the boat out through Ambrose Channel and into the ocean swells that rolled toward Sandy Hook. When I first met Keith, he seemed the typical Jersey shore kid, long and lanky with the typical blonde surfer hair and freckles, perpetually sunburned from growing up outdoors. Keith grew up in the 1950s in Bricktown, New Jersey, where the coastline for miles inland was mostly a sandy wilderness filled with pine trees and impenetrable bogs. After school he learned to hunt fox and muskrat and sell the pelts to furriers in Cape May. He learned to harvest wild rice just as the Indians had done from an open canoe, and he worked lobster traps and ran trotlines for catfish, all at a time when respectable New Jerseyans were buying their groceries wrapped in plastic from the supermarket. He attended the same high school as Bruce Springsteen and "Little Steven" Van Zandt, two icons of our popular culture. But I knew Keith mostly because of his proficiency as a hunter, a trapper, and an angler.

During the time that we worked together, we'd had some close calls. Once, we had been stranded on the open ocean with no steering wheel and nearly struck by lightning pulling in gill nets before a coming thunderstorm. Another time, Keith was almost shocked senseless while wrestling desperately with a battery in the bottom of our wallowing boat as a ship bore down upon us in the narrow confines of the Arthur Kill sluiceway between Staten Island and Bayonne. Yet we always came through somehow, thanks to Keith's ingenuity. But more important, it was his expertise as an outdoorsman and his unflagging devotion to the environment that helped us to alert the public about chemical contamination in food fish. These bioaccumulation studies showed significant amounts of polychlorinated biphenyls (PCBs) and dioxin in edible fish, both carcinogens that cause cancer and teratogens, which can result in learning disabilities and birth defects in children.

That cold day in April though, there were no recreational boats on the water, and looking about I realized we were all alone except for a freighter slowly pulling into the distance. I loved it when we were on the sea like that, New York City nothing but a low tangle of saw-toothed buildings in the haze. The world seems more open out there, the wave swells rising and falling as we wound our way past the buoys to where we knew the blue she-crabs, or "sooks," slept their frigid sleep, the winter months reducing their tiny hearts to quivers in the brown silt on the sea bottom. There they waited for the sluggish arc of the world to wend its way through the blue storms of November, into the white caps of January, only to return once again to the warming month of April. That's when the sooks sensed the warming waters above them, which softened the bottom mud with the promise of release. Only then would the gravid females dig themselves out and release their microscopic spawn by the millions into the outgoing floods of spring. The offshore waters nurtured the shrimplike larvae as they grew, the orphaned young eating and swimming their way to adulthood in that strange way of crabs, successively molting their exoskeletons, expanding their bodies into different metamorphic shapes as they flattened crablike, calcified, and hardened their shells. Eventually their swimmeret fins metamorphosed into spindly feet as they sank to the bottom and walked about, following the scent of their ancestral spawning grounds inexorably inland. A year of two later, their adult migration brought them back to the marsh where they were conceived, crawling ever upward into the brown water of the estuary. There they would stop in the grassy shallows of the salt marsh and mate. The females filled with fertilized eggs would then swim out through the estuary to sea, bury down for winter, then dig out and spawn in spring to repeat the whole natural cycle.

But we had a plan to interdict this process in the service of environmental science and public health. We were concerned that the crabs had picked up chemicals on their travels through the industrial waters of the New York–New Jersey harbor. We wished to pull the sleepy females from their muddy burrows with a crab trawl before they spawned, its steel-clawed fingers curling the bottom to troll them from their frigid beds. Our objective was to analyze their flesh for PCBs.

Bruce and I stood on the stern of our boat and played the drag ropes out to either side until the winglike otter boards spread the net like a pillowed sail along the bottom, its steel tongs digging into the sand as we motored along. Now usually with a bottom trawl on a small boat like ours, you dredge into the wind with the swell rising against you for stability. But the sea swell that day was a bit high, and it kept pulling the trawl off the bottom as Keith slowed the boat down to the marching pace necessary to dig in and pull the crabs out. Touching the towline, I could feel the rope hopping up and down like a skittering plate. So Keith decided to trawl with the wind behind us instead of against. That meant getting the swells to our stern, which kept the ropes from bouncing up and down.

And it seemed to work for a while as we felt the trawl dig in and pull smoothly along the bottom, but then something unexpected happened. The trawl snagged, perhaps on a wreck or a sunken cable, but nonetheless the trawl became an anchor. All of a sudden we were dead in the water with Keith yelling for Bruce and me to pull the trawl ropes up as he reversed and tried to maneuver us back over the snag to pull it free. And what happened next is one of those nightmare moments in time that never leaves you. I remember pulling on the trawl line as a massive swell came aboard the boat, burying the stern in its depths. My perspective became a bit vertiginous and unhinged then, as I distinctly recall staring intently past my boots as the rope came aboard and suddenly the deck disappeared into the water. For a moment it felt as if I was pulling the boat to the bottom instead of the trawl upward, as the cold water surged past my knees numbing me, a reminder that nothing stood between us and the unforgiving sea but a few inches of submerged fiberglass. Keith cursed as Bruce and I struggled in the wash trying to wrestle the trawl off the snag. It was then that the outboard motor coughed and spit black gouts of smoke before it died. We were now anchored by the stern, with the North Atlantic coming aboard and pushing us ever deeper with each swell.

That's when Keith shouted for us to get off the transom and onto the bow. Bruce and I sloshed back through the flooded boat and jumped onto its highest point, bringing our combined weights to bear, which flattened the boat's profile a bit before the incoming waves. I was aghast! In a few moments' time, we had gone from happy crabbers to shipwrecked sailors. I quickly surveyed the horizon for help only to realize that we were completely alone, just the April breeze and us. If we went into that water, I realized, we would freeze to death in about fifteen minutes, even with a life vest on. That's when I looked up and noticed Bruce holding a giant blue Igloo cooler on his lap.

"What are you doing with that?" I asked.

"It floats, my life preserver!" he said.

"Damn!" I remember thinking, "I wished I'd thought of that."

Keith by then was kneeling in the stern up to his armpits in green water that sloshed under the rocking motion of the incoming swells. I watched as he pulled the trawl lines that we had abandoned inboard and reached into a crab-filled bucket for his bait knife. With incredible presence of mind and flawless efficiency of motion he cut the lines and wrestled both of them around his shoulders before tying them off to a bright red marker and tossing them aloft and back over the side. He then scrabbled up and over to the console where he hit the ignition switch, muttering under his breath about "being damned if I'm going to lose a six-hundred-dollar trawl!" Meanwhile, Bruce and I sat helplessly on the bow as he fired up the engine, which coughed a few times before rumbling to life. He then threw the throttle into high gear, and the water-filled boat lumbered forward like a sunken tub as the wash slid back and over the transom into the sea. Bruce and I fell into the waist of the boat where we frantically bailed as the motor grumbled alive and gained speed, losing water with each second of thrust.

So we did not sink and we caught no more crabs that day either, but Keith did get his trawl back after we came about and grappled for the float. Suddenly we were driving inshore shivering, cursing, and alternately laughing hysterically at jokes that came to us unbidden in our joust with passing fear. For fear can be a peculiar thing. I always thought of fear as hot and bright, something that flushed you with adrenaline in the incendiary panic of a nightmare. But to feel fear as we had on a bright and sunny April day with its emissary only a broad expanse of freezing water, our boat miles from shore, that was indeed unexpected.

And a conundrum came to me as we motored ashore, made even more poignant as we skimmed the seawall protecting the wharfs on Shark River— namely, that commercial fishermen go out every day in both fair and foul weather. That they often faced the possibility of death, freezing in a swamped boat or run over by the myriad shipping vessels, with each morning bringing a new and imminent danger. Yet they go each day onto the back of the sea and drop their nets, pull their pots, carve great ripples of commerce in the swells far from shore. And I felt a bit ashamed at the thought of their labor and how our project might affect them if we found PCBs in their blue crabs. It would threaten their livelihoods and their families. For if we proved, as we suspected, that the seafood was contaminated, then fewer people might buy their fish.

But I realized that was only one side of the story. Looking homeward across the water, I also knew that fishermen were potential victims of the pollution as well. Their wives and children ate more seafood than anyone else. I was only the messenger. The source of this grief wasn't me or our puny boat out on the ocean but the lack of judgment by industries and the business and political compromises that allowed factories to release chemicals into the water in the first place.

I have found that when you start your professional life you are green but hope to get progressively smarter; otherwise you wind up disillusioned or dead.

I learned that April day that some jobs are more dangerous than others are an that New Jersey commercial fishermen command deep respect for what they endure to live life on the sea. I also learned that there is an unanticipated cost to being a field biologist that I had not appreciated before and that being attacked in the press, as I would be a few months later, after releasing our PCB fish consumption advisories, was less of a problem than being drowned.

Polychlorinated Biphenyls

Polychlorinated biphenyls, or PCBs, were one of the wonder chemicals of the early twentieth century. Shaped like a barbell, the two flat phenyl rings of carbon are held together by a strong bond; each ring is studded with a number of chlorine atoms. It is the array of the chlorine atoms that adorn each of these six-sided phenyl rings that gives the molecule much of its reactivity.[1] Such reactivity is that much more significant when you consider that there are 209 possible variants to the basic biphenyl form. These variants are called "congeners," based on the amount of ring chlorination. We can also group them into homologue classes of chlorination from one to ten, increasing from mono-chlorinated PCBs (one chlorine) to deca-chlorinated PCBs (all ten available carbon points on the rings hold a chlorine atom). Each PCB congener has different physiological properties, such as its ability to dissolve in water or oil, its ability to volatilize at room temperature, its ability to degrade by microbial action, and of course its toxicity (the more planelike and flat the congener's two phenyl rings, the more toxic).

Like the discovery of penicillin by Alexander Fleming and its subsequent mass production during World War II, PCBs became more widely available after that war ended and industries like the Monsanto Company sought wider commercial applications. Monsanto, founded in 1901, historically manu- factured agricultural pesticides such as DDT. More recently its specialty chemical, 2,4,5-T, a deforestation defoliant, was sprayed on the Ho Chi Min trail in Vietnam as a component of Agent Orange. We now know that during the manufacture of 2,4,5-T an unintended cocontaminant occurred, called "dioxin," which is believed to be one of the most toxic synthetic organic chemicals ever made by humans.

In 1935, Monsanto purchased the Swann Chemical Company in Alabama, which manufactured PCBs.[2] The major driver for the growth of PCB production was the electrification of American cities in the first half of the twentieth century and the need for fireproof electrical equipment by companies like General Electric (GE) and Westinghouse. From 1929 to 1977, Swann and then Monsanto produced PCBs, which found widespread use in thousands of applications because of their fire resistance and insulating capacity, especially in electrical transformers and capacitors. PCB-based products became central to many other American industries as well, such as the manufacture of inks and fabric dyes, lubricants, sealants, paint additives, and for softening caulk.

Yet the toxicity of PCBs was apparent almost from day one of their commercial manufacture. In the 1930s, Swann Company employees displayed distinctive health problems such as acnelike pustules on the face and body (chloracne) and a loss of energy, appetite, and libido. All are now considered classic symptoms of PCB toxicity. Currently Monsanto is a responsible party in more than fifty USEPA Superfund sites because of PCBs. In 1997, Monsanto spun off its industrial chemical division into Solutia Inc., effectively transferring financial liability away from the parent company for actions related to the production and contamination with PCBs at the Alabama plant.

Monsanto has since been sued and has settled multiple times for damaging the health of its employees or residents near its Superfund sites through pollution and poisoning. The most notorious of these cases was a class action suit by residents surrounding the Anniston, Alabama, plant where the Swann facility was located. The judge in that case awarded a multimillion-dollar settlement, finding that "Monsanto Company engaged in 'outrageous' behavior by releasing tons of PCBs into the city of Anniston and covering up its actions for decades." Under Alabama law, the rare claim of "outrage" typically requires conduct "so outrageous in character and extreme in degree as to go beyond all possible bounds of decency so as to be regarded as atrocious and utterly intolerable in civilized society."[3] The jury held Monsanto and its corporate successors liable on all six counts it considered: negligence, wantonness, suppression of the truth, nuisance, trespass, and outrage.

From 1929 until the mid-1960s, no one really knew that PCBs were getting into the environment because analytical chemistry techniques could not differentiate between PCBs in samples and other chlorinated chemicals like DDT. The world first became aware of PCBs as an environmental problem in 1966, when they were found in more than two hundred fish around Sweden, as well as an eagle that fed on them.[4] The study also showed that PCBs "bioaccumulate along the food chain," with little biodegradation. That is, the concentration and toxic dose increased by trophic (feeding-group) level from herbivores to carnivores. The food web includes humans as the top carnivores, much as the eagle in the Swedish study, which ate large amounts of fish.

By the early 1970s, PCB hazards to humans were recognized and linked to damage in the liver and in the neurological, immune, endocrine, and reproductive systems. The USEPA and the Agency for Toxic Substances and Disease Registry, part of the Department of Health and Human Services, also classified

PCBs as "probable carcinogens."[5] As a result, all production of PCBs was banned in 1977, as the USEPA developed guidelines and regulations for their control. This effort culminated in publication of a series of regulations on handling and disposal of existing PCBs.[6] In fact, to this day each of the ten USEPA regions has one staffer permanently assigned as the PCB coordinator for managing these regulations for waste haulers, disposers, and spill responders.

Yet the main reason that New Jersey was concerned about PCB contamination in the 1970s was because of fish contamination in the Hudson River. We were concerned that the General Electric Company in Fort Edward, New York, had discharged 1.3 million pounds of polychlorinated biphenyls from its capacitor manufacturing plants into the Hudson River from 1947 to 1977. The storage of these PCBs in sediments and their transport downstream, as well as their bioaccumulation in fish, resulted in the entire tidal Hudson River being declared a Superfund site by USEPA.[7] This "Hudson River PCBs Superfund Site" encompasses nearly two hundred miles of the Hudson River in eastern New York State from Hudson Falls, New York, to Jersey City, New Jersey. The PCB Site includes communities in fourteen New York counties and two New Jersey counties. The primary health risk associated with the site is the accumulation of PCBs in the human body through eating contaminated fish.

PCBs became the Dr. Jekyll and Mr. Hyde of the chemical world. On one hand and under the glory of discovery, PCBs were manufactured and distributed throughout the world as a new class of wonder chemicals meant to serve society. Yet under the surface, the monster hid, as company executives ostensibly knowledgeable about the chemical's toxicity allowed millions of tons of the poisonous material to be released into the environment. When I became involved in the "PCB Project" in New Jersey, seeking out the possible presence and sources of the cancer-causing chemicals in fish, little of the magnitude of these upriver actions were completely understood by regulators, although we did have our inklings. Some of that evidence came from Japan, other insights from across the United States.

In 1968, more than a thousand residents of Kyushu, Japan, fell ill after eating rice-bran oil contaminated with PCBs fluids. Since then, more than fifty of the affected people have died from internal tumors, irregular lymph nodes, and damaged livers. This incident also documented the first birth defects known from PCBs. At the time, PCBs were also being used here in America in the food industry. For example, the heating medium inside coils of deep-fat fryers in fast food restaurants contained PCBs, and cattle feed was found contaminated in an Ohio silo where PCB-based paints flaked off. Because of these food-borne contamination events, both countries moved to ban the manufacture and distribution of PCBs.

Here in the United States, Congress passed the Toxic Substances Control Act in 1976, which outlawed the manufacture, sale, and distribution of PCBs within three years. It was the only time the U.S. Congress ever banned a specific chemical. However, because of the adverse effect that a recall of all PCB electrical equipment might have on American industry, a phase-out approach was agreed to, which allowed the continued use of PCBs in closed systems (i.e., electrical transformers and capacitors) for the useful life of the operating electrical equipment. This was estimated to be approximately thirty to forty years. As a result, much of that equipment is still in use today, aging and leaking. In 1977, however, Monsanto voluntarily stopped manufacturing PCBs in the United States and GE stopped dumping PCBs into the Hudson River. At this same time, the federal Food and Drug Administration (FDA) proposed lowering the PCB tolerance levels from 5 parts per million (ppm) to 2 ppm for fish and shellfish, and Governor Brendan Byrne of New Jersey created the Science and Research Program in NJDEP. The commissioner of NJDEP, in response to this challenge, started the PCB Project.

THE PCB PROJECT

One of the first projects I managed for Science and Research was called the PCB Project. It entailed capturing finfish and shellfish and then analyzing the edible portions for contamination by the carcinogen polychlorinated biphenyl. The main objectives of the project were to evaluate whether fish and shellfish in New Jersey territorial waters were contaminated (states have jurisdiction over ocean waters out to three miles, the federal government from three to two hundred miles), to determine how PCB levels in fish varied with geography, and to assess the suitability of any contaminated fish we found for human consumption.

Keeping the third objective in mind, we analyzed only "edible fillets" of food fish and not the head and guts, as these were the parts most likely to be a threat to human health. Chemical analysis included not only PCBs but expanded over time to include chlorinated pesticides (DDT and chlordane), metals (mercury), and industrial contaminants (dioxin). Sampling locations included all the major freshwater, estuarine, and saltwater drainages in the state. We selected target species of finfish and shellfish based on their importance to commercial and/or recreational fisheries. At its inception in 1976, NJDEP's Commissioner David J. Bardin said: "If we find a river with contaminated fish, we will have to deal immediately to keep contamination off the market. The next step will not be regulatory, but investigative. The water pollution control staff will have to trace its sources. What New Jersey needs, and what the rest of the country needs is a systematic program, which will identify the most serious poisons that are liable to enter our waterways so we can prescribe practical limitations on production and transportation of such materials."[8]

The urgency behind Bardin's words proved ephemeral, however, as there was no immediate response when fish contamination was found, nor track-down of sources, and no attempt at systematizing the sampling into a routine monitoring network. When I took over the PCB Project in 1980, I reviewed data collected over the past four years and found hundreds of fish had been analyzed, many with elevated levels of PCBs. Yet nothing had been done about it. No alerting the governor's office or working with the Health Department to determine what the risks were to consumers—only a steady collection of more data from year to year with no public health follow-up. Part of this I attribute to bureaucracy and the designation of our Fisheries Division to manage the project. Their biologists looked at stocking issues and fisheries resource management, with no experience in evaluating public health risks. Yet as I took over, a paradigm shift occurred, which I attribute primarily to my boss, Tom Burke, who was an epidemiologist. He had one leg in the New Jersey Department of Health and the other in Environmental Protection, so we decided to take a new look at the data and compare it to the only regulatory action level available at the time, the FDA's PCB tolerance scale.

An FDA tolerance is a peculiar concept in governance, since it is not strictly a health-based action level for conservatively putting the consumer above all other concerns. Instead, tolerances allow consideration of potential impacts to the marketplace through a cost-benefit analysis.[9] That is, if a chemical tolerance value will put numerous fishermen or supporting industries, like canneries, out of work, the FDA can justify a number less protective of public health as long as it satisfies a greater economic good. A second mitigating factor in using the FDA tolerance scale was that it was limited in application, being a standard for evalu-ating only food fish involved in "interstate traffic." This restriction was of little help to coastal states like New Jersey, where significant amounts of seafood are captured and eaten primarily within state jurisdictional boundaries. In essence, New Jersey's recreational catch for many important species (e.g., bluefish) was almost as large as the commercial catch, which by statute FDA did not regulate. In spite of all that, FDA's PCB tolerance was the best number we had with legislative and regulatory power behind it, so we assessed our results against the tolerance value and found some surprising results.

Our 1982 PCB Project report showed that 75 percent of the finfish and 50 percent of the shellfish we collected had some detectable level of PCBs in their edible flesh.[10] Eleven percent of the finfish exceeded the FDA tolerance of 2.0 micrograms of PCBs in 1 gram of tissue (micrograms per gram) or 2.0 ppm.

The good news was that only a few species of fish had elevated levels of PCBs, and that freshwater fish had much lower levels than estuarine and marine fish. (This finding would reverse a few years later when we looked for mercury in fish and found certain freshwater species contaminated with mercury, ostensibly from coal-fired power plant emissions.) The bad news was that the most highly contaminated species, striped bass and bluefish, were important as both commercial and recreational fisheries, and brought millions of tourism dollars into the state. A geographical analysis revealed spatial differences in fish contamination, with the heavily urbanized northeast corner of the state (Hudson River–Newark Bay–Raritan Bay estuary) as the most PCB-impacted area. Of course we suspected that the Hudson River would be severely contaminated from the GE plant (Hudson River Superfund Site) upstream, but our data supplied the first solid evidence that health impacts from those PCBs could be felt far downstream in marine waters.

Yet here was the conundrum. Telling the public the fish were contaminated was easy. Telling them what to do about it was difficult. We needed a plan to protect public health but also a means to marshal the political will to expound and enforce it. For example, we had demonstrated in our analysis that PCB levels correlated with the fat content of our fish samples, and we knew that different species of fish stored body fat in different parts of the body. Some fish have oily flesh because they store fat primarily in their muscle tissue (e.g., bluefish, eel, striped bass), whereas other species store it in their livers (e.g., flounder). This allowed us, if need be, to advise the public on ways to reduce PCB contamination if they did choose to continue eating the contaminated fish. They could do this by simply trimming off the fat-rich skin and belly flap. We also calculated how many meals of each species of fish per month would result in an excessive risk for cancer and birth defects. The question was whether we could convince Governor Tom Kean and have him declare fish consumption advisories as a means to alert the public.

The NJDEP commissioner at that time was Robert E. Hughey. Bob Hughey was an unlikely bureaucrat. An independent consultant and urban planner from South Jersey before being tapped for commissioner, he once confided in me that he missed going to work in sandals and shorts and taking long walks on the beach whenever he felt like it. Governor Kean in his memoir, *The Politics of Inclusion*, said that he almost did not hire Hughey because "he had a strong independent streak, and he wondered how he would work within an administration." Kean was leery because he knew how hard a job it would be to run NJDEP. He also noted: "The job of commissioner of NJDEP could be the second most difficult job in New Jersey, because every issue under the department's purview is potentially explosive—from finding a proper storage site for toxic waste to reviewing industrial compliance with our air pollution laws, the toughest in the nation."[11] Kean went on to explain that the job requires someone who has the intellect to understand real science and the personality to deal with angry and often poorly informed constituents, along with a deep personal commitment to the environment.

In my opinion, Commissioner Hughey's independent streak made him a great asset to Kean's administration. Anyone can hire a yes-man to agree with his policy platform, but with science-based programs, politicians need someone who can say no—especially if the technical information does not support a policy initiative. It takes a good leader to hire smart, qualified staff and then let them go to work in an independent frame of mind, allowing frank discussion and agreeing to disagree on certain issues, but also willing to trust the scientists' conclusions when they tell you something is worth exploring.

I soon learned about Hughey's style when Tom Burke and I briefed him on the PCB Project results and laid out for him our recommendations for fish consumption advisories. We outlined how this might create political flashback from the recreational and commercial fishing industries. We also explained the problematic interstate commerce issues with FDA and how we would need to brief and integrate our actions with contiguous states that shared our fisheries (New York, Pennsylvania, and Delaware). After the briefing, Hughey suggested we take it to the governor, right away, and surprisingly, after a quick walk down State Street, the three of us were ushered past the State Police guard and into the governor's office. There he motioned us to a group of leather chairs surrounding a coffee table, where we spread out our maps and graphs and walked him through our rationale for closing some commercial fisheries and alerting recreational consumers to the risks of eating five species of fish caught in New Jersey waters.

Governor Kean was a pleasant surprise. On television he had, according to my Jersey City sensibilities, a peculiar accent that sounded more Bostonian and standoffish than *Jersey*. Yet in person, he was quite affable—quick to laugh at a joke and intellectually curious about what our data showed in spite the limits of his scientific expertise. I had forgotten that he started his career as an educator before becoming a politician and as a result was a good listener and a quick study. Tom Burke and I double-teamed the twin topics of ecology and public health, convincing him of the veracity of the data and the size of the threat. We told him about the FDA's PCB tolerance number and the advice we had developed with the state health department on how many meals of a specific contaminated fish one could eat before triggering a deleterious health effect. We especially laid out our recommendations for "no consumption" by nursing mothers and small children because of the birth defects and developmental risks associated with PCBs. Kean asked Hughey if he was convinced that the science was solid. When Bob replied in the affirmative, the governor told us to draft an emergency order for his signature to close the affected fisheries and advise the public.[12]

On December 13, 1982, in the midst of a driving snowstorm, Commissioner Bob Hughey and Dr. Allen Koplin, the commissioner of the New Jersey Department of Health, jointly announced fishing advisories for recreationally caught striped bass, bluefish, American eel, white catfish, and white perch and commercial fishing closures for striped bass and America eel, reflecting the inordinately high concentrations of the carcinogen.[13] The advisories warned the public to limit consumption to no more than one meal a week for fish taken from the designated waters. In addition, persons at greater risk such as pregnant women, nursing mothers, women of childbearing age, and young children were advised not to eat any of the indicated species at all. We also announced that both the FDA and the National Marine Fisheries Service were asked to review our data for appropriate federal actions in waters outside the three-mile limit of state jurisdiction. The migratory nature of the oceanic bluefish made localized health advisories problematic, since similar levels of PCBs might be found in bluefish caught in waters from Florida to Maine and the source of the contamination might be from any polluted estuary along the migration route. We believed that it was not necessarily a New Jersey contaminated fish issue but an interstate issue requiring the involvement of federal agencies.

Not surprisingly, the PCB Project results met with a lot of incredulity from the fishing industry and sportswriters who attacked us both on the accuracy and the timing of our assessment (they wanted to know why it took the state five years to release the results). Bob Duffy, the sportfishing writer for the *Newark Star-Ledger* said: "I personally, where it concerns my own dinner table, I am not all that concerned over this situation. I think there is a mountain being made out of a molehill. It just seems to be the age we live in."[14] Duffy then interviewed Jon Lucy, a marine scientist with the Virginia Institute of Marine Science, who said he thought bluefish in Virginia waters were safe to eat. Duffy responded in print with, "So what is going on here? Our Jersey bluefish warnings on *alleged* bluefish contamination are taken lightly, to say the least, by another state with equal if not better facilities for examining bluefish. Just how good are the studies on bluefish made by the Jersey DEP? Is our analysis correct? Were there enough studies made of individual fish to reach a valid conclusion? Were the people doing the Jersey evaluation competent to do this evaluation? Was their equipment reliable?"[15]

I cannot convey how gut wrenching it is to see your professional reputation slandered in the press, to see your competence called into question in the midst of a swirling national debate. However, I did not have the time to worry about it. I had to forget about personal reputation for the moment because the critical issue was that the accuracy of our study was being questioned. And more important from my perspective, the consumption advice we had given the public might be ignored. The advisories were in danger of being drowned out by media sound bites, resulting in a pregnant woman or a nursing mother making an ill-informed choice to eat contaminated fish. Tom Burke and I decided that the best way to move forward would be to collect and analyze more fish but also to keep the pressure on the federal agencies to perform a coastwide study of PCBs in bluefish.

The Coastwide Bluefish Study

A few weeks later we received letters reviewing our PCB Project report from all three federal agencies involved in the issue—FDA, the National Oceanic and Atmospheric Association (NOAA)'s National Marine Fisheries Service (NMFS), and the USEPA—telling us that they were gratified by the action taken by officials from the NJDEP to minimize, where possible, the exposure to PCBs. They added that the concept and procedures used to control the consumption of selected finfish for PCBs (advisories) appeared sound. They also agreed that artificial human boundaries such as state jurisdictional waters and federal waters were inadequate for managing public health impacts from contaminated and highly mobile species like bluefish and striped bass. However, all three agencies said they were unable to perform a coastal study of PCBs in bluefish because of a lack of money.

Not to be deterred, Tom Burke and I decided to organize a states-only task force workshop made up of environmental and public health officials from all the Atlantic coastal states stretching from Maine to Florida. This gathering took place on September 29, 1983, at NOAA's fisheries lab in Sandy Hook, New Jersey, and included more than fifty representatives from state health and environmental departments. Reluctantly, the FDA, National Marine Fisheries Service, and USEPA decided to attend. I began the meeting with an address pointing out that 4.9 million bluefish were caught a year for recreation in New Jersey and another 1.2 million pounds commercially.[16] Many of the states had the same kind of catch statistics. At the end of the workshop, a unanimous consensus was reached by the state representatives, with the federal agencies as well as representatives of the fishing industry (Atlantic Coast Fishery Management Council) concurring that a coastwide study of bluefish contamination was necessary. Unfortunately, no one stepped forward to lead such a study, as there was still no money to fund it.

Shortly after the PCB workshop, however, I received an unexpected phone call from New Jersey's Senator Bill Bradley. The senator had received angry messages from a number of commercial fishermen arguing that the imposition of a ban on fish consumption for the New Jersey side of the Hudson River was unfair since New York fishermen could still catch and sell their stock. Howard Bogan, a New Jersey charter boat captain claimed that the total state recreational fishery was worth some $551 million and its charter-boat business was valued at $82.7 million. Moreover, according to him, the 1983 summer charter business was off by 25 to 30 percent. He concluded: "Take away the blue fishing and you'll just close us right down."[17]

The senator therefore offered to use his senatorial privilege to seek special funding for a coastwide bluefish study and to have FDA, USEPA, and NMFS co-manage it. Tom Burke and I subsequently were asked by the senator to come to Washington, D.C., and defend a $2 million appropriation at a Senate subcommittee hearing. As a result, the National Marine Fisheries Service was directed to develop a study in collaboration with FDA and USEPA, with NJDEP and the other state environmental agencies acting in a supporting capacity by supplying manpower and resources when needed to capture the fish. Senator Bradley, fresh from this victory, decided to announce the appropriation at Liberty State Park in Jersey City with the Statue of Liberty behind him. Moreover, to show the commercial fishermen that he had heard them while still supporting NJDEP, he asked me to join him there for the press conference.

Today most tourists can identify Liberty State Park as the beautiful green retreat on the Jersey shoreline just behind the Statue of Liberty and Ellis Island. Many wedding photographers use the park for photos with the statue and the island of Manhattan and its skyscrapers as a spectacular backdrop. However, few realize that before it was developed, the area was an industrial wasteland composed of abandoned factories, fallen-down piers, and seeping chromium dumps. I, of course, remember it also as the site of the Liberty Yacht Club, which figures so prominently in the story with which I introduced this book.

All this went through my mind as I walked into Liberty State Park and watched the senator get out of his limo, surprisingly in the same way my dad used to, all six-foot-four of him unfolding out the door like a centipede. And as I shook his hand, I thought about Dad taking me to watch Bradley with the New York Knickerbockers back in the 1960s, playing alongside Earl "the Pearl" Monroe and Walt Frazier as they propelled the Knicks to two national basketball championships. So it was with a slight sense of awe and a bit of teenage hero worship that I greeted the senator on my home turf.

However, to be honest, Senator Bradley is one of the least prepossessing people I have ever met. He asked me to call him Bill as we strolled out along the promenade overlooking the Statue of Liberty, and I told him about the Liberty Yacht Club and my dad and the industries that once flourished there, which might have caused some of the legacy contamination in the fish. He listened politely and then asked me to make sure the commercial fisherman's concerns were addressed in the coastwide bluefish study. We stopped and had our picture taken shaking hands, and Bradley made a brief prepared statement. We then walked back to the limousine and he jumped in, followed by his staffers, and with a nod to me he was gone. I waved at the departing car, my hopes dashed for a private lunch with Bill Bradley, perhaps an invitation to discuss that incredible seventh game of the 1970 championship series, the Knicks shutting down Wilt Chamberlain to beat the LA Lakers. But then I thought about my dad teaching me to swim out beyond the river's edge and I felt a bit better. In spite of the excitement of having my work recognized, the thrill of shaking the senator's hand, nothing pleased me more than the idea that the Liberty Yacht Club was a ghost presence nearby, unseen by all but me, and maybe my dad was doing one more cannonball off that invisible railing of the barge as Jack, Joe, and I screamed in delight.

The Coastwide Bluefish Study and the Federal Response

After a series of planning meetings between the states and the federal agencies, the bluefish study finally got underway in 1984. Bluefish were collected from Florida to Maine over a twelve-month period by the National Marine Fisheries Service and summarized in a joint NMFS-FDA-EPA 1986 report.[18] It stated that PCB levels in large bluefish were elevated at every site sampled along the eastern seaboard, with many exceeding the tolerance. FDA qualified the severity of this finding, however, by announcing that only recreational fishermen and their families who consume contaminated fish day after day, year after year might have health concerns. They added that the levels of PCBs in bluefish—*in commercial distribution*—did not present a health concern for the general consuming public. This to me was an interesting policy statement if not outright regulatory obfuscation. FDA only regulates food in commerce, whereas bluefish because of their high fat content are not amenable to freezing for truck transport and other forms of processing (fish sticks). As a result, the recreational catch of bluefish is usually much larger and eaten more locally—within states—as opposed to transport between states for sale. The implication was that state health officials and environmental regulators were still on their own and forced to make local pronouncements about the Atlantic bluefish schools even though most of the larger and more contaminated fish moved through federal jurisdictional waters more than three miles offshore on their annual migratory runs. In fact, over the next few years almost every east coast state announced some form of health warning about eating large bluefish, especially for pregnant women.

A glaring deficiency in the NMFS-FDA-EPA 1986 report was that the agencies made no evaluation of the possible sources of the PCB contamination in the bluefish. Fortunately, other researchers obtained and used the data for some novel geospatial analyses. One study concluded that "based on relatively low PCB concentrations in the New York Bight bluefish during the spring and summer, we might speculate that some substantial portion of the New York Bight bluefish sampled during October/November were fish that had moved south from New England waters during the late summer and early fall. If this is the case, it would be unwise and premature to conclude that PCB sources in the New York Bight region lead to higher levels of PCB contamination in bluefish populations."[19] Thus it appeared that a large source of the bluefish contamination occurred in New England waters, which supported NJDEP's original position to Senator Bradley that the problem was not New Jersey's alone but coastwide, requiring a strong federal agency presence to deal with interstate transport and public health issues. Another study took the bluefish data and modeled fishery life history of the species with PCBs as a possible factor for developing a bluefish management plan.[20] This study concluded that alternative harvest strategies such as size catch restrictions for larger more PCB-contaminated fish could be incorporated into the plan to safeguard consumer health. As a bonus, stock replenishment would occur, because protected large females could spawn more frequently and contribute substantially more eggs to the stock. This would minimize dietary exposure to PCBs without closing the fishery or decreasing the pleasure of the sport. Yet in spite of this thoughtful analysis, the bluefish management plan developed by NMFS made no such provisions for size, nor do they currently do so.[21]

Thus Science and Research's strategy to compel these federal agencies to work together and outside their separate agency missions (NMFS to consider human health, FDA to think ecologically) may have been a one-hit wonder and more of an aberration than we thought. For once free of Senator Bradley's mandate to deliver a final report to Congress, NMFS and FDA went their separate ways and returned to being primarily responsive to their mission-specific constituencies. Only USEPA responded more definitively and in a way that addressed both source reduction and public health protection. Because of the many frenzied investigations into fish contamination in the 1970s and 1980s, USEPA moved to ban PCB production or the use of other equally toxic bioaccumulative pesticides such as DDT and Lindane. PCBs were replaced by other nonchlorinated mineral oils in electrical transformers without too much additional cost for manufactures. New generations of pesticides were introduced, especially organo-phosphorous materials, which are more biodegradable and largely do not bioaccumulate. Unfortunately, though, many of the legacy pollutants like DDT and PCBs left huge loads in soils, water, and sediments owing to their persistence and nondegradability. To meet this long-term public health challenge of continued uptake from these legacy pollutants, USEPA set up a persistent bioaccumulative toxics (PBT) program for tracking and assessing the risk from exposure to these compounds.[22]

EPA defines PBTs as highly toxic, long-lasting substances that can build up in the food chain to levels that are harmful to human and ecosystem health. PBTs include mercury, dioxins, and PCBs. The challenge to reducing the risks from PBTs stems from the fact that these chemicals can travel long distances, are transferred easily between air, water, and land, and also linger for generations in people, animals, and the environment. And although much has been done to reduce the risk associated with these chemicals, we still find them in our food fish supply. The total number of fish consumption advisories in the United States increased by 80 percent from 1993 to 1997, and the number of water bodies under fish consumption advisories increased from 1,278 to 2,299.[23] Some argue that this increase can be attributed in part to the fact that the states are now doing a better job of monitoring and setting protective levels, with many of them instituting pilot studies that grew into routine monitoring programs, much as what happened with NJDEP as a result of our PCB Project.

However, in the early 1980s when the press was criticizing me personally as an unprofessional Chicken Little screaming, "The sky is falling!" after the release of our PCB Project report, I was not so sanguine. As that time I found solace in my family, even though my dad was slowly slipping away while undergoing radiation and chemotherapy for his lymphatic cancer. After he died, I found a clipping from a local newspaper among his things—an editorial about my work with the PCB Project that I did not know he had cut out. It read:

These are the facts! They are not the predictions of "environmental extremists." This is what is! The DEP deserves applause for this study—a six-year project with more to come. New Jersey is one of the leaders in studying its environment. Sometimes that hurts because we know what's killing us while others live in the bliss of ignorance. Facts give people the information they need to make decisions. It is lately fashionable to talk of environmental extremists and clean water kooks. But what DEP found is what the so-called extremists warned us we would find one day. Studies don't solve our problems, and the problems won't go away by themselves. But studies can show us how to live with them, and we will have to live with PCBs in our fish for a long time.[24]

Dad was apparently happy that I had found a career, although until his dying day he was still puzzled over why I read Latin poetry. In fact, if he had lived, he might have found some of my other research projects quite interesting. For the question of toxic ingestion shifted from food to water in the 1980s, as regulators strove to develop standards for contaminants in drinking water. Science and Research played a central role in this quest, and once again Jersey City would be ground zero for the war on cancer as it related to safe drinking water. Potable water in Jersey City came from Boonton Reservoir some twenty-five miles away, pulled from the Rockaway River as it flowed into a dammed impoundment astride a craggy ridge in the Highlands and pumped back to the city in giant pipes. That's where I went next in my search for carcinogens that might have caused my brother's and my father's deaths. And I learned that the so-called pristine waters of Boonton Reservoir that we drank from everyday were not so clean nor the treatment methods as safe as we thought.

CHAPTER 3

The Quality of Water

I recently spent a few hours mapping the edges of a drinking water reservoir in Trenton, New Jersey, using a global positioning system (GPS). The GPS device was a small, handheld monitor that located my exact position by triangulating multiple satellite signals from thousands of miles above the earth's surface. As I awaited the satellite signals to synchronize and looked down into the bowl of the reservoir's catchment basin, my companion nudged me and asked, "Where's the water coming from?"

I glanced over at him, one of the mapping specialists that the department employed to develop digital computer maps from aerial photography, and I realized that he was probably rarely in the field. Then looking back into the reservoir I saw the source of his confusion. Rather than a placid blue lake, the reservoir was nearly empty. Yet the operators had opened a floodgate a few miles away to pump thousands of gallons of water from the Delaware River, which resulted in a huge cataract of water, plunging with a deafening roar to the bottom of the man-made impoundment. I realized that my companion's specialty in geographic information systems (GIS) only dealt with the earth as pixels, tiny dots on a computer screen. He had no substantive feel for the physical objects that he so meticulously mapped. He felt more comfortable transcribing aerial photographs taken from an airplane than walking in the woods. To technicians like him, the virtual reality game of a child lost in the forest was more important than the forest itself, with its subtle wind-brushed sounds of leaves, creaking trunks, and camouflaged squirrels and deer. The filling reservoir with all its noise and power was more overwhelming than the two-dimensional computer graphics he created, more disturbing than if he had seen Godzilla nesting at the bottom of the watery bowl.

As an environmental scientist, I know from well-traveled experience what reservoirs and swamps look like and how it feels to see the ocean from the back of a speeding workboat. A map is but a shadow of reality. It is a graphic approximation to get you near an object but not to guide your inquisitiveness, your fascination at how it functions once you arrive. Quite casually, I mentioned to my coworker that when I was a kid we used to swim in a reservoir by my house, usually late at night when the local cops could not see us in the dark.

"How would you get out?" he asked, looking back into the depths of that half-filled storage reservoir.

I pointed at a steel ladder along the far wall that descended all the way to the bottom. "The trick is not to jump into the end with the intake or the outlet. One pummels you to paste, and the other sucks you down so that you never come up."

The Search for Safe Water
(Boonton Reservoir, New Jersey—1904)

Bill Hoar was a hardhat diver from New York City, a specialty that involved placing a fifty-pound bronze helmet on his head, screwing it onto an air-tight rubberized canvas suit, and wearing shoes filled with pig iron weights. These usually carried him to the depths of the Hudson River, where he looked for lost items gone overboard or to inspect for cracks in pier supports and bridge pylons.[1] In 1904, he was contracted to dive in the newly constructed Jersey City Reservoir. The reservoir was built because the city's usual supply of water from the Passaic River had become contaminated by sewage, resulting in seasonal typhoid and cholera outbreaks. The city fathers decided to buy cheap land in northern Jersey on the Rockaway River, dam it up, and divert part of the flow through twenty-five miles of buried piping to deliver fresh mountain water to the growing metropolis.

Hoar was called into action because of a mishap during the filling of the manmade lake. When the reservoir was only half full, the sluiceway jammed and would not close. The sluiceway allowed the dam operators to control the level in the reservoir like a giant bathtub, raising or lowering the water for flood control. Rather than drain the lake, which could take a week, the operator decided to block the sluiceway and place a stopper in the tub. He had built a two-and-a-half-ton wooden ball, five feet in diameter and filled with lead, which he lowered on a crane to the mouth of the submerged sluiceway. That's when disaster struck as the harness snapped and dropped the giant orb where it stuck in the mud in front of the opening without sealing it.

Bill Hoar went into the water from a small barge while two men cranked fresh air into a pump that supplied him with oxygen on the bottom. Hoar was confident he could feel about in the darkness and surmise how to fix the problem. Unfortunately, as he groped about, he was sucked into the hole and under the giant ball. He was trapped with the full pressure of the lake squeezing him into the sluiceway, inextricably wedged tight. Up on the surface the crew of men turned and turned the air crank that fed Bill his steady supply of oxygen, and they would do so for more than four days as the operators tried to free him. They sent down another hard-hat diver who tried to pull Bill loose with no luck. They tied a harness around his waist and attached it to a team of mules, but that snapped as they tried to drag him from the depths. It was many days later when a plant mechanic found another way to clear the sluiceway from the other side of the dam that they pulled poor Bill's lifeless body from the depths.

It seemed that getting clean freshwater from pristine upstate rivers was not as simple as the engineers had predicted. There is risk associated with any construction project, but engineering safe drinking water relies not only on the dams and piping but also the infrastructure needed to filter and sanitize the source water. Filtration beds were built beside the sluiceways to remove debris and, it was hoped, any waterborne pathogens like those that caused the cholera epidemics in Jersey City. But sometimes the efficacy of these filtration systems was faulty or the upstream water quality was questioned, which again required diagnostic tools as primitive as putting a hardhat diver down to the bottom to take a look around. And for this reason, perhaps an ironic tear in the fabric of time, I led a scuba team to dive into Boonton Reservoir some seventy years after Bill Hoar had died under that gigantic wooden ball. My objective was to investigate the safety of the source water entering the manmade lake.

SOURCE WATER ASSESSMENTS
(BOONTON RESERVOIR, NEW JERSEY—1982)

The summer of 1982 saw one of the worst droughts in New Jersey history, and as a result the Boonton Reservoir shrank to a third of its size. So much had it dropped that an island appeared in the midst of the reservoir and the fieldstones of a dozen ancient drowned farms surfaced from the depths as the shoreline shrank and the Rockaway River—which fed the giant impoundment—slowed to a stream-size trickle. At the time, I was investigating the source water coming into the reservoir and the efficacy of the Jersey City Water Works at removing contaminants. We were not concerned with waterborne bacteriological threats such as typhus and cholera but with twentieth-century pollution in the form of synthetic organic chemicals coming from industries upstream.

Working with Gail Ashley, a Rutgers University professor of geology and her graduate student, Jacky DeLu, we had deployed suspended-sediment samplers a few weeks earlier throughout the reservoir by boat, carefully lowering them down to the bottom with marker floats attached. Jacky had ingeniously

Figure 4. Boonton Reservoir under drought conditions in 1982. The mouth of the Rockaway River enters into a cove at the upper left, where sediment samplers were deployed, across from the dam spillway. (Source: Jacqueline DeLu for the New Jersey Department of Environmental Protection.)

devised these samplers from cigarette butt urns she had purloined from the graduate student lounge at Rutgers. She then retrofitted them with special footings to stabilize on the bottom, a lever to automatically close the lid when we pulled them up, and a rope attached to a float. The samplers were a true mark of mechanical genius, I thought at the time, and benefited her classmates by removing reminders that smoking was once allowed in most public buildings.

We had planned on retrieving them in a few months' time to measure the amount of suspended sediment that deposited on the bottom and to gain an empirical measure of sediment load to the reservoir under baseline (low-flow) conditions. Then it started to rain—and it rained nonstop for three weeks! Soon the waters rose, covering the ancient farm walls; the island sank beneath the waves, as did the floats to our samplers. Unfortunately, we had deployed them with only enough slack to deal with the drought levels that we had encountered in the halcyon days of August.

Without the floats to latch onto, we had no way to retrieve our samplers. Therefore, with youthful exuberance, I suggested to two of my coworkers at Science and Research that we scuba-dive on the samplers and pull them out. The three of us, Robert Mueller, Theresa "Tessie" Fields, and I, were all certified open-water divers but with little experience in the kind of technical diving we so blithely agreed to undertake. We dove at the inlet, which was then dumping tons of suspended sediment from eroded mudflats upstream. The water was turned a chocolaty brown by the current, which was so strong that we had trouble pulling our boat up against the mouth of the Rockaway River that fed the reservoir.

To accommodate for the strong current we used two anchor-lines to keep our boat from drifting off-station. That's when Tess realized we did not have enough weights for three dive belts. Bob, being the largest and heaviest, suggested that he simply pull some rocks off the shoreline and stuff them down his wetsuit (not a great idea as I realized halfway through our first dive). To keep within the planned search radius emanating from the bottom of the anchor line we agreed to go down in a single file, attach a tether to the anchor line, and the three of us would circumscribe its axis, fanning out along the bottom in pursuit of the sampler. I was in the lead and going down hand-over-hand as the visibility was reduced to nothing within a few feet of the surface. The high volume of sediment discharged by the river had clouded the water and the cone of light from my diver's lamp went from amber to dark brown to pitch black as we descended. I felt like we were diving into a box of Count Chocula breakfast cereal.

Nevertheless, we continued downward hand-over-hand along the anchor line until I noticed something coming toward me in the darkness. With a shock I let go of the rope and watched the thing disappear back into the depths. It was the anchor. By hauling on the line we had been pulling it up, instead of us down. I realized that the boat above us must have drifted off-station as well. It was then, hanging upside down in the water, that I felt a huge clang against the bottom of my steel tank, and then another. Glancing up I sensed more than saw a pair of rocks whip by my face and head for the bottom. Mueller's makeshift weights were shaking loose of his wetsuit and dropping on Tess and me like a biblical rain of stones.

Returning to the surface a bit bruised but not drowned, we all agreed that *that* wasn't such a great idea. Yet with the tenacity and stoicism of youth we decided to try again, but this time only Tess and I went down to complete the search. We repositioned the boat and dropped our two anchor lines as we returned to the water. Lightly touching the rope so as not to repeat the last fiasco, Tess and I descended through the photic zone into the darkness that swallowed the sun. I pressed on, kicking downward until eventually my outstretched hand met the bottom mud in such absolute darkness that I could not see my depth gauge with my diver's lamp pressed fully against it. I spun about and knelt on the bottom tying my tether to the anchor in anticipation of Tess joining me to begin our search. Holding my diver's lamp at full length up along the rope I hoped to guide Tess. But no Tess! I spun around and shone the light around me in a complete circle. No Tess!

For the life of me, I couldn't figure out where she had gone. Fearing that she might have gone back to the surface or be in trouble, I reluctantly unhooked my tether and ascended in search of her. As I gained the surface, I found Tess bobbing in the water beside me, her mask pulled back and her mouthpiece out, shouting angrily, "Where were you?"

Aghast, I shouted back, "I was on the bottom waiting for you!"

"So was I!" she replied quizzically.

Then it occurred to us that we must have gone down the two separate anchor lines into the chocolate soup and knelt not five feet from each other, invisible because of the tons of sediment propelled past us in the deep water. We started laughing then, as we bobbed in the lake, the silty water creasing our eyelids like muddy mascara, the spray splashing into our mouths. By then we were totally exhausted from our two dives, being pummeled by falling rocks, and the bone-numbing cold of the mountain water, so we agreed to give up the ghost on our search and motor back to shore, where we stripped off our wetsuits and fell blissfully asleep in the warm sunshine.

My dad used to say when confronted with folly, "Find another way, Tom." In this instance, I decided to be patient and wait for the drought to return (which it did!) and the water to go down (which it did!). And the floats from the sediment samplers popped to the surface and we retrieved them.

Waterborne Chemicals (Synthetic Organic Contaminants)

Potable drinking water can be pulled from rivers, lakes, groundwater aquifers, and even seawater if desalination technology is available to remove the salt. Yet universally the raw, untreated, potable water is referred to by custom as source water. And one of the underlying concerns of water treatment plant operators and public heath officials alike is the quality of this source water. This affects how much treatment (and its related expense) is needed to remove the waterborne contaminants, as well as the risk to consumers if they are not removed. The main reason for our study of the Boonton Reservoir was to evaluate the quality of the raw water being drawn into the Jersey City Water Treatment Plant. By the 1980s, water quality and safe drinking water research, to some extent, had moved away from waterborne diseases (fecal coliforms and other bacterial pathogens) to the chemical toxins in the water column. Our goal was to evaluate the drinking water supply for some of these synthetic organic chemicals and the potential for the contaminants to pass through the treatment plant. As is typical with environmental investigations, ours was an interdisciplinary study, merging the expertise of a geologist from Rutgers University with an environmental chemist from Drexel University in Philadelphia.

The team included Gail Ashley and Jacky DeLu, tasked with mapping out the hydrological and geomorphologic characteristics of the Rockaway River. DeLu successfully mapped out the fluvial characteristics of the Boonton Reservoir for Science and Research and also used it as her research dissertation for gaining her master's degree in geology from Rutgers.[2] In addition, I. W. (Mel) Suffet, an environmental and analytical chemist from Drexel University's Environmental Studies Institute, was tasked with isolating the synthetic organic chemicals in the reservoir source water, the results of which were piggybacked onto Ashley's hydrology study. Mel and his graduate student, Kathy Hunchak, also devised and placed unique water quality samplers near the mouth of the river feeding into the reservoir and another set near the intake of the water treatment plant. Kathy's device pumped source water at each location through a series of specially built filtration-adsorption columns filled with plastic polystyrene beads called XAD resins. These were designed to filter-adsorb only molecules with a certain molecular weight and size (a midweight class of organic compounds that we suspected to be in the water but for which there were no good isolation techniques). Our final assessment compared the results for raw water from the river mouth against the intake water, which had traversed the reservoir and ostensibly lost some of its suspended sediments and adsorbed contaminants (contaminants gathered in a condensed layer on the surface) to gravity, dropping to the bottom of the reservoir before being sucked into the treatment plant.

For as Mel explained to me, adsorption by suspended soils is an important mechanism for the transport of organic contaminants in flowing waters. Back in his lab Mel found different chemicals in the aqueous dissolved phase of the source water as opposed to what was on the suspended sediments or soil phase. Most notably on the suspended solids, we found alkyl phenols and plasticizers (phthalates). These chemicals were known to be toxic to aquatic organisms at the time but with unknown toxicity to humans.[3] Specifically, we found nonylphenol and octylphenol, as well as paper mill wastes (produced primarily by the bleaching of wood pulp to make paper white). Nonylphenol is an organic chemical produced in large quantities in the United States to manufacture detergents. It is also used in lubricants, antistatic agents, high performance textile scouring agents, emulsifiers for agrichemicals, antioxidants for rubber manufacture, and lubricant oil additives. Its toxicity to freshwater and saltwater animals was unknown in 1982, but twenty years later in 2003, USEPA developed an Ambient Aquatic Life Water Quality Criteria for Nonylphenol.[4] However, there is controversy over its human health impacts, and USEPA has not generated a safe drinking water standard, even though nonylphenol is both estrogenic (hormone-like compounds that may hinder the reproduction, growth, and survival of organisms) and commonly found in source waters owing to the detergent's incomplete degradation in sewerage treatment plants.

In addition, we found butyl phthalate and butyl glycolate ester, both primary plasticizers in the polyvinyl chloride manufacturing industry and very controversial in the current regulatory climate. Phthalates are added to plastics to increase their flexibility and can be found in many consumer products, including detergents, food packaging, and personal-care products such as soap, shampoo, and hair spray. Phthalates are also widely used in children's toys, which has generated a lot of discussion between regulators and children's public interest groups based on the toxicological uncertainties. Phthalates are known to produce negative health effects in animal studies, including testicular damage, liver injury, liver cancer, antiandrogenic activity, and teratogenicity. Some phthalates have recently been restricted for use by the State of California and in the European Union for children's toys.[5] However, in the United States the National Toxicology Program's most recent evaluation concluded that there were too many significant uncertainties in the exposure database to regulate phthalates in spite of its expert panel's high confidence in the toxicology effects database. In essence, the institute was confident that phthalates are toxic but less confident at what concentration an effect might be expected.[6]

THE NEW JERSEY DRINKING WATER QUALITY INSTITUTE

The environmental fate studies we carried out at Boonton Reservoir were part of a national trend in the 1970s and 1980s to identify contaminants of concern, using novel analytical techniques on ambient samples of water, air, and soils. The goal was to see what kinds on chemical contaminants might be present and available for human ingestion or ecological effects. For example, we knew through the efforts of the Industrial Survey what kinds of chemicals were commonly used in New Jersey industries (see chapter 1), but little was understood as to how they were transported or degraded once released into source water from discharge pipes. In fact, little or no toxicological information was available for many of the compounds we identified in those early days . Therefore regulators were blind to what it meant when we found them.

Often, as was the case with Boonton Reservoir, the analytical chemists and field biologists were far in advance of the toxicologists, who could not determine the hazard to public health when new contaminants were found in food or potable water. For example, in our 1982 study we had isolated two new compounds in the water supply, nonylphenol and butyl phthalate, but because of the meager toxicology available on them we did not know if it was cause for concern. Years later, however, these same chemicals were identified as important toxicants in need of regulation and reduction in the environment. Sometimes it worked the other way around; toxicologists first identified negative health effects from lab rat exposure studies and it was only later, after new field sampling and analytical techniques were developed, like Dr. Suffet's XAD resin sampler, that we could determine if they were common in the environment.

In 1984, New Jersey addressed this disparity by amending the State Drinking Water Act (Amendment 280 or A-280) to assure that all New Jersey public community water supplies were monitored on a routine basis for the presence of twenty-two soluble chemicals (which became known as the "A-280 Contaminants") identified in a comprehensive field study of drinking water carried out in Science and Research by Robert Tucker.[7] These included volatile organic compounds (VOCs), chlorinated pesticides, and industrial solvents. This broad sampling program was the most extensive of its kind in the United States at the time.

Amendment 280 also mandated the establishment of maximum contaminant levels (MCLs) for the contaminants in drinking water. These MCLs were epidemiological and risk-based, and set at a level that would cause no more than one cancer in one million persons if consumed on a regular basis over a lifetime. The amendment also established a Drinking Water Quality Institute to provide external peer-review of the MCLs. Between 1987 and 1994, the institute recommended MCLs for the contaminants based on toxicology performed by Science and Research staff and which were adopted in 1996.[8] NJDEP's Bureau of Safe Drinking Water now uses these MCLs as drinking water standards to ensure that public water supply systems in New Jersey are safe.

The development of these state-specific MCLs is an example of where state science programs stepped in when the federal government failed to act. The USEPA was tasked in the 1970s to develop safe drinking water standards for these same A-280 chemicals but had fallen far behind in its toxicological studies and technical abilities.[9] New Jersey took up the task willingly, with Science and Research toxicologists and risk assessors in the lead. They first classified each chemical as a carcinogen or noncarcinogen, based on a weight-of-evidence approach. Then after an exhaustive literature review they published a "Basis and Background" for each chemical to document their approach. They then performed an implementability analysis to determine whether analytic methods existed capable of reaching the often-low detection concentrations in an MCL. The institute also evaluated treatability, the efficiency and practicality for using the only two known treatment technologies available at the time for removing low concentrations of VOCs from source water (air stripping and adsorption to activated carbon). For it would be senseless to saddle water purveyors with standard concentrations so low that they could not be met by conventional potable water treatment technologies. Since then, other water treatment technologies have been developed, each one evaluated by the institute.

From a toxicology perspective, many of the A-280 chemicals found in drinking water were either liver or kidney carcinogens. This made sense considering the oral mode of exposure and the role these two organs play in processing, detoxifying, and excreting metabolic products from the human alimentary canal. Yet benzene was different—it alone of the A-280 chemicals commonly found in drinking water was a *leukogen*, a known cause of human leukemia.

I must admit I was particularly intrigued by this fact during the development of the Basis and Background document for the A-280 benzene MCL, primarily because of my family history and my brother's leukemia. I couldn't help but wonder if there were deadly sources of benzene in my old neighborhood when we were growing up. My brother, Jack, reminded me that there was indeed a sprawling industrial laundry on the next block. There it poured the sickly sweet smell of solvents into the air just a few hundred yards from where we lived. And benzene was up until the mid-1980s the solvent of choice for dry cleaning. Indeed, dry cleaning means not using water; industrial solvents are used instead, many of them carcinogenic. However, as with all such hindsighted speculations, the scientific question remains unanswerable. It could have been exposure to benzene that triggered a latent mutagenesis. Or perhaps Joe would have died from leukemia anyway owing to a congenital disposition or genetic weakness that none of us could detect. In fact, it could have been precipitated by interaction with a number of contaminants inadvertently placed into our drinking water by one of the twentieth century's greatest innovations, chlorination as a disinfectant in our drinking water supplies.

BOONTON RESERVOIR, NEW JERSEY—1908 (CHLORINATION)

A hundred years ago the Boonton Reservoir and the Jersey City Water Company factored into another important and epochal change in how the world treats potable water. By 1904, the year of Bill Hoar's fatal dive, the massive dam had backed up enough water from the Rockaway River for the treatment plant to filter in its huge sand beds and send fresh water the twenty-five miles to Jersey City through huge cast-iron pipes. Yet there was a problem. The designers of the reservoir had failed to factor in towns upstream of the reservoir. In 1906, a typhoid epidemic hit Jersey City, killing fifty-three people in a single month.[10] The Jersey City health inspector traveled to Boonton and found three cases of typhoid in towns above the reservoir. These towns all discharged their sewerage into the Rockaway River above the water treatment plant.

This led to a near-riot in Jersey City as politicians tried to lay blame on those whose absurd idea it was to seek clean water anywhere in New Jersey. The mayor insisted that the contractor responsible for building the dam and operating the Jersey City Water Treatment Plant, fix it. However, rather than build an expensive filtration system, the contractor tried something novel. He had heard about a new approach being used to treat water for cattle in the Chicago stockyards. The animals had failed to gain weight when given the sand-filtered water of Bubbly Creek, a stream so polluted with meat waste that it bubbled with noxious gases.[11] George A. Johnson, a consulting engineer for the stockyards, analyzed the water and found that while sand filtration cleared the water of visible particles, the levels of invisible bacteria remained high. Yet when he added chlorine to the water, the bacteria counts dropped to the point where the livestock water was more sanitary than the water used for human consumption.

Meanwhile the mayor of Jersey City demanded that the Boonton Reservoir contractor provide expensive sewer treatment for the communities upstream of the lake or else increase the size of the reservoir's own sand filters to improve the water quality. John Leal, an adviser to the Jersey City water company, was also experimenting with disinfectants and believed that he could rid the city water of bacteria by using very low concentrations of chlorine as a disinfectant. Calling Johnson in from Chicago to consult with him, Leal devised a system to chlorinate the drinking water as it left the Boonton Reservoir for the journey to Jersey City.

On September 26, 1908, U.S. public health history was made as chlorine was added to the Jersey City water supply, delivering the first chlorinated drinking water to American homes. Another advantage for the contractor in using chlorination was that it was cheap. Small applications of chlorine could significantly reduce bacterial levels in drinking water at a cost of only fourteen cents per million gallons (in 1908 dollars this was a mere $5.60 per day for Jersey City's forty million gallon a day usage). By the summer of 1908, a full-scale chlorine plant had been built near the outlet of the Jersey City reservoir, holding three giant tanks filled with eleven thousand gallons of chloride of lime for bleaching the water before it entered the distribution pipes. Instead of filtering, the water was disinfected and made nonpathogenic.

In a matter of years, many water treatment facilities in America followed New Jersey's lesson and built chlorine treatment plants for a fraction of the cost of building a filtration plant. Others that had filtration plants added chlorination to supply an extra measure of protection against waterborne pathogens that might periodically break through the sand filters. Within a few years, half the water treatment plants in the United States were using chlorination. By 1924, thousands of American cities had turned to chlorine (mostly in the form of chlorine gas), and serious epidemics of waterborne diseases became quite rare.

DISINFECTION BYPRODUCTS (DBPs)

Yet nothing is ever as good as it seems. By 1970, evidence began to accrue that something was wrong with chlorine-disinfected water. With increasing development of both urban and suburban lots, and the transition of small agricultural plots into industrial farms, most potable water companies were increasingly treating more sewage at their intakes from dischargers somewhere upstream. Even groundwater supplies faced this situation if their wells were not sufficiently deep enough and downstream of subsurface contamination. In the twentieth century, as raw water supplies became more contaminated or filled with heavy suspended solids, potable water purveyors responded by increasing chlorination. This led to water that often smelled like bleach and inadvertently caused chemical reactions with the organic loads in the water. These reactions created new chlorinated compounds, reactive chemicals that proved upon toxicological analysis to be carcinogenic.

These chemicals that result from water treatment are known as disinfection byproducts (DBPs). The first DBPs were regulated in 1979 and called trihalomethanes (THMs). Later, USEPA reevaluated these chemicals along with others and on February 16, 1999, issued a final rule on disinfection byproducts.[12] THMs include chloroform, bromodichloromethane, dibromochloromethane, and bromoform, some of which are known and others suspected carcinogens. Other DBPs such as chlorite, bromodichloromethane, and certain haloacetic acids also cause adverse reproductive or developmental effects in laboratory animals. Today more than two hundred million people consume water that continues to be disinfected with chlorine, making it one of the largest populations ever exposed to known or suspected carcinogens, and therefore the health risks associated with DBPs, no matter how small, need to be taken seriously.

In response, USEPA developed a "Stage 1 Disinfectants and Disinfection Byproducts Rule," which applies to all community water systems that treat their water with a chemical disinfectant. The rule reduced exposure to three disinfectants and many disinfection byproducts by requiring enhanced coagulation treatment or enhanced precipitative softening of the water for certain types of water treatment systems. USEPA also recommended that water purveyors transition to other less toxic disinfectants such as ozone, chloramine, or ultraviolet radiation. None of these reacts with suspended organic matter in water to form DBPs.[13]

Ironically, when the Jersey City water treatment plant operators added chlorine to potable water for the first time in 1908 to solve a problem, they inadvertently created another unanticipated threat to public health. This is an instance of catastrophe management gone awry, or maybe as the noted modernist, Buckminster Fuller once aptly said: "Every technical solution to one of man's problems creates four more technical problems that need resolution." In the case of chlorination the water purveyor chose a cheap and apparently effective disinfection approach with unexplored toxicological risks hidden in the details. But we cannot fault the utility too strongly, since the annual occurrence of waterborne bacteriological epidemics in the United States virtually ceased after this technological advance.

In fact, I can be sympathetic to the fog that accompanies technological advancements, based on my own experience. We had no idea until recently that the contaminants we found in our Boonton Reservoir source water study of the early 1980s, nonylphenol and butyl phthalates, were potential health threats. We needed to wait in the mist for the toxicology to become strong enough to extrapolate consumption risks to safe concentrations. In a similar fashion, our inadvertent synthesis of THMs and DBPs during water disinfection was not known until analytical chemistry methods evolved to meet the low levels of analysis needed to detect them. Unknowingly, the water-consuming public has become a natural epidemiologic experiment for DBP exposure. Over a ninety-year period, people throughout the developed world have been drinking low levels of carcinogens. Only time and close scientific scrutiny will tell what this may mean in terms of our population's cohort for cancer morbidity and mortality. It was not until USEPA's Disinfectants and Disinfection Byproducts Rule passed in 1999 that our daily dose of chlorine was reduced.

New and Emerging Contaminants

In spite of the increased surveillance and MCLs devised by state and federal authorities, and the improvements in our water treatment technologies, the largest waterborne disease outbreak in the United States occurred as recently as 1993 in Milwaukee, when a mysterious epidemic caused more than four hundred thousand people to become ill. After an intensive investigation by the U.S. Centers for Disease Control and state health officials, the source of this sickness was identified as *Cryptosporidium parvum*, a protozoan parasite for which there was no MCL.[14] Ironically, Milwaukee had experienced the largest outbreak of waterborne disease in the history of the United States, and yet the water in question had not violated any state or federal drinking water standards. Yet half a million people were sickened and a hundred dead.

Milwaukee is served by two water treatment plants that pull source water from Lake Michigan. Before the outbreak, severe spring storms caused the lake's suspended sediment load (turbidity) to rise, which increased the amount of particulates passing through the plants. This upsurge in particulates also allowed more *Cryptosporidium* oocysts, a dormant form of the parasite that is so small it can pass through most filtration beds, to enter the public water supply. The hard and egglike oocyst is also resistant to chlorine and other disinfectants, but once ingested, it hatches and infects the human gut wall.

Cryptosporidium causes severe diarrhea and is related to the malaria parasite, *Plasmodium malariae*. Yet unlike *Plasmodium*, which is transmitted through mosquitoes, *Cryptosporidium* completes its life cycle within a single host. This results in the oocyst form, which is excreted and transmitted to a new host in drinking water. Since the 1993 Milwaukee outbreak, USEPA has issued guidance to water purveyors on how to protect against *Cryptosporidium* under the Interim Enhanced Surface Water Treatment Rule.[15] The rule established performance standards for filters in drinking water treatment to restrict turbidity levels. This decreases the risk of infection by limiting the level of particulate material and oocysts in the finished water. Yet the more sobering aspect of USEPA's decision to manage *Cryptosporidium* primarily via a "treatment technique" instead of an MCL is that there are neither technical nor economically feasible methods to measure such pathogens in either the source water or the treated water. These are research and analytical challenges for the future.

Gloria Post, a toxicologist in Science and Research, and author of many of the Basis and Background documents for the original A-280 contaminants, stays abreast of these emerging chemicals for NJDEP and advises the Water Quality Institute on their toxicological importance. Recently, she specifically alerted the institute and urged the USEPA to develop drinking water MCLs for a number of these chemicals of concern, including perfluorooctanoic acid, or PFOA. Perfluorooctanoic acid is a synthetic chemical that does not occur naturally in the environment. Companies use PFOA to make fluoropolymers, substances with special properties that have thousands of important manufacturing and industrial applications, including fire resistance and the ability to repel oil, stains, grease, and water. They are used to provide nonstick surfaces on cookware and waterproof, breathable membranes for clothing.

In 2004, USEPA's Office of Enforcement and Compliance Assurance took administrative action against DuPont de Nemours and Company (DuPont), one of the main producers of PFOA, charging that DuPont illegally withheld evidence for twenty years that PFOA endangered human health and the environment.[16] In 2005, DuPont paid $10.25 million in damages for violating federal environmental statutes, which is the largest civil administrative penalty USEPA has ever obtained. Subsequently, on January 9, 2009, USEPA issued a drinking water MCL advisory value for PFOA at 0.4 micrograms per liter.[17]

In New Jersey, however, the issue of perfluorooctanoic acid in drinking water became increasingly important before USEPA acted. In 2004, PFOA was found in two New Jersey public water systems at concentrations up to 0.19 micrograms per liter. Subsequently, a larger study of twenty-three water suppliers in 2006 detected PFOA in fifteen of them, or 65 percent of the systems. To assess the significance of these data, Gloria Post calculated a health-based drinking water concentration that would be protective for lifetime exposure to PFOA at 0.04 micrograms per liter.[18] This NJDEP number is ten times lower and more protective than USEPA's advisory number of 0.4 micrograms per liter. Currently NJDEP and USEPA are in discussions as to which number should be used. Many in the federal agency and the academic toxicology community argue that NJDEP's health advisory for drinking water is based on defensible science and that the more protective MCL is warranted.

The Future of Safe Drinking Water

Safe drinking water to a certain extent is taken for granted in the United States. The water supplies are often out of sight, far away, or deep underground. In addition, the treatment technologies are often unknown to most consumers except those who read the detailed explanations of their water quality in reports delivered periodically by their purveyors. Robert Morris, a physician and environmental epidemiologist who serves as an adviser to USEPA, the Centers for Disease Control, and the President's Cancer Panel on drinking water issues, summarizes the ever-changing dilemma of safeguarding our potable water supplies. He observes: "The operation of our water supplies is, to most of us, invisible. Invisibility encourages complacency. The technology we rely on for treating most of our drinking water is almost a century old and many of our water treatment plants have been in operation since the early twentieth century. In addition, much of the source water pulled into treatment plant intakes today are [sic] already contaminated with recycled sewage, agricultural run-off, and/or industrial waste."[19]

These are sobering thoughts. Yet in addition to these infrastructure concerns we must contend with new and emerging pathogens like *Cryptosporidium* or chemicals like nonylphenol, which require constant vigilance and research to keep abreast of what lies just over the horizon. How will we know what hovers below our radar screens for years without a proper defense? Some of these contaminants are old villains like arsenic; others are surprisingly new. Today we worry about pharmaceuticals like birth control pills (estrogens) and antidepressants flushed down the toilet, which can cause unanticipated health problems. These include endocrine disruption, which can cause population-wide shifts in male-to-female sex ratios in aquatic organisms and perhaps humans as well. In fact, R. Lee Lippincott from Science and Research performed a study with the U.S. Geological Survey to look for the occurrence of pharmaceuticals and other wastewater-related compounds in New Jersey's surface water supplies. They sampled thirty streams downstream of potential sources of human wastewater and found that more than 90 percent of the samples contained one or more of the target compounds. These included caffeine, pharmaceuticals, flame retardants and plasticizers, fragrance compounds, steroids, and pesticides.[20] The number and concentration of target compounds correlated significantly with the percentage of stream-flow contributed by sewage treatment plants, indicating, as expected, that the likely source for many of these compounds was the effluent from the wastewater treatment process. This finding points to the unsettling conclusion that a new threat awaits us in terms of water treatment technology and the need for more aggressive wastewater technologies to remove these emerging contaminants from the source water.

Since 1971, the Centers for Disease Control, the USEPA, and the Council of State and Territorial Epidemiologists have maintained a collaborative surveillance system for the occurrences and causes of waterborne-disease outbreaks. This monitoring is the primary source of data concerning the scope and effects of waterborne diseases in the United States. In a report released in 2002, the agencies found that during 1999–2000, there were a total of thirty-nine outbreaks associated with drinking water supplies as recorded by twenty-five states.[21] One of them spanned ten states. The proportion of drinking water outbreaks associated with surface water increased from 12 percent during 1997–1998 to 18 percent in 1999–2000. The CDC noted, however, that the increase in the number of incidents probably reflects improved surveillance and reporting at the local and state level, as well as a true increase in the number of waterborne-disease outbreaks.

It is hoped that things will improve as a result of recently passed federal legislation, constant monitoring vigilance, and continued research that employs innovative analytical methodologies and sampling procedures to identify new contaminants of concern, much as we did at Boonton Reservoir years ago. The application of chemical disinfection and filtration to drinking water in the United States has successfully controlled the transmission of disease-causing organisms (for example, bacterial pathogens) through drinking water supply systems. Waterborne diseases such as typhoid and cholera have been virtually eliminated as a result. Yet we are still vulnerable to waterborne pathogens, as demonstrated by the 1993 *Cryptosporidium* outbreak in Milwaukee.

Disinfection will continue to be a critical element of drinking water treatment, but recent research confirms that disinfection can create its own health risks from disinfectant residuals and disinfection byproducts. As a result of this concern, USEPA in 2002 released interrelated regulations called the M-DBP cluster of rules to control health risks from *both* microbial pathogens and disinfection byproducts. The Long Term 1 Enhanced Surface Water Treatment Rule supplies guidance to purveyors on how to control microbial pathogens (specifically, the protozoan *Cryptosporidium*) while at the same time addressing the risk trade-offs associated with disinfection byproducts.[22] The American Water Works Association, a professional group representing the interests of water purveyors, agrees with the provisions of this rule and points out that the future of water quality will require the multiple barrier method for supplying safe drinking water. This method relies on a multipronged battery of defenses to safeguard potable water, including source water protection, coagulation with sedimentation, filtration, and disinfection. It is highly unlikely that pathogens could get past all four barriers.[23]

The Boonton Reservoir story may be a paradigm for water quality development throughout the United States and the world. And that story demonstrates that we should learn from our mistakes and recognize that research is necessary in any vigilant management strategy for supplying safe drinking water. Many of the professionals I work with are trained to see and measure the workings of a microscopic world filled with chemicals and pathogenic creatures like THMs and *Cryptosporidium*. They worry about organisms so small that special procedures are needed to guess their presence, since they cannot be seen under a microscope. Sometimes we know they are there simply because they graze holes in a lawn of bacteria on a petri dish, much like a herd of cows gone to pasture. Or we pursue toxic molecules so miniscule that only through high-volume sampling can we isolate enough to identify. In hindsight and after seeing all the subsequent issues related to DBPs and *Cryptosporidium*, we must be humble and realize that any regulatory measures we employ may be imperfect and based only on the information available under existing conditions and the limits of current scientific knowledge.

And this lesson should be remembered in our vigilance for other contaminants as well, although the source might be the soil beneath our houses. For in New Jersey this is exactly where the next threat came from, a colorless and odorless subterranean gas that crept into basements and seeped upstairs with deadly consequences. The culprit is radon, and the health threat is radiation poisoning. The discovery of this danger caught New Jersey and the country by surprise in the mid-1980s, as another national emergency played out on our doorstep. This time, though, it affected not just those who lived in a smog-choked city or next to a hazardous waste site. It concerned millions of people who live over naturally occurring uranium deposits. Here in New Jersey it had a name, the Reading Prong geological formation, which begins near Reading, Pennsylvania, and runs under the Delaware River through the Highlands geo-province (and Boonton Reservoir) to end in lower New York State. The radon emergency would force the states and USEPA to consider indoor air pollution for the first time as a new environmental threat. For this threat there was no immediate remedy, since the Clean Air Act passed by Congress dealt only with outside air. Once again, states like Pennsylvania and New Jersey were on their own while the federal agencies played catch-up.

CHAPTER 4

Radiation Protection

I would like to tell you a nonlinear story about my introduction to radiation protection as an occupational and environmental issue. Just as in *Alice in Wonderland*, my journey was fraught with conundrums that pitted logic—with unexpected consequences—against my desire to be a scientist. Physics was the most difficult university subject for me. To some mechanics, the intrinsic forces moving the physical world are as simple to read as the nightly baseball scores. For me it was more like trying to reassemble the family clock after I had pulled it apart as a child to see how it worked. Every piece came away with superb logic on disassembly, but the reconstruction eluded me. It might have been easier to make a time machine than figure out what matched what without a diagram. I could not see the obvious mechanical connections to recreate time's swift passage in a box. I might as well have gone outside and looked at the sun.

Training to become a field biologist, I was more likely to look at the big picture, the great uncertainties in nature surrounding animal instincts as conditioned to habitat, rather than a few pat thermodynamic laws. Yet in spite of this shortcoming, when my wife and I were broke in graduate school and needed money to keep the wolf from the door, it was a job as a radiation safety technician at the University of Pennsylvania that kept us from penury. The Radiation Safety Office was tasked by the federal Nuclear Regulatory Commission to inspect labs and affirm the safe use of radionuclides in every academic and medical department. There was the miniparticle accelerator under the Palestra basketball court that nightly sent neutrinos through unsuspecting fans. In the basement of the university hospital I stumbled on a hermetic molecular biologist who injected isotopic iodine-137 into nanny goats, then studied kidney failure when she subsequently deprived them of essential amino acids. At the physics department I measured isobars of invisible radiation leaking from lead-encased sources of thorium and radium.

This job proved to be the best all-around education that a budding scientist could ever hope for. In my daily inspections I observed every possible permutation of inquiry devised by the scientific community and their unique modes of application to physics, chemistry, and medicine. Each day I went to class carrying my trusty Geiger counter and a pack of toluene-soaked papers to take wipe samples on lab benches. It was a great icebreaker for making new friends, or meeting maniacs, as I chatted with hundreds of curious people who wanted to debate the ethics of dropping the bomb on Hiroshima or the perils of nuclear energy. Some just wanted my useless advice on how granny's latest CAT scan might pan out. I myself relished these willy-nilly amateur discussions but found the more interesting anecdotes coming from the researchers I visited. Some described how radio-pharmaceuticals would become the diagnostic tool of the century (which they did), while others prophesied how the boundaries of physics would be pushed into the development of cheap and safe nuclear fusion reactors (which they were not).

My first environmental experience in radiation protection outside of academia, however, came in 1979 when we heard over the office radio that a nuclear meltdown was underway at the Three Mile Island nuclear power plant. Three Mile Island was just ninety miles upwind of Philadelphia, located just outside of the Pennsylvania state capital of Harrisburg. The nuclear incident was a partial core meltdown of the pressurized water reactor in Unit No. 2, which resulted in the most significant accident in the history of the American commercial nuclear power generating industry.[1] We later learned that the accident could be attributed to a stuck valve in the reactor that was compounded by operator error. Owing to inadequate training and a poorly designed control room, the nuclear event released an estimated forty-three thousand curies of radioactive krypton and twenty curies of the more dangerous and gaseous iodine-131 into the atmosphere. Iodine-131 can cause thyroid cancer at dosages much lower than this.

The "curie," named after the French scientists Marie and Pierre Curie for their famous research into the nature of radioactivity, is a standard measure for the intensity of radioactivity contained in a sample of radioactive material. The basis for the curie is the radioactivity of one gram of radium. A picocurie is one-trillionth of a curie. To put the relative size of one-trillionth into perspective, consider that if Earth were reduced to one-trillionth of its diameter, the "picoEarth" would be smaller in diameter than a speck of dust.[2] USEPA recommends that no one be exposed to concentrations of iodine-131 in excess of one hundred picocuries per cubic meter of air.[3] Needless to say, twenty curies is a lot of radiation.

The U.S. Nuclear Regulatory Commission (NRC) seemed paralyzed during the ensuing five days of the national emergency, trying to simultaneously understand the problem, communicate about the relative risks, and decide whether the accident required a widespread emergency evacuation of those downwind. All of the health physicists in my office at Penn immediately began debating the repercussions if the protective containment around the reactor core cracked and the impact on human populations in the atmospheric fallout zone. I, on the other hand, saw the world much differently, since I had been studying marine biology. I recognized a much bigger issue with more long-term impacts from a meltdown. The reactor was built on Three Mile island in the middle of the Susquehanna River that flows through central Pennsylvania. The Susquehanna is the primary drinking water source for many communities downstream and supplies half the freshwater flow to Chesapeake Bay. The Chesapeake Bay is the largest estuary in the United States and an incredibly complex ecosystem. Its watershed stretches across more than sixty-four thousand square miles, encompassing parts of six states—Delaware, Maryland, New York, Pennsylvania, Virginia, and West Virginia—and the entire District of Columbia. What would happened to Chesapeake Bay, I thought, if the meltdown sent tons of fissionable materials downstream to this waterway, the source of seafood for millions of Americans? It would kill millions of animals outright but also bioaccumulate isotopes in the tissue of those that survived. The half-life for many of these fissionable nuclides was in the hundreds if not thousands of years. We could lose the Chesapeake Bay as a natural resource for generations.

That's when our office received a call from the Nuclear Regulatory Commission in Washington asking for help. The commission was mobilizing all the available assets in Pennsylvania to perform downwind monitoring and to seek advice on plume meteorological calculations. We found out that day that the shortcomings shown in the blockbuster movie *The China Syndrome*, released only twelve days before the accident occurred, were not far off the mark. The 1979 movie thriller with Jack Lemmon, Jane Fonda, and Michael Douglas tells the story of a reporter and a cameraman who discover safety cover-ups at a nuclear power plant. The title refers to the idea put forth by nuclear engineers that if a nuclear plant melted down and breached its containment, it would melt straight through the earth until it reached China.[4] The parallels with the events going on in central Pennsylvania were disheartening and colored our perceptions of the regulator's deliberations over the next few days as we listened to the emergency response personnel in Harrisburg on our office shortwave radio and helped plan with the potential evacuation of the fifth largest city in the United States.

Uncertainty reigned in those chaotic days as the Three Mile Island disaster paralyzed the nation with fears of nuclear fallout and communities across the United States mobilized for safety reviews at every nuclear plant. Even President Jimmy Carter, a former nuclear engineer in the U.S. Navy, visited the reactor facility to calm the nation. Eventually the TMI accident was contained and no further amount of radioactive material was released to the environment. Overnight, though, nuclear energy as an acceptable technology for safe electrical power generation became a target for anti-nuke environmentalists and apple-pie politicians alike. Following the TMI calamity, nuclear power plant construction in the United States virtually ended, a self-imposed industrial moratorium that lasts until this day.

This may change in the twentieth-first century, however, as politicians debate weaning the country from oil addiction and the negative global warming effects of fossil fuel combustion. Only time will tell. My own belief is that nuclear energy, if managed wisely and with proper regulatory oversight, is a safe and efficient means for the United States to become energy independent. A cautionary note, however, is that we must not neglect the concomitant need for a national high-level radioactive waste disposal strategy. Currently, spent nuclear fuel rods are typically stored onsite at each generating station with no centralized depository to receive them. For more than twenty years the nuclear industry has been waiting for the U.S. Department of Energy to complete its studies at Yucca Mountain, Nevada, designated by past federal administrations as the nation's only high-level nuclear waste repository. This hiatus may prove all for naught, however, as President Obama recently announced that he would not fund further studies at the Yucca Mountain site.

The project has already burned through $7.7 billion. It was supposed to start accepting spent material from the nation's operating nuclear reactors (now numbering 104) in 1998. The logic that Congress used in proposing the siting of the facility at the heart of a desert mountain, and one thousand feet underground, was that it was better and safer than the current practice of spreading storage over 121 above-ground sites located within seventy-five miles of more than 161 million people in thirty-nine states.[5] President Obama's administration has not proposed an alternative location for the waste repository and will seek other potential host states. Unfortunately, the fact that it took an act of Congress to get it sited in Nevada, and twenty years of studies and delays, without accepting one ounce of high-level radioactive waste does not bode well for a solution to this vexing environmental problem.

We have four nuclear power plants in New Jersey, including the Oyster Creek Nuclear Generating Station—the oldest in the country—on the Atlantic coast. The others are clustered along the Delaware River and are called Hope

Creek, Salem 1, and Salem 2. New Jersey ranks tenth in power generation among thirty-one states with nuclear capacity. In fact, nuclear power is the leading source of electricity here. Therefore, if you study the environment in this state, radiation is always a concern. In fact, one of my fish studies at Science and Research was to place baskets of the commercially important hard clam, *Mercenaria mercenaria* in the hot water plume emanating from the Oyster Creek Nuclear Generating Station on Barnegat Bay and analyze the tissue for radionuclides. Yet the nuclear industry sent me another curve-ball on a par with TMI that affected my research plans. This time though it came from a power plant a world away.

As part of this Oyster Creek study, Bruce Ruppel and I collected more than a thousand hard clams from another bay to the south and then carefully weighed, measured, and marked each shell with a big black identifying number before transplanting them into three locations around Barnegat Bay. We then retrieved some of the clams monthly to see if these filter-feeding organisms bioaccumulated any radionuclides from the plant's discharge plume. We had convinced NJDEP's radiation laboratory to analyze our samples, which were collected from three sites throughout the bay. However, on April 26, 1986, as we dropped our clams off at the lab, I found the technicians glued to a portable television set watching a spectacular fire in the Soviet Union at a place called Chernobyl.

The Chernobyl nuclear power plant in the Ukrainian Soviet Socialist Republic exploded that day, causing the "graphite moderator" to catch on fire, which sent plumes of radioactive smoke high into the atmosphere. The firemen, at odds on how to put out a radioactive fire, brought in helicopters and repeatedly dumped liquefied concrete until the run-away reactor was buried beneath an ugly ziggurat. Unfortunately, the plume of highly radioactive smoke blew over an extensive area, dropping an estimated four hundred times more fallout than had been released by the atomic bombing of Hiroshima, Japan, in 1945.[6] Chernobyl, by international consensus, remains the worst nuclear power plant disaster in history. The reason for this had to do with engineering. Unlike most Western-designed nuclear power plants, the Soviet reactors had no containment vessel over them, so when the roof collapsed, it exposed the fission pile, sending radioactivity high into the atmosphere on the rising heat and smoke. This plume drifted over large parts of the Soviet Union, Europe, Asia, the Arctic, and as far as North America. Fifty-six people died fighting the fire, many as a result of radiation poisoning and thyroid cancer. It is estimated that an additional four thousand cancer deaths occurred among the approximately six hundred thousand most highly exposed people. A chilling legacy to this nuclear accident is the realization that since the end of the Soviet Union, there remain dozens of nuclear reactors designed just like the one at Chernobyl both in the former Soviet republics and in eastern European bloc countries.

My own regret about the Chernobyl fire was more personal. The accident increased the worldwide background levels of the exact radioisotopes my research was measuring. This created a problem for us, since we now needed a means to measure and somehow subtract this increase in background radiation from our measurements beside the Oyster Creek nuclear plant. With no accurate way to make this measurement, I decided to abandon the Barnegat Bay research and pursue something different. Little did I realize that it would take me even farther back in time, past the rise of commercial nuclear power and even the atomic bomb, to an era when this country's legacy of mismanaged radiation protection included painting objects with radium to make them glow in the dark.

The Radium Girls of South Orange, New Jersey

My wife's Uncle Nick is one of those unique individuals whom every family seems to cherish. Although not related by blood to my wife, Bernadette, having married her mother's sister, he is a central and loving figure in our lives. When Bernadette wanted to learn how to drive, it was Uncle Nick who came to the rescue, because her dad worked nights as a firefighter. When she banged up his car on the first outing, it was their secret—Aunt Barbara is still in the dark about it to this day. Later, when our kids came along and Bernadette's mother died young, it was Aunt Barbara and Uncle Nick who became surrogate grandparents. We often celebrate Thanksgiving and Christmas at their house.

Nick loved our kids so much that he asked my son, Dan, to accompany him on a cross-country road trip to Las Vegas that they have not stopped talking about. When my daughter, Laura, needed softball coaching, it was Uncle Nick, a famous South Jersey umpire, who stepped in and taught her how to cock a throw from behind her ear and peg a runner at home from the outfield. His quirky sense of humor always managed to rise up at family gatherings. Presents were delivered with mock long-winded speeches, and some gifts were tricks, like the roll of money all taped together that Dan had to unravel or the briefcase he gave Laura along with a multiple-choice quiz that provided the lock combination.

One year he hid Laura's Christmas present and had her look for it with a treasure map. This took the whole family throughout the house following clues and then outside, where Laura found a shovel in the backyard for digging up a treasure chest filled with South American gold Krugerrands. Nick is one of the most cherished and loved people by those fortunate to know him, but to some extent he is lucky to be alive. Not because of anything that happened to him but because his mother, Mafalda Cuccarese, lived long enough to give birth to him after working for the infamous United States Radium Corporation in the 1930s.

The history of industrialists' indifference to worker safety was always axiomatic in New Jersey's working-class neighborhoods. The epitome of this indifference can be found in the bizarre story of the Radium Girls. Uncle Nick's mother was one of the innocent victims of that terrible moment in American industrial and environmental history. A young Italian American woman from Union City, New Jersey, she got a job with United States Radium along with hundreds of other women, many too fresh to this country to ask questions about their employers. Mafalda was hired to work at the dial plant, where she applied radium-based paint to the faces of watches and later altimeters used in military airplanes.

From 1917 to 1926, the United States Radium Corporation extracted and purified radium from carnotite ore to produce luminous paints in Orange, which were marketed under the brand name Undark. As a defense contractor, the company was a major supplier of radioluminescent watches to the military. Its plant in New Jersey employed more than a hundred workers, mainly women, to paint these radium-lit watch faces and instruments. The women were directed to handle the radium while the owners and their scientists, familiar with the effects of radium, carefully avoided any exposure to it themselves. The chemists at the plant used lead screens, masks, and tongs. An estimated four thousand workers were hired by corporations in the United States and Canada to paint watch faces with radium.

The Radium Ladies received no training or education as to the serious health hazards associated with radioactive materials. Therefore, Mafalda, like the many new women on the production line, wetted her small paintbrush between her lips whenever she sought a fine tip for the delicate work of painting tiny watch hands. Reportedly, the Radium Girls painted their nails, teeth, and faces with the deadly paint produced at the factory, sometimes to surprise their boyfriends or husbands when the lights went out. The radioactive paint coated their gums as they swallowed deadly doses of bone-seeking nuclides in the luminescent paint. It wasn't long, however, before the women started to suffer. Mouth and throat cancer, lung cancer, bone cancer—all hastened the early demise of these poor immigrant workers. Yet the cover-up that followed and the denial of the U.S. government's involvement in this enterprise opened a new page on the irresponsible nature of the military-industrial complex.[7] Many of the women later began to suffer from anemia, bone fractures, and necrosis of the jaw. The ingestion of the paint by the women, brought about while licking the

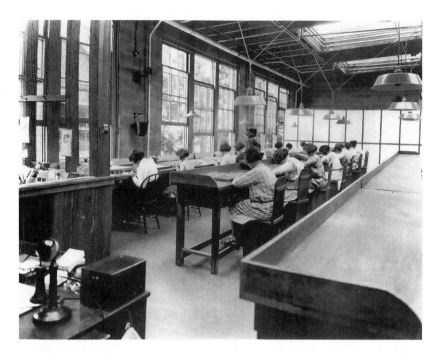

Figure 5. "Radium Girls" working in a U.S. Radium Corporation factory. (Source: U.S. Environmental Protection Agency.)

brushes, resulted in a condition called "radium jaw," a painful swelling and porosity of the upper and lower jaws, and ultimately led to the deaths of many of these women. United States Radium and other watch-dial companies rejected claims that the afflicted workers were suffering from exposure to radium. Worker deaths were attributed by medical professionals to other causes—even syphilis—in an attempt to smear the reputations of the women.[8]

One plant worker, Grace Fryer, decided to sue, but it took her two years to find a lawyer willing to challenge United States Radium and its federal government backers. Five factory workers, dubbed the Radium Girls, joined the suit. The litigation and media sensation surrounding the case established legal precedents and triggered the enactment of regulations governing labor safety standards. In fact, the right of individual workers to sue corporations for damages resulting from labor abuse was established because of this case (though the combined settlement for the Radium Girls was only $10,000).

Subsequently, Robley D. Evans measured exhaled radon and radium excreted by former dial painters and in 1941, using data from 1,346 subjects, established a National Bureau of Standards tolerance level for radium in the workplace of 0.1 microcuries. In addition, the radiation poisoning of the

Radium Girls served a legal precedent. Evans's study set a legal standard for what is known in labor law as a baseline of "provable suffering." That is, through their suffering a provable link was established between the internal doses of radiation and cancer. The Radium Ladies' case also led to the passage of a congressional bill in 1949 that made all occupational diseases compensable for damages and extended the time during which workers could discover illnesses and make a claim. This was important because environmental-based cancers may have a latency period of many decades before a tumor appears.

Ironically, in 1928, Sabin von Sochocky, the inventor of radium-based paint, died of aplastic anemia resulting from his exposure to radioactive materials. He became a victim of his own invention. Of course, this was of little value to the thousands of Radium Girls, including Uncle Nick's mom, Mafalda, who died of jaw cancer years later. They all went back to their lives and sought other employment, not realizing that a ticking radioactive time bomb had been deposited in their bones.

United States Radium: The Superfund Site

The United States Radium Corporation processed approximately two tons of carnotite ore every day for the eleven years that the plant operated, which created numerous uranium tailings spread around the plant. The ore, mined in Colorado and Utah, was shipped east to South Orange, New Jersey, by train. It typically contained about 4 percent uranium dioxide. The extraction process was extremely wasteful, as a ton of carnotite ore yielded only about five grams of radium. As a result, large amounts of radioactive waste piles called "tailings" were discarded on the plant property and at various satellite properties surrounding it. The ore processing facility closed in 1926, although the dial painting operations continued until approximately 1940, when the company moved to New York City.[9]

The inhalation of radon gas is of special concern for any residents with houses built on top of uranium tailings. In fact, radon gas is the major source of background radiation exposure in the United States. The decay of radon-222 releases extremely radioactive alpha particles and other types of radiation. Alpha particles are highly unstable and unusual atomic configurations composed of two protons and two neutrons, which if inhaled or ingested into the body can cause massive tissue damage. The many short-lived atoms into which a radon atom decays are collectively called radon daughters or progeny. The radon progeny float around in the air during their few moments of existence, often attached to dust particles, which if inhaled can irradiate the lung wall, damaging the tissue to create a protocancerous cell as a prerequisite to lung cancer.

In 1979, the United States Radium plant property was unearthed as a potential environmental threat during a desktop file review of former uranium processing sites in New Jersey. In 1981, an aerial sensor survey confirmed radioactivity in the soils at the former facility and surprisingly in residential sites surrounding it. Apparently during the intervening years of suburban expansion many houses were placed atop the tailings. NJDEP requested that USEPA place the plant site on the National Priorities List as a Superfund site, as well as these peripheral properties. The United States Radium Superfund area of concern includes the former plant site and more than 350 residential, light industrial, and commercial properties located within a few miles of the abandoned ore processing facility. In December 1983, NJDEP went public and announced that more than one hundred homes in Montclair, Glen Ridge, and West Orange contained unsafe levels of radon from radioactive fill under the houses. Then, with very little public input, NJDEP senior management decided not to tear the houses down or buy and demolish them outright as USEPA had recently done with dioxin-contaminated properties in Times Beach, Missouri. Instead the state opted to perform an in-place remedial demonstration project on twelve of the houses in Montclair. This involved jacking them up onto supportive pilings, removing the radon-contaminated material from underneath, and then replacing it with clean fill before dropping the houses back into place at a total cost of $8 million. If it succeeded, NJDEP planned on carrying out the same procedures on the other 138 radon-contaminated houses for a total cost of nearly $100 million.

The fatal flaw in this logic was what to do with the excavated dirt. As work began in early 1985, Richard "Dick" Dewling, who had replaced Bob Hughey as commissioner of NJDEP, planned on sending it to a waste disposal facility in Nevada (after short-term storage in New Jersey). Unfortunately, the governor of Nevada did not like the idea, nor did the locals living near the disposal facility, resulting in separate lawsuits in federal court to prohibit the transfer, which they won. New Jersey now had fifteen thousand barrels of excavated radioactive soil piling up onsite but nowhere to send it. Thus began a political game of hot potato, driven by a not-in-my-back-yard (NIMBY) sentiment that whiplashed across the state from one municipality to another. Each town refused to be a storage site. This resulted in a clamor that converted even the most complacent of New Jerseyans into rabid social activists mobilizing to protect home and family. There were soccer moms lying down in front of trucks, local activists descending on Trenton to picket the State House dressed as mushroom clouds, and even little babies dressed in handmade radon costumes with Xs painted across the spinning electrons.

I became involved in some of these deliberations on what to do with the radioactive dirt as a science adviser along with my boss, Thomas Burke. They were typically those "cast of thousands" emergency response meetings in the commissioner's conference room, with two dozen people seated at a huge mahogany table and another two dozen sitting in chairs along the walls, with representatives from every operating division in the department. It was during one of these meetings that Commissioner Dewling wanted to know why we couldn't just take the radioactive soil, fly it out over the ocean, and dump it into the sea. Serendipitously, I had an answer to this question, but not because of the Montclair situation.

A few months earlier Science and Research was asked to help with a putative cancer cluster investigation in Cape May near South Jersey's peninsular tip. At the public meeting a local claimed that the U.S. Air Force had run an airfield during World War II near where the cancer cluster was now centered. He also alleged that after the war the Air Force stored radioactive waste on the site from the Manhattan Project, which was placed in drums, loaded onto Air Force bombers and dumped offshore at some unspecified distance. The Manhattan Project was the code name for a vast, yet secret, industrial project related to the manufacture of nuclear weapons.[10] NJDEP knew that there were, indeed, a half-dozen Manhattan Project sites in New Jersey where uranium-235 had been processed for the war effort, so this claim was taken seriously. Therefore Tom Burke sent Science and Research's Site Investigation Unit (SIU) down to Lower Township to look around.

They found no military airport or radioactive soils in the area, just a patch of pine barrens overgrown with thick shrubbery. Yet the field crew who performed the reconnaissance sensed it might have been a strategic military site because of the metallic debris scattered throughout the woods. A few hours later, Randy England from the SIU came back into the director's suite and slammed a large conical piece of metal on Tom Burke's desk. It was the nose cone cover of a Navy bomber engine, which had been left to rot in the swamps of Jersey. We subsequently learned that a Naval Air Station had been built in Lower Township on an existing municipal airport in 1942. It was used to train naval aviators for carrier duty, with as many as 443 officers and 2,497 enlisted men onsite throughout the war and 154 planes. In 1946, the Navy returned control of the station to Cape May County, which currently serves as its commercial airport.[11]

There was no record of radioactive waste being stored or disposed of at the site, however. Therefore finding the lost naval air station did not move us one jot closer to affirming the claim that radioactive waste was dumped in the ocean from that location. Yet because of the SIU's investigation, and my research into the Manhattan Project in New Jersey, I knew and informed Commissioner Dewling that it was currently forbidden by federal law and international treaty to dump radioactive wastes into the ocean and that it would take an act of Congress to get approval.

Yet the shocker at this meeting was yet to come! That's when a representative from the Division of Radiation suggested that we simply entomb the dirt at one of those abandoned Intercontinental Ballistic Missile (ICBM) silos in Fort Dix, like the one that was already filled with radioactive waste from the fire. "What fire?" the commissioner asked. I remember there was this long, communal held breath in the room, as everyone just stared at him. It became apparent that no one else knew about this military secret.

The "Fort Dix nuclear accident" occurred in 1960 during the height of the Cold War with Russia. ICBMs were placed in remote locations along both seaboards to intercept, or launch, nuclear attacks. Unknown to the citizenry during the late 1950s and early 1960s, missiles were placed in underground silos around most major American cities, this as a last line of defense against nuclear attacks. In hindsight it seems kind of incongruous to position nuclear bombs around American cities as a *defense*, but that was the nature of Cold War logic. The fire started on June 7, 1960, in a nonnuclear explosion in Missile Shelter 204, which burned uncontrollably for thirty minutes.[12] The force of the explosion destroyed the missile, sending its plutonium-containing warhead and portions of the shelter roof skyward, as flames rose to twenty feet and black smoke blanketed the area. Firefighting crews responded and contained the fire with water, much of which ran into a tributary of the Toms River, while the smoke blew into the surrounding forest.

The missile contained not only weapons-grade plutonium but also enriched uranium and tritium. Although no nuclear explosion occurred, the force of the explosion damaged the warhead, releasing some of its nuclear material with the smoke. The missile shelter and the immediate area around it had radiation readings of greater than 2 million counts per minute (background is generally less than 5 to 10 counts per minute). The missile wreckage was subsequently removed and disposed of offsite, while the silo was filled with the contaminated soil and sealed with concrete. The entire Fort Dix ICBM facility was deactivated in 1972, and all the missiles were removed from their shelters to other locations, although the Missile Shelter 204 site was remediated and is still under the control of the U.S. Air Force.

Commissioner Dewling subsequently did ask for military help. He approached the U.S. Army to transport the Montclair soils to Fort Dix, and mixed with clean soil for lowering the radioactivity. The Department of Defense said no, claiming it was a nonmilitary issue. I thought this disingenuous of them since it was United States Radium luminescent paint that coated most of the Air Force's flight instruments throughout World Wars I and II.[13] By December 1986, Dewling was taking so much heat over the perceived closed-door nature of his decision making that he appointed a Radon/Radium Advisory Board. Its ten members included representatives from municipalities, environmental watch groups, and state regulatory agencies. They were tasked with suggesting places to dispose of the soils with a carrot of $6 million to any community willing to take the thousands of drums of soil. No takers stepped forward. At one desperate point, a Wildlife Management Area in the federally protected Pinelands Preservation area was suggested. That got the conservationists up in arms as well.

Finally a solution was found, which involved sending the waste to Oak Ridge National Laboratories in Tennessee for $4 million dollars. There it was mixed with highly radioactive material and then sent to a federally approved depository in Richland, Washington.[14] In essence, the low-level waste had to be blended with high-level radioactive waste for a much higher disposal cost. By the middle of 1988, three years after the excavation began, all the barrels were removed from Montclair. USEPA, however, would not complete remediation of the other two hundred United States Radium sites until 2005 for a total cost of $250 million.

In his book *Elements of Risk: The Politics of Radon* on the political aspects of the 1980s radon scare, Leonard Cole, a professor of political science at Rutgers University, looked critically at how NJDEP handled itself during this crisis.[15] He argued that Commissioner Dewling and Governor Kean seemed unwilling to accept the blame for the Montclair remediation demonstration project. He noted that Dewling believed politicians and the press stoked a NIMBY mentality, which was "the single major cause of environmental gridlock" and that Governor Kean agreed with him.[16] Cole admits that exaggerated fears doubtless helped undermine what may have been a scientifically sensible plan but added: "Popular rejection was largely primed by the DEP's manner of informing, that is, it failed to consult and educate the local communities *before* announcing its policies." Cole concluded: "The Montclair experience is unarguably a consequence of a radon mitigation program not carefully thought out. It is a reminder of the need for circumspection; that well-intended policies may lead to terrible consequences."

THE READING PRONG AND RADON

The last chapter in my odyssey through radiation protection brought me back to the seemingly pristine forests of the Highlands in New Jersey. This is the same geologic province that contains Boonton Reservoir, where I had conducted my drinking water studies a few years before. Now the issue that confronted us was much bigger and tougher to address and would require presenting to the public the same kind of risk information that got the state into so much trouble with the United States Radium cleanup in Montclair. It became a litmus test for NJDEP to see if we had learned our lesson on communicating risk and successfully getting people to institute environmentally safe practices in the home. For it appeared that the source of the radon was beneath their feet this time, naturally occurring, and as deadly to them as living inside a uranium mine.

In December 1984, while NJDEP was still planning its pilot study for digging up and remediating the twelve Montclair houses, Stanley Watras, an engineer assigned to the Limerick nuclear power plant under construction in Pennsylvania, set the radiation monitors off. This might have been an understandable event if he was exiting the plant after a full day's work, except for the fact that the nuclear rods had not been delivered yet and the alarm went off as he *entered* the plant. He asked Limerick's owner, the Philadelphia Electric Company (PECO), to check the radiation levels at his house a few miles from the plant. There technicians discovered the highest concentration of the colorless, odorless, and tasteless radon gas ever found in the United States.[17]

The Pennsylvania Department of Environmental Resources estimated that by living in the radon-tainted house for one year, Watras and his wife, Diane, had been exposed to the equivalent of 455,000 chest X-rays, which increased their risk of contracting lung cancer by 13 to 14 percent.[18] They immediately vacated the house and did not move back in until PECO completed a $32,000 cleanup. The Watras house, as geologists later determined, sat on the Reading Prong, a granite formation that extends like a river of stone from near Reading, Pennsylvania, on through a wide section of northern New Jersey and into a narrow band of New York State and Connecticut. This whole formation was known by mining operators to have high uranium content.

Both Pennsylvania and New Jersey moved quickly to deal with this finding by mapping out the thousands of houses that lay atop the Reading Prong and sampling the interiors for radon. New Jersey was primed to perform this work because of the increased monitoring capabilities we had acquired during the United States Radium investigation. Yet we were surprised by the results. NJDEP's health physicists estimated that roughly 30 percent of all the houses over the Reading Prong in New Jersey had radon levels that exceeded a USEPA-calculated action guideline of 4 picocuries of radiation per liter of air. In response, the state legislature passed two laws in 1986 appropriating more funds to sample and locate areas of radon risk, to develop remedial strategies, and to determine whether there were any measurable relationships between elevated lung cancer incidence and radon levels in contaminated homes.[19] The mapping and sampling was done by NJDEP with help from the health department. At the time, we knew very little about the pathways and exposures of radon in a nonmining context. Don Deieso, the NJDEP assistant commissioner in charge of the studies admitted at the time: "We do not adequately understand the scientific principles governing radon. Pathways into the home, geological factors and remedial techniques remain in large part a mystery."[20]

Science and Research helped distill this information and focus it into regulatory responses. We organized an Indoor Air Pollution–Radon Workshop at Ramapo State College in the Reading Prong area, where experts from all over the country came to speak and give advice. We also held a series of public outreach sessions with small groups, using some of the risk communication strategies we had developed. Peter Sandman, a professor from Rutgers University who coauthored a risk communication guidance manual for NJDEP, assembled a radon panel for the department, composed of physicists, journalists, and health professionals who were given the task of devising uniform messages targeted at homeowners for allaying their panic while at the same time mobilizing them to test and mitigate their homes, if necessary. An immediate problem was a lack of test kits, as well as snake-oil charlatans who sprang up like weeds to offer door-to-door, supposedly accurate, radon home testing apparatus. Many of these turned out to be no more than mayonnaise jars stuffed with litmus paper.

The second New Jersey bill established funding for NJDEP to develop a licensing program for both testing and mitigation consultants. As further testing in New Jersey proceeded, we became aware that homes outside the Reading Prong had elevated radon levels as well. We declared radon a statewide health issue and recommended that all homeowners should test for radon and, if levels were elevated, to consider remediation. This produced a new wrinkle in our investigation. Realtors began calling NJDEP for the results in houses we had sampled for radon. Potential buyers in northern New Jersey wanted to make these results a prerequisite for sale, not so much for public health reasons but for the potential drawdown on the resale value if radon mitigation was needed to make a future sale. As a result, the state legislature passed a bill making real estate transactions contingent on a radon test and required an escrow account set up with funds allocated by the seller to mitigate if testing revealed concentrations of 4 or more picocuries of radon per liter of air.

Subsequent to the Reading Prong emergency NJDEP created a Radon Program in its Bureau of Environmental Radiation, which regulates radon testing firms and mitigators and conducts extensive outreach to the citizens of

New Jersey to inform them of the risks. In 2008, the bureau released statistics that showed approximately six million people in New Jersey living in moderate- to high-risk radon areas, with 2.4 million homes in those areas still needing to be tested. The good news is that the radon message is out and understood: more than two thousand public schools have been tested (51 percent in the state) and more than four thousand child-care centers, which are now required by regulation to test every five years. In addition, 60 percent of the homes mitigated had radon levels reduced to 1 picocurie per liter, or less, and 84 percent of the homes mitigated reduced to 2 picocuries per liter, or less. So effective has NJDEP's Radon Communication Program become that in 2007 the USEPA presented it with a Radon Leaders Saving Lives Award, noting that New Jersey was selected because it "demonstrated quantifiable results for radon mitigations and radon resistant new construction; high performing collaborations; and a core capacity to sustain results into the future."[21]

THE FUTURE

I could never have envisioned my own future back in 1979 when I joined the Radiation Safety Office at the University of Pennsylvania—a decision that impelled my career into a winding trajectory through nuclear power plant disasters, the Manhattan Project, exploding ICBMs, the Radium Ladies, and the precedent-setting moments in radiation regulation for indoor air pollution and hazardous site remediation. Along the way I learned a lot about radiation as yet another possible source of my brother's leukemia. For along with benzene, ionizing radiation is one of the strongest environmental leukogens. Perhaps it was Joe's misfortune to grow up during the Cold War, when aboveground nuclear testing of hydrogen bombs was at its highest. This and the coincident fallout of leukemia-causing radionuclides, like that from the plume over Chernobyl, might have influenced the onset of his cancer. But no one can say definitively that's what occurred, for millions of others survived the same fallout. It might be that only those with a genetic predisposition to the carcinogenic radiation became symptomatic, a game of nuclear dice played out on a worldwide scale, with unsuspecting human lives the environmental stakes.

I look back on my fear of failing physics in college now and find that in spite of its arcane formulas of subatomic particles and nuclear fission that it offered some simple philosophical tools to support an environmental detective. For it was Isaac Newton who proposed a new dynamic and mechanical description of the world in which energy and motion are characterized by acceleration, inertia, and the concept of conservation of momentum. And perhaps it is in his concept of momentum, with events moving ever forward, that I find a simple explanation, one that makes the universe understandable to me. Even such a small part of the universe as New Jersey.

Newton's first law states that "a body remains at rest or moves in a straight line of constant velocity as long as no external forces act upon it." He called this lack of momentum "inertia." Inertia is a good metaphor for government bureaucracy, burdened as it is with meaningful but often unenforceable rules that move inexorably in one direction without the means for recalibration unless there is some sort of tragic emergency like TMI, United States Radium, or the Reading Prong.

Newton's third law is perhaps the most famous and my favorite. It states that "for every action there is an equal and opposite reaction." This fundamental concept of opposites could stand as a paradigm for environmentalism. The world is a balancing act of protons and electrons holding the material universe together. My professional life as a researcher is perhaps a momentary pulse of energy, pushing back with science against bureaucracy and public disinterest to create a counterbalancing effect of environmental protection for the citizens of New Jersey.

To some extent this pushing back has occurred repeatedly over the years, taking me to unusual places that few citizens see—mostly to cities distressed by too much pollution, too many people in too small a space, and few environmental regulations. This lack of regulation before 1970 allowed companies like United States Radium and many others to blithely walk away from tons of hazardous debris. Many old factories were abandoned as their owners went bankrupt. Regulators call these "orphaned sites," since there is no parent company or owner to pay for the cleanup. Many of them presented significant technical and sociological difficulties. Indeed, working to develop mitigation and cleanup strategies for these abandoned sites became a problem that Science and Research was often asked to engage. Thus, over the next decades we worked on some of the most difficult hazardous waste sites, filled with myriad contaminants with tongue-twisting names like hexavalent chromium, azo dye, or tetrachloro-dibenzo-dioxin, that often challenged both our ability to detect and remove them. In addition, many of these sites were in cities filled with street urchins that reminded me of my own neighborhood near the Junction in Jersey City. There we found the businessmen and the politicians too, those who often thought it appropriate to dump toxic wastes wherever they wished and those who were paid to ignore it.

CHAPTER 5

Environmental Crime

When presidents and presidential candidates came to Jersey City to speak at public rallies, my father was often assigned to guard them. He assumed this had something to do with his six foot, four-inch frame, which allowed him to look out over the crowd like a towering Praetorian Guard. I have a front-page photo of him guarding John Fitzgerald Kennedy in his run for the presidency and another of him with Richard Nixon. I was too young to see him escort President Kennedy, but I do remember when he escorted President Nixon onto the Saint Peter's College campus that I was attending in the 1960s. And what a circus it was!

I remember Dad hovering over Nixon's sweating face as he waded through a massive crowd into our auditorium filled with antiwar protestors, shrieking fans, and fawning Jesuits. One of the antiwar activists held up a sign with an unflattering picture of Nixon and the adage, "Would you buy a used car from this man?" Another sign held up by a Black Panther—in the requisite Huey Newton uniform of black leather and wrap-around shades—was a poster of a pregnant black woman with the candidate's slogan, "Nixon's the One!" printed across her extended belly.

Politics in Jersey City was rough and always filled with street theater, the historically corrupted nature of our hometown politics making it extremely difficult to get anything done without the attendant carnival atmosphere. The term "pay-to-play" may have been invented by William "Boss" Tweed in Tammany Hall, the political machine across the river in New York City, but it quickly marched into Jersey under the guidance of Frank ("I am the law!") Hague, the autocratic leader of the New Jersey Democratic Party. Even Franklin Delano Roosevelt came hat-in-hand to Hague for delivering a majority at the polls so he could win his first New Deal presidency.[1] So complete was Roosevelt's win in 1932 that Hague was rewarded with money to build (with extortion) a massive medical center complex in town with a maternity wing that Frank named after his mother, Margaret. With typical élan and a sense of invulnerability before the law, Hague then had a penthouse apartment built on the top floor where he enthroned his revered mother with the best view of the New York skyline for its day.

Frank Hague served an unparalleled eight consecutive terms as the mayor of Jersey City from 1917 to 1947, including the critical years of the Great Depression and World War II. At his death, he was reportedly worth $10 million, even though his city salary never exceeded $8,500 a year. So complete was graft under the Hague organization that my father had to donate every year to the Democratic Party fundraisers, whether he voted Republican or not, just to keep his job. In addition, his gun, his uniform, even his shoes had to be purchased from distributors who routinely kicked-back payoffs to the Hague machine. My father was so paranoid about being perceived as anything but a loyal Democrat that if anyone asked him whom he was voting for, he would always say with a chuckle, "Mickey Mouse!" He knew that if it ever got back the ward bosses that he voted any other way, he would find himself either on foot patrol in the worst slum of the city, or worse, without a job and seven mouths to feed.

A sign of how corrupt politics could be in Jersey City was the fact that industries typically made deals with city officials to release chemicals into the sewers and to mix toxic slag with building fill. And it was not just small-time grifters and midnight truckers involved in illegal waste disposal. In its most blatant form, legitimate corporations were allowed to do as they pleased while city health inspectors and county engineers looked the other way as industrial waste was dumped into empty lots beside children's playgrounds. This changed in 1976, however, once the cradle-to-grave provisions of the Resource Conservation and Recovery Act (RCRA) became law.[2] RCRA was a federal law managed by USEPA that established mandatory record keeping and inventory manifest tracking by generators and haulers of hazardous waste. It also banned the dumping of these wastes in unregulated or poorly engineered structures such as sanitary landfills and unlined lagoons. Most states, including New Jersey, subsequently enacted their own laws and promulgated regulations that were at least as stringent as the federal regulations.

After 1976, it became harder and more expensive to dispose of toxic waste. Suddenly industrial plant managers found that cheap disposal in landfills and dumps was off-limits and the cost of sending a drum of hazardous waste for treatment or incineration went from a few dollars to hundreds of dollars. As a result, organized crime in New Jersey quickly transitioned from controlling the trash and garbage hauler industries to illegally disposing of hazardous materials. Sensing an opportunity, the Mafia moved in. Mob-controlled garbage trucks started picking up drums at factories and combining regular trash with chemicals as plant managers put on blinders as to what was happening once the material left their premises (even though the drums and paperwork had their corporations' names attached). Small gang wars followed as the lucrative trade was consolidated. Vincent "the Chin" Gigante reportedly put a gun to a competitor's head in 1979 over the rights to illegally dispose of Ford Motor Company's paint wastes from its Ringwood, New Jersey, plant.[3]

The mob found willing compliance in some places where graft was a common part of people's lives in those early, confusing days of environmental regulation. Moral reflexes were different in many factory towns, where corrupt politicians sent messages down to their departmental administrators and the staff they managed to take as much as they could. This created a Wild West way of thinking, where every open-services contract was a big score, especially to someone who only made a few bucks at the bottom of the ladder, like building inspectors or permit writers. Organized crime was much more than municipal graft across the entire New York–New Jersey metropolitan area. Goodfellas, as they called themselves, existed all around New Jersey in the 1970s. My dad and his cop friends called them wiseguys, because that's exactly how they acted, "making wise" as if the world was a joke only they had figured out. And it wasn't just the Italians, for there were many mobs: Irish mobs, Jewish mobs, Chinese *tongs*. Graft flowed upward, and hazardous waste flowed downward for years into the streets and onto our lawns.

One of the most blatant of these mob-controlled hazardous waste sites in New Jersey was the Chemical Control Corporation hazardous waste storage, treatment, and disposal facility in Elizabeth, New Jersey. Starting out as a legitimate business, it was eventually infiltrated by the mob, and hazardous wastes were collected at such a phenomenal rate that the facility could not process the materials fast enough. So the operators just piled them up, making pyramids of drums in gigantic proportions. So high was the pile that when NJDEP inspectors went to visit, they found overflowing pallets placed dangerously close to one another, corrosives stored next to flammables, and acids atop explosives. Eventually, on April 21, 1980, as New Jersey State Police were closing in and NJDEP was cataloging the owners of the millions of drums, a fire started.

The ensuing explosions sent drums of flaming toxic waste spiraling high into the sky for two days as firefighters from a dozen surrounding communities tried to get close enough to spray down the witch's brew of toxic chemicals without breathing the black smoke that engulfed them. Many were overcome and developed lifelong health problems from exposure to the smoke. The drums took off like rockets, some actually landing across the Arthur Kill in

New York. Burning tank cars filled with chemicals rolled into the Elizabeth River, bleeding poisons into New York Harbor for months. The chemical plume, stringent with corrosives, poured over sections of Elizabeth that were evacuated, and thoughts were given to evacuating the entire city.[4] At the time of the fire there were more than fourteen thousand residents living within a mile of the site.

The Chemical Control fire was one of the most dangerous chemical fires ever fought in the United States, and its toxic legacy of leached and windswept pollutants lasted for decades as NJDEP initiated a cleanup of the devastated site and the surrounding waterways. Eventually the mob takeover of the Chemical Control Corporation was traced in part to a wholesale fish dealer at the Fulton Fish Market in lower Manhattan, according to materials presented at a congressional subcommittee investigating Mafia links to the hazardous waste trade.[5] It was a terrible travesty that the mob-controlled business was allowed to operate for so long. Equally sad was the fact that the conflagration destroyed most of the manifest records of which companies sent wastes to the facility. Yet many in law enforcement suspected that something like it was bound to happen. Only months before the Chemical Control fire exploded, two detective sergeants with the New Jersey State Police, Dirk Ottens and Jack Penny, presented evidence before the U.S. Congressional Committee on Interstate and Foreign Commerce tying several waste disposal companies in New York and New Jersey with Mario Gigante, one of the important leaders of a major organized crime syndicate known as the Genovese family.

In the summer of 1979, the Genovese syndicate moved some of its hazardous waste disposal operations from Mahwah to Edgewater, New Jersey, on the banks of the Hudson River and others to Newark. By the spring of 1983, these facilities had long lists of hazardous waste violations in the state. From Edgewater, NJDEP enforcement inspectors tracked PCB liquid wastes sent to incinerators without permits to handle such material. The mob-run business also initiated a massive waste oil operation, in which hazardous chemical wastes were mixed with heating oil and then sold to the public for home use. The FBI and the U.S. Attorney subsequently found that the Mafia had "siphoned millions of dollars in cash from these businesses using a number of intermediaries to 'launder funds' for other nefarious purposes."[6] Murder was also a management tool. Crescent Roselle, a general manager for one of these mob-controlled waste disposal businesses, was found brutally murdered in a gangland-style execution, shot numerous times while sitting in his car outside his company office.[7] Yet corporations did not really need the Mafia to dispose of wastes illegally after RCRA passed in 1976. Many legitimate businesses had been doing so for decades, finding ingenious ways to dispose of their wastes, sometimes hiding them in plain sight. Many years later this would come back to haunt Jersey City. The biggest culprit was chromium.

THE HUDSON COUNTY CHROMATE SITES

Chromium waste was everywhere in Jersey City when I was growing up. I just didn't have a name for it. I later learned its official title, hexavalent chromium (chromium-6), as a toxic byproduct in chromium ore processing residue (COPR). This COPR was strewn all over the city, left behind by three companies or their predecessors: AlliedSignal, Pittsburg Plate Glass (PPG) Industries, and Maxus Energy.[8] From 1905 to 1976, Jersey City was the center for chromate chemical manufacturing in America, which typically involved mixing 50 percent chromium ore with lime and soda ash, then heating it and leaching with water. The waste material from this process was commonly called "mud," and it is estimated that a total of two million to three million tons were generated by the processing facilities. Yet in spite of its known toxicity, mud was given away, or sold, for reuse as fill material in construction, road grading, building foundations, and the filling of wetlands. In its most despicable guise, mud was offered to municipalities for high school running tracks; the Roosevelt Drive-In movie theater, where I spent many nights walking over the yellow mud to the snack bar; or, more insidiously, in baseball fields and public parks, where small babies learned to crawl in sand boxes that hid the unseen hazard.

One of the chromate plants lay aslant a beeline path from my home to the Hudson River. That's where my friends and I went on wilding expeditions as kids, trips to the wetlands—where we reenacted Robinson Crusoe fantasies amidst the rushes. The grasses were so high that it was easy to forget that we lived in a congested metropolis. Usually, to get to the river we would circle around the chromium factory and make our way along its barrier fence to gain access to the waterfront. However, a few times, with the impatience of youth whispering in our ears, we would take a shortcut and in one synchronized jump hurdle over the cyclone fence and fall into the factory lot. There we would make our way surreptitiously past the buildings and the high, smoking mounds of greenish-yellow mud that billowed a pungent acidic odor into the summer air.

I remember once there were jibes of "I dare you to run up that pile!" before a friend of mine took the bet. Unfortunately, halfway up the smoking mound his legs sank up to his knees, and he began screaming, swatting at his legs as he stumbled down again, his sneakers and socks stained yellow, his calves toasted red. In fact, that's how my mother usually knew if we had taken a shortcut through the chrome yard: my Keds would be sickly yellow near the edges with a whiff of brimstone and burnt rubber on them. This just from walking across the surface puddles! What did we know? We were just kids out for adventure. At least the toxic exposure we experienced when trespassing was our own fault and not the result of subterfuge by some of the Hudson County chromate corporations. They knowingly distributed toxic wastes for so-called beneficial reuse just to save a few dollars on their quarterly operating budgets. Thus, when I came to work as an environmentalist and learned what that yellow mud really was, it became a symbol for me of greed at its ugliest, where profits were more important than the health of children.

My friend and boss, Tom Burke, the director of Science and Research, also grew up a few blocks from these sites when they were operating in the 1950s and 1960s. However, twenty years later, as environmental scientists and regulators, we were in a position to investigate. In 1991, Burke coauthored an important review paper on the Hudson chromate sites that brought many of the health issues to the public's attention.[9] He noted that in November 1988 the state medical examiner listed chromium toxicity as a contributory cause of death for a man who worked at a truck-loading facility built atop a chromium dump.[10] This stimulated NJDEP to look for other waste piles that might be "hidden" right out in the open.

Figure 6. Chromate waste dumping sites in Jersey City, New Jersey. (Source: New Jersey Department of Environmental Protection.)

The chronic affects of chromium exposure were first examined in the 1800s in occupational studies. Chromium is a steely gray metal that exhibits a wide range of possible oxidation states. The hexavalent state (chromium-6) acts as a powerful oxidant, with many industrial uses. It is also the most toxic form. Chromium-6 can cause ulcers of the skin and irritation of the nasal mucosa and gastrointestinal tract; it also has adverse effects on the kidneys and liver. Chromium-6 is listed as an inhalation and ingestion carcinogen in humans by the USEPA and the International Agency for Research on Cancer. Industrially, hexavalent chromium is used in wood preservation, leather tanning, and the production of stainless steel, textile dyes, and anticorrosive coatings.[11]

NJDEP found 106 of these COPR sites throughout Hudson County, most of them in Jersey City. Our immediate concern was the large number of residential properties and schoolyards built on chromate residues, which continued to leach yellow water. These yellow "chromate blooms," as they are called, were corrosive and allergenic exudates of chromium interacting with groundwater and migrating upward over time. Yellow stains were even found on basement floors and walls built atop the mud. Drainage ditches and waterways around the dumps also ran with this bright chromic water from the buried yet still mobile contaminants.

Burke felt that the large number of Hudson County chromium sites presented a perhaps unprecedented complex web of exposure pathways that could challenge the limits of current exposure assessment technology. In fact, we are still performing risk assessments on past exposures to chromium and may never know retroactively the true extent of public health impacts from this indiscriminate spreading of hazardous waste beneath a densely populated community. With determination and detailed searching, NJDEP's Site Remediation Program made investigative headway throughout the 1980s. This was followed up by field sampling, which identified the 106 COPR sites at various residential, commercial, and industrial locations. Unfortunately, the tons of mud had been used in a variety of ways that frustrated easy remediation. We found COPR in building foundations, for the construction of tank berms and roadways, the filling of wetlands, and even mixed with concrete for large public works projects. It is predicted that the cost, cleanup, and containment of this chromium waste could ultimately be in the billons of dollars.

Moving quickly, NJDEP triaged the sites and moved to clean up or enclose those presenting the most immediate risk. By 1997, most of the residential properties were remediated by the state, with two-thirds of the remaining non-residential sites under investigation by the three principal responsible parties (PRPs). Initially NJDEP covered, fenced, and/or restricted access to site, and then in a second phase sought more permanent solutions, including excavation and removal of the mud, groundwater treatment, and in some cases in-situ entombment by capping. For many of the nonresidential locations, COPR was left on site with interim remedial measures in place. These included long-term institutional (i.e., deed restrictions limiting subsequent uses) and engineering controls (i.e., capping, fencing, and monitoring).

Yet after these initial steps, there was little action at these partially remediated sites, as the PRPs fought in court to delay performing any further removals or offsite treatment of COPR wastes. This was unfortunate and untimely, as interim remedial measures are by definition temporary and not meant to hold for protracted periods of time. Asphalt caps and cyclone fences alone would not protect the public's health. This PRP recalcitrance was about to change, however, in some measure goaded by a chromium-based lawsuit three thousand miles away.

The Pacific Gas and Electric Company (PG&E) in California used chromium-infused water as an anticorrosive coolant at some of its natural gas compressor stations, where it discharged the tainted water into unlined ponds at the site, which then percolated into groundwater supplies. In 1996, and because of her involvement in this case, Erin Brockovich became a household name in America. At the time, Brockovich, a former Miss Pacific Coast beauty queen, was an unemployed single mother of three children who, after losing a personal injury lawsuit against a doctor in a car accident, asked her lawyer for a job as a file clerk. She found an overlooked case in his files involving real estate and medical records against PG&E. Digging deeper, she exposed a systematic cover-up of industrial poisoning of a nearby town's water supply by hexavalent chromium. Julia Roberts subsequently won an Academy Award for Best Actress for her portrayal of Brockovich in the movie docudrama named after her. The California courts awarded the class-action litigants $333 million for tainting their drinking water, the largest settlement ever paid in U.S. history.

Meanwhile, in New Jersey the management of these remaining COPR sites was fraught with the "fog of war." For example, the analytical chemistry method used to isolate hexavalent chromium was still being refined, and the toxicology was based on occupational outcomes, not readily extrapolated to exposures from playing fields and buildings. As a result, the early risk-based cleanup numbers developed by NJDEP to declare "no further action" at a site were based on broadly interpreted exposure scenarios and conservative toxicology. Yet it was the best available science of the time.

Ten years later in 1998, the risk numbers were reevaluated and lower cleanup numbers proposed, based on new toxicology and a review of former exposure assumptions. Moreover, what made this confusion even worse were the actions of the lawyers and scientists hired by the PRPs. They flooded the department with briefs and remedial work plans that capitalized on these uncertainties. Their game plan was to delay for as long as possible, to keep remedial actions at any site to a minimum, and to keep only interim measures in place rather than pay for more costly removal and offsite treatment of the waste. NJDEP was in a bind, since by policy law we were required to pursue a known responsible party with adequate financial resources as long as possible before doing the work ourselves. To the public, however, these delays smelled of mendacity, an elaborate attempt by NJDEP to lie or drag its feet in support of the PRPs, when in fact it was only environmental science slowly evolving before their eyes.

CLASS ACTIONS SUCCEED WHERE GOVERNMENT FAILS

Significantly, it took action by a nongovernmental organization to redress this impasse. The Interfaith Community Organization (ICO) in Hudson County filed a class-action lawsuit against AlliedSignal (now Honeywell International) to clean up its old manufacturing site on Route 440. ICO, founded in 1986, is composed of religious congregations whose original mission was to improve the urban environment with park renovations, community policing, and the exposure of fraud in federally funded job-training programs. Its greatest success, however, came when the pastors learned that some of their parishioners' homes were located on or near the chromium dumps. ICO developed an ingenious legal strategy based on the "citizens' suit" provision in RCRA. This provision states that a person may commence a civil action against a generator of solid or hazardous waste that may present an "imminent and substantial endangerment to health or the environment." It also allows that person to obtain injunctive relief to address the contamination, as well as the recovery of attorneys' fees and the costs for expert witnesses.

ICO sued AlliedSignal in 1995 to compel cleanup of the largest chromium waste site in Hudson County (under the Roosevelt Drive-In and surrounding areas). In 2003, ICO won the lawsuit in federal court, but two years of appeals by Honeywell delayed resolution. After the U.S. Supreme Court refused to hear another appeal, the largest environmental cleanup in New Jersey's history finally began.[12] In the original decision, Judge Dennis M. Cavanaugh wrote that the chromium at the Honeywell (AlliedSignal) site represented "a substantial risk of imminent damage to public health and safety and imminent and severe damage to the environment."[13] Cavanaugh added that the corporation used its vast resources to frustrate government efforts to bring a resolution to the matter. "I find that Honeywell was less than cooperative and embarked on a dilatory, foot-dragging scheme for 20 years." He pointed out in his decision that the company officials made proposals on how to clean up the site, took them to NJDEP, were told what was wrong with the plan, and would then come back with essentially the same plan, frustrating the efforts of the agency. Cavanaugh ruled the site be excavated immediately and to move things along, he appointed former U.S. Senator Robert Torricelli as a "special monitor" for the court-ordered cleanup.

ICO's struggle with Honeywell was a testament to the ability of community activists to move effectively against environmental injustice. The ICO ruling's legacy was not only for the remediation of that COPR site but also for developing litigation strategies that could be used by other communities as a model for future cleanup negotiations and decisions. It also set a precedent for "complete and effective" measures at the outset of a remediation instead of just using interim measures, and will discourage delaying tactics on the part of PRPs for the numerous other COPR sites similarly contaminated.

Class-action lawsuits related to these COPR sites also accelerated other cleanups as NJDEP struggled with PRPs in court. In 1992, Honeywell Corporation was compelled to sign an agreement with NJDEP to clean up a contaminated park in Jersey City because of a class-action suit filed by users of a baseball field at the site. Honeywell never produced chromium in Jersey City but inherited the liability because in 1954 Allied-Signal had bought the stock of the Mutual Chemical Company, which operated one of the world's largest chromium processing plants nearby. The baseball field was closed down after NJDEP found chromium levels more than four hundred times higher than considered safe. Honeywell subsequently removed more than fourteen thousand tons of contaminated soil from the Metro Field site at a cost of more than $4 million.[14]

The plaintiff attorneys also tracked down a former Mutual Chemical plant worker in Arizona who gave a sworn deposition that the company "dumped chromium waste, a known carcinogen, on the site to create a playing field for the company softball team. Workers used the field for about two years and then stopped after complaining to the company that team members were developing chrome sores. Once they found out their people were getting sick on the field, they held the field for awhile, then turned it over to the city without telling them.[15] Subsequently, Hudson County Superior Court Judge Mark A. Baber certified a chromium-exposure class-action lawsuit for all participants of recreational activities at Metro Field and the adjoining playground on West Side Avenue. Any individual who played on the site for an equivalent of at least ten ball games (approximately twenty hours) prior to the cleanup of the site was eligible to be included in this class action. The initial litigants included eighteen children who claimed they suffered ailments such as rashes, stomach pains, sinus and respiratory problems, chronic colds, sore throats, and severe headaches. The lawsuit sought damages in the form of medical monitoring expenses, as well as personal injury damages for exposure to chromium.

THE CHROMIUM WORKGROUP

In 2004, then NJDEP Commissioner Bradley Campbell met with irate residents from Hudson County because of the litigious impasse with the responsible parties. The citizens were primarily concerned about safety near the sites where chromium wastes were left behind. Campbell created a Chromium Workgroup in response to their concerns and appointed the director of Science and Research, Eileen Murphy, to chair it. Murphy managed this process transparently, using an open stakeholder process that called on the technical expertise of scientists both within and outside government. Subgroups met to address a number of technical issues, including analytical chemistry (earlier cleanup decisions were largely based on weaker methods), environmental chemistry (how much chromium-6 was present in samples as opposed to less toxic forms of chromium), and risk assessment (the original toxicology only assumed lung cancer and inhalation pathways, whereas newer data showed cancer from drinking water ingestion).

A series of reports followed the activities of the Chromium Workgroup.[16] One of these addressed a reevaluation of NJDEP's soil cleanup criteria for chromium, which is used by the agency to start a cleanup if exceeded, and then to end a remediation if soil levels drop below this critical value. Some of the public felt the existing soil criteria were not low enough and that residences were thus insufficiently protected. After an exhaustive analysis and vetting at public meetings, and in response to technical comments, the workgroup determined that the existing criteria were based on valid science; however, a reassessment of the ingestion route of exposure being performed by the federal government might result in these levels being lowered in the future. This gave NJDEP the green light to continue remedial activities at the COPR sites, which had been put under a moratorium while the workgroup sought technical consensus. Neighbors and community groups living in the shadow of these facilities wanted to wait until the federal ingestion study was completed, which might lead to a more intensive remediation.

Subsequently, on May 3, 2005, Commissioner Lisa Jackson, who was appointed by Governor Jon Corzine in that year (and is currently serving as the head of USEPA under President Barack Obama), lifted the moratorium and directed that remediation and soil removal begin anew based on the conclusions of the workgroup. Simultaneously, New Jersey Attorney General Peter C. Harvey filed lawsuits naming Honeywell, Occidental Petroleum, and PPG Industries liable for the COPR sites and sought reimbursement for the cleanups.[17] At the time, Harvey said: "Clean water, air and land are a right, not a privilege and . . . for too long, the residents of these communities have lived with the threat of this highly toxic chromate waste. Our lawsuit will compel the responsible companies to clean up the remaining chromium contamination."

Attorney General Harvey's directive also demanded reimbursement for the cost of a study to assess the health risks to residents exposed to dust near chromium waste sites. Although funded by NJDEP while the PRP lawsuit moved forward, this study was subsequently developed by NJDEP's Science and Research staff, the N.J. Department of Health and Senior Services (DHSS), and the Environmental and Occupational Health Sciences Institute (EOHSI) of the University of Medicine and Dentistry of New Jersey. We knew from previous exposure studies conducted by Alan Stern of Science and Research and EOHSI in the 1990s that levels of total chromium (hexavalent plus trivalent) in house dust were related to the proximity of known Hudson County chromium waste sites. The studies also showed elevated levels of chromium in the urine of young children in these houses. After remediation of those waste sites, however, follow-up studies showed that the levels of chromium in house dust had returned to background levels.[18]

In the 2008 study, the methods remained the same as in the 1990s, focusing on house dust as an indicator of exposure potential to hexavalent chromium from the waste sites. More than two hundred dust samples from a hundred households near the sites showed hexavalent chromium at all locations investigated. However, nearly all concentrations were below the current NJDEP soil remediation criterion of 20 ppm.[19] The data showed that the households surrounding the COPR sites were not currently impacted by chromium dust. To help the state in conveying this information, Science and Research also developed a simple pamphlet called the *Citizens Guide to Chromium Exposure and Health Effects Dust Study*.[20] This guide asked and answered key questions for the public, such as "Should I move?" The answer: "The results are reassuring that risks are low and people do not need to leave their homes because of chromium levels." In line with similar questions raised during the Reading Prong Radon Emergency, another question posed was: "Will my property values go down?" The *Citizens Guide* responded: "The presence of the chromium sites is a matter of public record. Interested buyers may already be aware of any former chromium waste sites located near your home. Having your home tested may provide reassurance that chromium levels in the home are below safety guidelines."

Although the result of this 2008 dust study reassured the public as to the safety of the current situation, a persistent question remained that was asked frequently at public meetings: "What is the long-term carcinogenic legacy of the chromate sites for the residents in Hudson County and Jersey City?" To answer this question, researchers at Science and Research and the Department of Health devised an interesting study. Ironically, the approach mimicked the methods used in the 1970s Mason and McKay cancer atlas for plotting mortality on a map. This time, however, the cancer incidence data used were from a more detailed state database, and the mapping that we utilized was digital information on a computerized geographic information system (GIS). Gail Carter, a cartographer at Science and Research, played an important role in compiling this mapping information, using U.S. census blocks and population grids at a fine scale in Jersey City neighborhoods. This allowed the health professionals to evaluate the relationships between historic exposures from chromium ore processing sites and the incidence of lung cancer in Jersey City over a twenty-five-year period.

The investigation included the population residing in Jersey City from 1979 through 2003, a period when most of the COPR manufacturing sites ceased operations but when exposures during interim and final remedial activities would be significant. Using historic information on the location of known COPR sites along with their contaminant levels, census block groups were characterized as to their potential for residential hexavalent chromium exposure in Jersey City. The results showed an increase in the rate of lung cancer incidence for populations living in closer proximity to historic COPR sites (although the increases were not statistically significant).[21] The results suggested that living closer to COPR sites was a potential risk factor for the development of lung cancer. The study cautioned that results could not prove a definitive cause-and-effect relationship. Yet, in spite of the statistical shortcomings, the findings were important, since they showed a refined spatial relationship, no matter how small the significance. This is in contrast to the broad associations gleaned from the cancer atlas of the 1970s.

Yet by the end of 2008, even with the release of these cancer and exposure studies, the PPG Industries' Garfield Avenue facility was still only partially remediated. The buildings were demolished and the mud piles removed, yet tons of "heaving chromium" still move under the interim cap. Heaving chromium is caused by groundwater interacting with the waste and binding it into hard layers that push upward, breaking the surface layer and possibly breaching the protective cap.[22] Unfortunately, most of the clay caps constructed in the 1980s at COPR sites were temporary and not designed to last twenty years. They were stopgap measures put in place until a more permanent remedy could be initiated.

Thus in early 2009, the Interfaith Community Organization in Jersey City rose to the challenge and sued PPG Industries to permanently remediate the Garfield Avenue site. This time ICO collaborated with the Natural Resources Defense Council, again using the citizens' suit provisions of the federal Resource Conservation and Recovery Act.[23] Ellen Wright, a leader of ICO who has lived near the site for forty-three years, said in an interview: "We've tried everything else. We've asked every governor and every Department of Environmental Protection commissioner since 1989 to get this site cleaned up. We've asked PPG Industries directly to clean up the wasteland they created and protect the health of the people who live and work in this community. But so far none of the people with the power to clean up this site have been able to feel the same sense of urgency that I feel living blocks away from it."[24] So ICO and NRDC asked the federal court to get the job done. Perhaps as a result of this lawsuit and the lesson of how AlliedSignal was directed to dig down forty feet to remediate the Roosevelt Drive-In COPR site, PPG signed a settlement one week later. On February 12, 2009, the attorney general announced that PPG would clean-up the Garfield Avenue and numerous chromium-tainted sites throughout Hudson County.[25] The $193 million settlement would be used to remove an estimated half-million tons of contaminated soil. An additional incentive for PPG's signing of the agreement might have been real estate pressure, as the Garfield Avenue site is now traversed by a light rail commuter line that funnels thousands of commuters daily to New York City. There are redevelopment plans for the land along the railway, and developers wait anxiously for the remediation to be completed so they can build residential houses worth tens of millions. It seems the only thing in their way is the heaving chromium that lies just beneath the surface trying to break free.

COMMAND AND CONTROL: POLLUTER PAYS

When I was a young boy, the Jersey City Police Department still had a mounted patrol. The horses were stabled in a wide-ranging paddock behind Frank Hague's towering medical center, the horses' exercise yard built on a strange slag that bubbled with yellow water whenever it rained. The Police Athletic League softball field was right next door to the stables and lay atop this same scratchy material. My dad used to take us to the field on Saturdays to watch his buddies play ball. I loved watching the softball games, as dad's buddies dressed in hokey uniforms and drank beer in the dugouts, shaking off the grind of being a cop with some fun, their kids tagging along like puppies. I remember once sitting on an outfield fence with my brothers Jack and Joe, the mounted patrol horses nuzzling our backs, begging us to feed them sugar cubes and carrots we had brought from home. The smell of horse sweat and dung were overpowering as the blacksmith hammered a tattoo on his anvil in the barn, the line of mounts sidling and snorting along the split-rail fence outside the stable. Once, Jack suggested we sneak over and peek through the double doors to watch the blacksmith work. I can still see him now, wearing his leather apron and hat, blue shirtsleeves singed by the iron sparks that flew from his hammer, the red glowing horseshoe against the black anvil that he pounded, his beetled brows squinting against the smoke that rose from the hearth, beating and bending iron shoes to match the feet of his charges. But there too, inside his domain, we saw the yellow pools coming up from the dirt floor, staining the anvil's base with a bilious yellow color where it had settled into the mud.

I didn't know until years later what this staining meant. The hexavalent chromium heaving from the ground, its puddles filled with toxicants. And to be honest, even my dad and the other cops didn't know; the blacksmith didn't know. But someone knew! Someone made a deal that we were not aware of, a deal bartered for a few dollars of seemingly innocent graft to distribute the chromium mud across the city. The legacy of that arrangement was 106 Hudson County chromate sites spread throughout the most densely populated land in the United States, half a million people potentially and needlessly exposed to carcinogens, and the millions of dollars spent to make the land safe. This immoral and unfair bargain still elicits outrage at its cold, calculated intent.

Yet even more amazing are the extraordinary lengths to which corporations go in order to protect against liability. Many of the chemical and manufacturing firms whose names appear on Superfund dockets or court orders for emergency cleanups are the same cast of characters. Sometimes the names are changed as a result of mergers, acquisitions, or divestures; sometimes these reorganizations are specifically designed to siphon off liability from a parent company's assets. For example, the Occidental Chemical Corporation, one of the three PRPs for the Hudson chromate sites, bought the Diamond Shamrock Chemical Company in 1986 (formerly a Diamond Alkali Corporation holding).

Diamond Alkali was incorporated in Delaware in 1929 to produce soda ash for the manufacture of glass. By the mid-1960s, the company's line had grown to more than 1,400 products. Eventually it became one of the largest chemical, oil, and gas companies in the United States. After World War II, the company expanded its range of products to include plastics like polyvinyl chloride and chemicals for the agricultural industry. Diamond Alkali merged with

Shamrock Oil and Gas Corporation in 1967, creating the Diamond Shamrock Company. In 1983, Maxus Energy of Dallas became owner of Diamond Shamrock Chemicals through a stock transaction. Three years later, Maxus sold the company to Occidental Chemical, also of Dallas. But as part of the transaction, Maxus was contracted to indemnify Occidental for a pesticide manufacturing facility in Newark, New Jersey, and Tierra Solutions was created as a subsidiary of Maxus to own properties associated with that indemnification.[26]

Yet under state and Superfund regulations, Occidental Chemical Corporation (one of the Hudson County chromate responsible parties) still bears a share of responsibility for any cleanup activities at the Newark site because it purchased the company and inherited the liability. The Diamond Alkali plant is on Lister Avenue in Newark surrounded by the old Portuguese section on the waterfront called the Ironbound. There in the early 1980s, NJDEP discovered that for two decades the operators intentionally discharged pesticides like DDT and Agent Orange into the nearby Passaic River. And the one chemical that went unnoticed in spite of all these corporate mergers was not even on the inventory list, a deadly chemical byproduct of the chlorinated pesticide manufacturing process called dioxin.

CHAPTER 6

Environmental Warfare

Dioxin in Newark

Governor Thomas Kean said in his memoir, *The Politics of Inclusion*, that the most serious potential crisis of his governorship occurred in June 1983, a few months after the USEPA purchased the entire town of Times Beach, Missouri, as a result of dioxin contamination. He said that his environmental commissioner, Bob Hughey, had taken Kean's warnings about crisis management to heart, had dusted off an old federal survey of eleven New Jersey companies that manufactured dioxin-related products, and had begun to visit the sites and test the soils. Kean notes: "The result from the very first site the 'DEP technicians' visited was startling. The amount of dioxin in the dirt was so high that the test couldn't measure it. Subsequently we found that the dioxin levels were two times the levels found in Times Beach."[1]

These levels were found at the Diamond Alkali pesticide plant in the Ironbound section of Newark. One of the chemicals manufactured at the site was 2,4,5-trichlorophenoxyacetic acid (2,4,5-T). Dioxin was formed as a byproduct of the process, and up to 15 percent of the total national output of 2,4,5-T was produced at this Newark site, with an average output of approximately eight hundred tons per year. Yet unlike Times Beach, this plant was in the middle of a densely populated neighborhood in the largest city in New Jersey. Kean could not buy it and move the people out, as the USEPA had done in Missouri. Instead, he had us draft an executive order for his signature (EO-40-17), declaring a state of emergency and authorizing NJDEP "to engage in emergency measures necessary to fully and adequately protect the health, safety and welfare of New Jersey citizens." We also drafted a press release to inform the public, which read in part: "High concentration of dioxin had been discovered in a factory and . . . we did not know if the chemical was in the river and surrounding neighborhood. Newspapers from Texas to Florida immediately picked up the story, calling Newark the new Times Beach, Missouri. Kean said in his book that the people in the community acted with restraint. I would say they were more numb to the situation, having lived in the shadow of the plant for so many years, and they did not adequately understand the threat at first. This changed after we held our first public meeting.

Kean acknowledges that panic did set in that night: "Some people questioned whether they could drink the water or whether they should burn their clothes." He therefore decided to visit the Ironbound himself, even though his staffers counseled otherwise. And I must agree that this was the proper thing to do. He walked in and talked to the people, surrounded by television crews and news photographers. But he was not abused by the angry citizenry. He was welcomed with typical New Jersey perseverance and humor. As Kean noted, one old gent called out to him: "Get right into the dioxin with everyone else, Governor Kean. Just don't breathe too deep!"

After a few weeks of street dust samples that showed dioxin localized around the Diamond Alkali site, it seemed to Kean that the dioxin crisis had been diffused. Yet from my perspective, it was just beginning. As with my concern for radiation at Three Mile Island—that the more widespread danger was in radionuclide transport downstream to Chesapeake Bay—I knew that the bigger threat from the Diamond Alkali plant was to be found in the Passaic River. A few miles below the facility was Newark Bay and one of the largest freight handling and container ports in the world. Its shipping channels were also routinely dredged and the spoils dumped offshore in the Atlantic Ocean. Dioxin I knew, like PCBs, binds strongly with suspended sediments, and if transported to these shipping channels, it could be dumped offshore, potentially contaminating thousands of species and millions of tons of seafood with the most toxic synthetic substance known to humans.

In his memoir Kean recalled that the night he walked the streets of the Ironbound, he accepted the responsibility and prevented panic. Indeed, the media treated his visit well, and his human touch for talking to the common man on the street was pitch-perfect. He felt that some columnists traced the beginning of his popularity to that night he spent in a bar in the Ironbound kibitzing with Newarkers. Yet what actually happened before, and after, Tom Kean walked the streets of Newark is another story, one that is still going on today.

Rosemarie Tuccillo, who worked for Ed Stevenson on the New Jersey Industrial Survey, was perusing newspaper clippings one day in 1983, looking for information on chemical manufacturing facilities that she was to visit as part of the survey work. She noticed a brief squib in the newspaper that the Diamond Alkali facility in the Ironbound section of Newark had received a contract to manufacture 75 percent of all the Agent Orange pesticide used in the Vietnam War. Agent Orange is a broad-spectrum herbicide blended from two other pesticides, 2,4-dichlorophenoxyacetic acid (2,4-D) and 2,4,5-T (discussed above). Ed Stevenson decided to drive up to Newark that day and visit the Diamond plant, where he sampled a spillage area beside the river where rail tanker cars were off-loaded. However, only a few labs at that time could perform dioxin analysis, mostly specialized P3 or "clean labs" with the ability to protect against unintended releases of toxic contaminants. Commercial P3 labs are typically used for Department of Defense studies of chemical weapons or by the National Institutes of Health for screening for the deadly hemorrhagic fever virus called Ebola. The most reliable dioxin analytical laboratory at that time was run by Christopher Rappe at the University of Umea in Sweden.

Not letting the Atlantic Ocean stop us, Tom Burke called Sweden and convinced Rappe to process our soil sample. Serendipitously, one of his postdoctoral students was in the United States on vacation. Rappe called him and he agreed to take our sample back. Ed Stevenson met him at Newark International Airport and handed over a paint can filled with Diamond Alkali dirt. They shook hands, and the postdoc got on the plane, arrived in Sweden eight hours later, and then drove to Umea. There the sample was placed on a lab bench and screened, filtered to remove rocks and glass, ground down and extracted, boiled in solvent, then reduced in volume and shot into a gas chromatograph. The results were confirmed on a mass spectrometer.

A few days later Burke received an angry call from Rappe. It turned out our sample was so highly contaminated with dioxin that it had effectively contaminated his entire laboratory. Rappe had to shut it down for a month to clean up all the residual background traces of our sample. "And oh, by the way, the result was 50 milligrams per kilogram!" he added. This was one of the highest ambient levels of dioxin ever recorded. It was comparable to levels in the denuded forests of Vietnam where Agent Orange was used in Operation Ranch Hand to defoliate the Ho Chi Minh trail where the Viet Cong smuggled weapons to insurgents in the south. My brother, Jack, who spent a year in Vietnam as a soldier, told me about walking through these ghost forests without a leaf or a blade of grass visible for miles, the ground a foot deep in black, decaying vegetation and puddles of "Orange Crush" on the ground, the name the GIs gave to the herbicide, which reminded them of the popular orange soda sold at the base commissary.

Revisiting the Diamond Alkali facility a few days later with NJDEP's Division of Hazardous Site Remediation staff, we noticed an open-air food market across the street from the plant and a nearby public housing project, both filled with people. Dust clouds arose every few minutes in the August heat as trucks rolled by from industries up and down the river. We called USEPA for an emergency meeting and briefed its staff on our findings. Within hours, Richard (Dick) Dewling, the Region 2 administrator for USEPA, ordered an emergency Superfund response after meeting with Governor Kean (Dewling would eventually become Kean's second commissioner of NJDEP).

Men in Level-A protective suits with taped sleeves and cuffs descended on the Ironbound like aliens from Mars. The moon suits, as the local kids called them, were impermeable white Tyvek that ballooned out over the hazmat workers' self-contained air-packs. They also wore full-face respirator masks that glinted in the hot sun. The bright yellow rubber booties over their work boots reduced their mobility so much that they walked in a roly-poly fashion that the projects kids mimicked as the workers walked up and down Lister Avenue with hoses hooked to vacuum trucks for cleaning the streets of dioxin-laden dust. Mystified by all the fuss and soon bored under the August sun, some kids in T-shirts and cutoffs opened a nearby hydrant to cool off, sending cataracts of rusty water rushing through the contaminated hot zone. This led to comic slow-motion scuffles, as red-faced men in moon suits chased barefooted kids and attempted to shut off the hydrants. Irate parents came rushing out of the projects, wanting to know what was going on.

Dioxin Toxicity

The kind of emergency remedial response we did in the Ironbound for those first few days was peculiar for a hazardous waste cleanup and primarily driven by the urgency of working in a crowded city neighborhood. Investigations of contaminated sites are typically evaluated more slowly and in a choreographed manner following NJDEP's Technical Requirements for Site Remediation.[2] However, when the contaminant of concern is extremely toxic and the possibility exists for broad public exposure, the process is accelerated. Dioxin, like PCBs, is not one chemical but a class of chemicals; their official name is polychlorinated dibenzo-dioxins or PCDDs. There are seventy-five possible configurations (or congeners) of PCDD. The most toxic of these congeners is 2,3,7,8- tetrachlorodibenzo-p-dioxin (2,3,7,8-TCDD), considered by many toxicologists to be the most deadly synthetic chemical ever developed. In animals, it is teratogenic, embryotoxic, carcinogenic, and co-carcinogenic. In other words, it can cause birth defects, mental retardation, cancer, and can interact with other carcinogens to increase cancer severity. It is remarkably stable, non-biodegradable, and, owing to its extreme toxicity, the cumulative effects of even extremely small doses are a major concern.[3]

Ironically, dioxins have no industrial uses but occur as byproducts in the manufacture of other organochlorine chemicals (e.g., the two pesticides blended into Agent Orange), during the incineration of chlorine-containing substances such as PVC (polyvinyl chloride), in the bleaching of paper, and even from extreme natural phenomena such as volcanoes and forest fires. The toxic, chronic, and sublethal effects of this chemical are borne out by studies from the Centers for Disease Control and evidence from studies of Vietnamese and Vietnam-era veterans, decades after tons of Agent Orange were air-dropped onto the jungles in wartime. As previously noted 2,3,7,8-TCDD was a common contaminant in Agent Orange. The U.S. Army called it Operation Ranch Hand with typical American insouciance, as if killing off thousands of acres of virgin tropical forest were no more than a cutting for a right-of-way in a brushy swale down in the Texas panhandle. And to this day, the putative deleterious health affects of Agent Orange on exposed U.S. veterans continues to be studied by doctors of the National Academy of Sciences' Institute of Medicine, and its research conclusions are still fraught with emotional controversy for veterans seeking disability compensation for perceived health affects from Agent Orange exposure.[4]

DIOXIN IN THE WATER

The Diamond Alkali facility sat on the banks of the Passaic River. One of the first things that concerned me when we drove our workboat past the facility's bulkhead was the number of hoses and pipes running out of the processing buildings and into the river. Having just completed a year of sampling these same waters for fish contaminated with PCBs, I knew that dioxin, once released into the open environment, showed similar physiochemical properties as a persistent bioaccumulative and toxic compound. The river emptied a mile downstream into Newark Bay, where the Port Newark and Port Elizabeth marine terminals operated the largest container port in the world. And to facilitate this constant traffic in shipping, the channel sediments were routinely dredged and barged offshore to be dumped at open-ocean disposal sites managed by the U.S. Army Corp of Engineers.

The nearest disposal site to Port Newark in operation at the time of the Diamond Alkali investigation was called the New York Bight Dredged Material Disposal Site. It was euphemistically called the "Mud Dump" by local fishermen because of its soft bottom and mounded profile as seen in relief on their depth finders. Other materials such as acid waste, industrial waste, municipal sewage sludge, cellar dirt, and wood were also dumped in these waters. The Mud Dump was twelve miles offshore in federal waters and in use for more than a century. State jurisdictional boundaries extend only three miles offshore whereas federal waters go from three to two hundred miles seaward. Between 1976 and 1995, the Mud Dump received on average about six million cubic yards of dredged material annually. Unfortunately, the Mud Dump is in the midst of the same offshore region where bluefish and other important commercial fisheries migrate and feed. These fish are sold at every stand and supermarket from Montauk on the tip of Long Island to beautiful Victorian Cape May in New Jersey, an imaginary triangle in the ocean between New York and New Jersey called the New York Bight, a navigational term indicating a recess or bite into a coastline.

When the dioxin emergency took off, NJDEP serendipitously had a number of recently collected fish, crab, and Passaic River sediments samples left over from the PCB Project. We supplied these to Christopher Rappe for analysis, but this time we used an international commercial carrier. What quickly came back did not surprise us. We found the river bottom highly contaminated with dioxin, especially the surficial sediments adjacent to the Diamond Alkali plant. This pervasive contamination existed in spite of the fact that the plant had not operated for twelve years.[5] Our fish and crab samples were contaminated not only in the Passaic River but in Newark Bay and the ocean waters of the New York Bight as well. Fish and shellfish from all three locations showed con-tamination with TCDD that exceeded FDA "levels of concern." Dioxin toxicity was so new to environmental science that FDA had not developed a tolerance level yet. Instead it advised actions according to two possible scenarios. "No consumption" for fish exceeding 50 parts per trillion and reduced consump-tion for results between 25 and 50 parts per trillion (no more than one meal a week for infrequent consumers and no more than once or twice a month for frequent consumers). It is informative to compare these levels to our PCB-based fish advisories, which were based on levels in the parts per million. The dioxin levels of concern (in parts per trillion) triggered carcinogenicity and other adverse health affects at a much lower concentration in food fish. To put parts per trillion into perspective and the incredibly small amounts that might cause cancer, one part per trillion can be considered equal to one square foot of floor tile on a kitchen floor the size of Indiana, or one drop of detergent in enough dishwater to fill a string of railroad tank cars ten miles long.[6]

The results showed dioxin in both resident and migratory species of edible fish and shellfish including carp, catfish, American eel, striped bass, and blue crab. Fish caught in freshwater upstream on the Passaic River above a dam showed no detectable levels of TCDD. We therefore surmised that the source of the dioxin contamination was confined to the tidal section of the river and probably from the vicinity of the Diamond Alkali plant. Our sense of urgency then shifted from the Ironbound neighborhood and focused on getting a new health food consumption advisory out to the public as quickly as possible, especially since the blue crabs we caught near the pesticide plant showed the highest levels of TCDD found in food fish anywhere in the world.[7] Subsequently Kean's dioxin Executive Order (EO-40-19) was amended to "prohibit the sale and consumption of all fish, shellfish, and crustaceans from the Passaic River and Newark Bay," which remains in effect to this day.

We were equally concerned that bluefish and lobsters collected in the ocean waters of the New York Bight also had elevated levels of TCDD. Significantly, we found similar levels of dioxin in lobsters caught at the mouth of New York Harbor and many miles out to sea, indicating a possible secondary source of exposure to TCDD, possibly from offshore dredge spoils. To test this hypothesis we initiated a second investigation off New Jersey's coast. A NJDEP lobster tagging study carried out by the Division of Fish, Game, and Wildlife in the early 1980s showed three geographically separate lobster populations in the New York Bight, with only limited migratory movements between them. Our follow-up field sampling collected lobsters at all three of these fisheries, which coincided with sea bottom inshore of the Mud Dump, atop it, and farther seaward. Our analytical results showed TCDD in the flesh of all three populations, indicating widespread dioxin contamination for New York Bight lobsters across the continental shelf at concentrations exceeding the FDA levels of concern. As a result, New Jersey issued food consumption advisories for American lobsters caught in New Jersey waters, and the federal government soon followed, but for areas outside of state jurisdictional control.[8]

The Lobstermen

The American lobsterman, like his prey, is no less changeable and predatory in his behavior. Typically a church-going and family man ashore, once on the water he will do anything to get his pots set, lobsters in the hold, and products to market. "Katy, bar the door" should anyone get in his way, for in the past years there have been repeated shootings on the grounds, with disputes over unspoken rights to ancestral sets resulting in shotgun blasts across gunnels and waters stained red with boatman's blood. I did not know any lobstermen when I was growing up in Jersey City, a wayward sliver of land across from New York City, except possibly those I had seen at the Clam Broth House in Hoboken chowing down after a long trip offshore. The Clam Broth House was a favorite among the locals, a place where lobstermen, longshoremen, and local politicians all rubbed elbows on the shell-strewn bar, loudly discussing sea currents, stevedoring, and crime bills in the legislature.

It was not until Governor Kean signed his dioxin Emergency Order that I was introduced to this fiercely competitive world of seamen. Governor Kean may have a patrician accent and a lisp that Cary Grant would have envied, but it belied his sixth sense for saying the right thing to the working men and women of New Jersey. He knew that in such a small and built-out state that environmental protection was not only good sense but good politics. He also believed in the personal touch and was never nervous about mingling with the public to explain his policies. Thus when we briefed him about dioxin in lobsters and the possible linkage with ocean dumping, he insisted that we hold a meeting with the Lobstermen's Association before he alerted the public. He also insisted that we do it on their turf at a closed fish factory on Sandy Hook Bay and without any State Police protection. He felt that the presence of uniforms would send the wrong signal. A call was then made on shortwave for the lobstermen on the water and those ashore to come in for the meeting.

Tom Burke, Bruce Ruppel, and I then drove across the state to the factory unescorted to talk toxicology and risk assessment with a collection of salt-hardened men. We were nervous because we knew they would be angry, because the lobster advisories would negatively affect their industry, their pocketbooks, and probably take food out of their children's mouths. The lobstermen came in like irate locusts from their offshore sets and gathered on the top floor of the factory in a wood-paneled conference room. We could hear them before we could see them as we looked up, the building's only light casting shadows onto the window of the hundred men that pressed into the wood-paneled room. As we drove up the driveway, the darkened Belford fish factory looked penitential and threatening to me, like a shadowed cathedral filled with drowned fishermen. Across the bay we could see the glittering lights of the Verrazano Bridge in the gathering dusk, the skyscrapers of New York City barely visible through the bridge's pylons. This added to the surreal nature of our mission, as the distant city looked like a toy snow-globe on a child's bookcase. The fish factory stink was overwhelming as we walked into the silent building, wandering among the fish oil rendering equipment and the troughs filled with depurating clams.

The only way into the meeting room was through a door clogged with men in faded yellow rain slickers and black rubber boots. We pressed in through in the bodies sideways, passing men in flannel shirts and watch caps, their hard looks a harbinger to "talk straight" and "keep it simple" or don't talk at all. We edged into the front of the room single file and turned to meet their gaze. Introduced by a lawyer who represented the Lobstermen's Association, I suddenly realized that the only way out of that room was back though the angry crowd of men. Not a good beginning!

What ensued then was an extraordinary bit of rhetoric on Tom Burke's part. He tap-danced his way through the details of what our dioxin data showed and how we only wanted to alert the public in an "advisory capacity" and that we were not there to shut down their fishery. What followed was a lot of shouting and ugly looks until someone shouted "Bullshit!" Burke took up this challenge with a quick riposte and said: "I know a friend of mine who spent some time in Vietnam wouldn't think so." He told them about Operation Ranch Hand and the veterans who waded through denuded jungles sprayed with Agent Orange and the debilitating health effects that they experienced when they got home. Then he added that the factory that made the pesticide was the one that might have contaminated their lobsters. This caused a galvanic shift in the demeanor of the men, a stiffening of their bodies and a more intense gaze. I surmised that many of them were probably Vietnam-era veterans. And the more Tom talked, the more their anger deflated as heads began to nod and a less vehement stare came from under their watch caps. What followed was less shouting, more questions, and eventually a begrudging conversation about the health of their own children, who ate more of the contaminated seafood than anyone else in New Jersey.

A few minutes later we pressed through the body of men and out into the darkened factory to our car. It had snowed while we were inside, covering the shoreline with a white scarf of snow and a slick of ice on the dirt road that sent our car skidding onto the highway. So icy was the road that we decided to stop and wait it out at a local diner. It was then I noticed it was Valentine's Day, as the menu had sweetheart specials scrawled in chalk on a board as we sat down. Bruce Ruppel mused that he felt terrible, as if we had just delivered our own version of Al Capone's Saint Valentine's Day Massacre, lining the lobsterman up against a wall and shooting them all down. I agreed but suggested it was still the right thing to do. I just hated being the messenger!

THE MUD DUMP

The lobstermen were as frustrated as we were because they too suspected that offshore dumping of dredge spoils at the Mud Dump astride their lobster grounds was a factor in the contamination. During the meeting we told them there were plans afoot to close it down. That was good news to them, as they told us they had complained for years about how New York City and New Jersey dumped their wastes at sea. "Out of sight—out of mind!" one of them said. "And nobody's expecting it to bite them in the end!" They told us about lobster pots lost on the "Cellar Dirt" dump site, where structural debris like

Figure 7. Staff from Rutgers University Marine Field Station deploying a sampler to collect bottom sediments and aquatic organisms at the dredged material disposal site (Mud Dump) for development of an index of ocean water quality. (Source: Thomas Belton.)

concrete was disposed of, and navigating around the anchorage for the burn barges, where countless wooden boats and pilings were doused with gasoline, lit with flares, and the ashes fed into the rolling waves. Twelve miles farther out was the "Sludge Dump," where tons of solids from all of New York City's sewage treatment plants and ten of North Jersey's plants were barged offshore daily and released into the ocean.

Our suspicion about dredge spoils from harbor sediments as a source of dioxin was confirmed by a study of sediments in Newark Bay commissioned by Science and Research in the late 1980s. At that time, Fredrika Moser and

I approached Richard Bopp of Rensselaer University to collect deep sediment cores for NJDEP throughout the Newark Bay and the surrounding waters in order to create a geomorphologic sedimentation record of dioxin contamination. The analysis of sediments can give valuable information concerning the spatial variation of contamination, and sediment cores are useful for investigating historical trends. Bopp analyzed these sediment cores and suspended matter collected in the Passaic River near Diamond Alkali and in Newark Bay. He found historical levels of 2,3,7,8-TCDD at concentrations up to 21,000 parts per trillion (ppt) and concluded that the chemical manufacturer was the dominant source in the area. More recently, in 2003, one of Bopp's students, Damon Chaky, reanalyzed these cores and calculated the loadings and timelines for the releases of dioxin. He concluded that the Diamond Alkali Agent Orange plant was responsible for fully half the dioxin beneath the New York Harbor Estuary and that Newark dioxin may have gone as far as twenty-six miles *upriver* in the Hudson River, owing to strong tidal flows from the Atlantic Ocean.[9]

Our fear in the early 1980s, while open-ocean disposal was still going on, was that this contamination was being transported offshore. Yet the restriction of dumping at the Mud Dump and other sites would not occur until years later when the Ocean Dumping Ban Act was passed in 1988.[10] By then much of the damage was done. The inner harbor pollutants in these dredged sediments were transported offshore for decades and into the pathways of major fisheries such as lobsters, bluefish, and striped bass. However, as is typical with much environmental legislation, it would take a direct and dramatic threat to human health to get Congress's attention. This was precipitated by an incident in which medical waste with vials of blood and syringes washed up along beaches in New Jersey and Long Island during the summer of 1988. This incident pressured Congress into passing the Medical Waste Tracking Act of 1988. It was not until September 1997, however, that the Mud Dump was officially closed as a disposal site. The entire region around it was designated the Historic Area Remediation Site (HARS), and the sea floor around it (approximately nine nautical square miles in area) was remediated by systematically placing a three-foot cap of clean dredged material atop the sediments contaminated from previous disposals.

In some small way I would like to think that our dioxin in fish and sediment studies were integral to the banning of ocean dumping off New Jersey's coast. For until our offshore lobster results became known, there was insufficient evidence to imply that open-ocean disposal of sewage sludge and contaminated dredged material might be a significant source for the bioaccumulation of persistent toxics in marine fish. Of course we already knew about PCBs in offshore bluefish, but the potential sources of PCBs were so widespread it was difficult to link any offshore contaminant in fish to any one waste disposal activity such as dredge spoils. Yet with 2,3,7,8-TCDD as indicated by Bopp and Chaky's studies, we had a unique marker for a specific contaminant (dioxin) in a specific part of the inner harbor (Passaic River), which was now found offshore (surrounding the dumps) in a species of food fish that never came into the estuary (lobsters).

The Diamond Alkali Remediation

On September 21, 1984, USEPA placed the Diamond Alkali site on the Superfund list, but it was not until 1987, after a series of studies were completed, that EPA selected an interim remedy for the property, including the construction of a clay slurry wall around it, the installation of a cap, and the pumping and treating of groundwater to reduce the migration of contamination to the river.[11] Construction began in April 2000 and was completed in December 2001. Subsequently, workers gathered the contaminated soil and debris from around the area then buried and capped it onsite with concrete. The Diamond Alkali Superfund site today can be seen from the Port Authority commuter train heading into New York City as it runs along the Passaic River from Newark's Penn Station. Immediately your eye is drawn to an incongruous grassy mound with a huge set of potted trees lining the waterfront, as if it were a bit of gardening done by an industrial landscaper with no eye for aesthetics. To me it looks like a pustule about to burst and spray its pestilence all over downtown Newark. This bit of landscaping charade encapsulates the entire contents of the pesticide factory dismantled brick-by-brick and carefully buried onsite as an urban hazardous waste site. The impregnable clay slurry wall was poured into a thirty-foot deep trench that encircles the site like a clay bathtub and the groundwater treatment system installed to cleanse what little rainwater infiltrates the site.

The human drama this parklike landscape hides, however, is the years of intensive policy and political work that the dismantlement took. This included years of environmental provocateurs and flamboyant politicians at pubic meetings deriding the owners, as well as community activists who lobbied that the dioxin be hauled offsite. But no disposal facility existed that would accept dioxin, so onsite it remained. Glancing at the green lawn covering the impermeable cap there is no indication of the attempts to track down and evaluate the health of workers and surrounding community members. And more important, what is left unseen to the citizenry is the stalling by the owners to delay and spend as little as possible on cleanup, especially as it pertains to the river. Until recently the toxic material in the river sediments remained relatively untouched by remediation. In fact, the Army Corps of Engineers and USEPA suspended dredging for a while in the late 1980s while they devised a method to assess the safety of the dioxin-contaminated mud dumped at the offshore ocean disposal site. This threatened Port Newark and Port Elizabeth downstream of the plant, since the shipping channels filled with silt and threatened to choke off commerce until a plan was devised to remedy the disposal of the contaminated dredge spoils.

This came to a head in 1992 when a New Jersey appellate court handed down a scathing opinion against the responsible parties associated with the Superfund site. The three-judge panel found that for the almost two decades ending in 1969, the Diamond (Alkali) Shamrock Chemicals Company and its predecessors had polluted the Passaic River. "Diamond's management was wholly indifferent to the consequences," appellate division judge David Baime wrote. "Profits came first." This decision gave the USEPA the leverage to order in 1994 that Diamond's corporate successors (Tierra Solutions) clean up the river pollution.[12] In 1994, under USEPA pressure, the companies signed an administrative order compelling them to study pollution along six miles of the Passaic River flowing past the former Diamond plant and then clean it up. They did this study, but it took an inordinately long period of time with few practical results. Between 1990 and 2005, scientists retained by the Diamond site PRPs published at least thirty-five papers on Passaic River pollution in academic journals, presented papers at conferences, and even wrote a general interest book titled *A Common Tragedy: History of an Urban River*.[13] Yet no dredging and clean-up followed!

In 2005, then NJDEP Commissioner Bradley Campbell (under Governor McGreevy), dissatisfied with this slow USEPA Superfund approach, took harsher enforcement actions against Diamond's successors and issued a directive giving them thirty days to pay for a $2.9 million study—by a consultant the state would hire—on how to clean up the river, ostensibly by dredging up to ten million cubic yards of dioxin-contaminated sediment. In the lawsuit, Campbell argued that the companies had "orchestrated and implemented a strategy to delay and impede the cleanup and restoration of the Passaic River." Three years later under yet another NJDEP Commissioner (Lisa Jackson had replaced Campbell) Occidental and Tierra Solutions agreed to pay $80 million to at least remove a hotspot of dioxin-contaminated sediments from the river near the old pesticide plant.[14] The plan was to drive metal sheets into the river around the hotspot, dredge the sediments, and barge them to a nearby location for processing and decontamination. In June 2007, USEPA announced it was considering six options to accelerate the cleanup of pollution from dioxin and other contaminants in the entire seventeen miles of the lower tidal Passaic River. For the purpose of this study a governmental partnership was formed, including the Army Corps of Engineers, USEPA, N.J. Department of Transportation, N.J. Department of Environmental Protection, the National Oceanic and Atmospheric Administration, and the U.S. Fish and Wildlife Service. This group is currently managing a remedial investigation funded by more than a hundred companies at a cost of $50 million, which will result in a comprehensive solution for the entire lower Passaic River basin. The alternatives under consideration include dredging and capping the sediments of the lower eight miles, which could carry a price tag of $1 billion to $2 billion.[15]

Professionally, I am relieved that the Passaic River, even in a limited capacity, will be cleansed of its dioxin load after twenty-five years of study. It was also satisfying to see how the "command and control" nature of our actions in the 1980s had national significance, as dioxin sources were aggressively investigated nationwide and remedial strategies finalized. We identified the threat, alerted the public, and removed the contaminant as expeditiously as possible. The success of this approach was validated by a 2006 USEPA report that summarized the results of a comprehensive inventory of the sources and environmental releases of dioxinlike compounds in the United States from typical activities, including combustion; metal smelting, refining, and processing sources; chemical manufacturing sources; natural sources; and environmental reservoirs.[16] It estimated a 90 percent reduction in the release of dioxin into the environment of the United States between 1987 and 2000 from all known sources. This stands as testimony to the aggressive campaigns in New Jersey, other states, and the federal government to track down and remediate or remove known sources of environmental contamination during those intervening years.

However, this aggressive "polluter pays" and "command and control" approach to environmental protection had some unexpected consequences. Following Superfund's lead, New Jersey laws mandated "strict and several liability" for all PRPs associated with a newly discovered hazardous waste site. This was the provision that allowed NJDEP and USEPA to pull current owners into cleaning up the chromate and dioxin sites and to accept liability for companies they bought or managed. Yet when NJDEP included this provision in the Environmental Cleanup Responsibility Act (ECRA) of 1983, it sent shockwaves throughout the banking and development community. Under ECRA, specified industrial properties where hazardous materials were commonly used and possibly abandoned were required to perform environmental assessments as a prerequisite for sale. Unfortunately, the legislature did not provide NJDEP with enough funding to enlarge the bureaucracy to support these transactions, especially real estate deals that were often time-sensitive.

As a result, backlogs grew in the days before desktop computers, and a mountain of paperwork trailed behind each deliberation.

By the late 1990s, a few hundred NJDEP professionals managed tens of thousands of sites. Some of these were straightforward, whereas others were quite complicated with air, water, soil, and groundwater contamination spread over acres. For these large sites, subsets were cut out called areas of concern and managed as nested sites within the much larger ones, adding to the complexity. The ECRA management model ran into so much red tape that it became known as the "Environmental Consultant Retirement Act," since all it seemed to do was generate mounds of paper by consultants for industrial property owners. Unfortunately, owing to this deluge of paperwork, few decisions were made, and it became increasingly difficult for a developer to get a "no further action" letter and proceed with the transfer of property. As a result, many of these stagnant sites languished or were abandoned in disrepair. More often developers shied away from these industrial locations for redevelopment, labeling them "brownfield" sites and preferring to shift their activities to more suburban "greenfield" locations. Therefore, many critics claim that ECRA went too far and inadvertently accelerated urban decay and suburban sprawl.

In response to this phenomenon another pollution cleanup paradigm came about in the mid-1990s to replace the "polluter pays" and "command and control" strategies. This involved "voluntary cleanups" by responsible parties and a reduction in "strict and several liability" provisions for banks and developers through a concept that has become synonymous with twenty-first-century urban redevelopment, namely, brownfields remediation. Some applaud the brownfields concept as a release from the economic gridlock of the 1980s, using a more business-friendly model for remediation, whereas others question whether the paradigm shift is equally protective of human health and the environment. This remains to be seen, for reasons I will explore in the next chapter.

CHAPTER 7

The Lure of Brownfields

NEW WAYS OF THINKING ABOUT POLLUTION

I went to see Buckminster Fuller speak in graduate school at the University of Pennsylvania on the topic of "progressive thought." Fuller was one of those under-the-radar geniuses of the twentieth century's technological pantheon, known more for his invention of the geodesic dome than for his radical ideas about the educational conformity that dimmed students' brilliance. That day he talked about how he came up with the idea of the geodesic dome by watching trees in his yard sway with the breeze, some bending over in a stiff storm yet never breaking. He eventually devised equations to show how tensile strength, when applied to slim structures like a tree trunk, which radiates growth outward in sequential layers, could be harnessed to make three-sided pyramidical structures. He linked these forms by interlocking triangles to create immense domes of glass panels and feather-light materials that allowed sunlight to penetrate the open spaces below.

Fuller was also renowned as a cultural radical. When I was an undergraduate, he published a book whose text was presented numerically from front to back only on even-numbered pages; one was then expected to flip it over and read the rest of the book ostensibly upside down on odd-numbered pages. This approach to printing, he argued, was as valid as the Chinese custom of *shupai*, or vertical scriptwriting, where text was printed from top to bottom in columns instead of lines across a page. He wished to show that the world is hampered by cultural biases and that we should not be impeded by static worldviews. He felt we should be open to other perspectives and perhaps more utilitarian ways of describing the world around us. He argued that as a result of this blinkered mode of thought many technological solutions were too conventional and answered only proximate questions while ignoring long-term consequences. And there for him was the fatal flaw in societal thinking.

These unsustainable solutions often created other problems that needed solving. Perhaps not apparent at first, these drawbacks could multiply over time and create more tangled and apparently irresolvable issues.

In this book, *Operating Manual for Spaceship Earth*, Fuller says, "If you are in a shipwreck and all the boats are gone, a piano top buoyant enough to keep you afloat that comes along makes a fortuitous life preserver. But this is not to say that the best way to design a life preserver is in the form of a piano top. I think that we are clinging to a great many piano tops in accepting yesterday's fortuitous contrivings as constituting the only means for solving a given problem."[1] His point is that many scientists and professionals lumber along not seeking change primarily because of how we are trained to build on known systems of thinking. I mention this anecdote because Fuller's insight into the need for innovation that is tied to constant reassessment can act as a means to explore the evolution of New Jersey's hazardous waste management laws from the 1970s until today. Admittedly, many legislative acts and environmental regulations were extremely useful in their time and resulted in positive changes to the state's landscape. In contrast, a number of piano tops drifted by that held us afloat for a while but in hindsight were mere flotsam and jetsam that precipitated other regulatory crises, with little thought given to how to map a sustainable way out. For example, the "command and control," enforcement-centered regulations of the 1970s and 1980s ran into roadblocks as the century progressed. As I have described in previous chapters, many of the events that overtook us in those early days were catastrophic, a series of crisis management moments that drove legislators and regulators to intervene with new laws and regulations only when confronted by calamity. Thus, New Jersey moved forward environmentally as a "state of emergencies," turning from one crisis to another with limited forethought and based only on what we knew at the time. These incidents included cholera epidemics, tainted drinking water, radon leaking into basements, and explosions of illegal hazardous waste over residents cowering in their houses. However, with time, experience, and introspection, New Jersey did shift the paradigm for action and pass new and more circumspect legislation, although sometimes with the same unforeseen consequences.

Hazardous Site Legislation in New Jersey

On December 11, 1980, the U.S. Congress passed the Comprehensive Environmental Response, Compensation, and Liability Act (CERCLA), commonly known as Superfund.[2] This law created a tax on the chemical and petroleum industries and provided broad federal authority to respond directly to releases or threatened releases of hazardous substances that could endanger public health or the environment. Superfund established "strict, joint, and several liability" for all present and former land owners and operators of a site, which meant anyone who had ever owned or operated on it could be found liable for a portion of the cleanup costs. The only exemption from the strict liability statute was an act of god, or war, and in some limited circumstances the act of a third party. "Strictly liable" also meant that the government did not require proof of negligence or deliberate misconduct to hold a responsible party liable for the cleanup costs. In addition, Superfund held that if a responsible party did not clean up a site, then the government could and would seek punitive damages for triple the costs. The treble cost would act as an enforcement hammer to seek up-front cooperation.

Building on this approach, New Jersey passed the Environmental Cleanup Responsibility Act (ECRA) in 1983.[3] ECRA was considered the country's most stringent environmental cleanup law when it was enacted. It required that certain industrial and commercial sites be cleaned up before they were sold, transferred, or closed. It was designed to regulate property transfers in such a way as to redress the laissez-faire economic policies of the twentieth century, which endorsed minimal government intervention for industrial activities and hazardous waste disposal. It established preconditions on the transfer of specific types of industrial properties that were meant to assure buyers and the state that the land was not contaminated. If hazardous substances were found onsite, then the owner had to clean it up based on a closure plan approved by the state or else pass the remediation costs on to the buyer. This typically involved an escrow account established by the seller.

In 1986, Congress amended Superfund with SARA, the Superfund Amendments and Reauthorization Act. SARA made several important changes and additions to the program, including a stress on "permanent remedies" in remediation, and it increased the focus on human health problems associated with these sites. It also provided exemptions from strict and severable liability, using an "innocent landowner's defense." This allowed property owners who did not know and had no reason to know of any contamination at a site before it was purchased to be held free from liability as long as certain conditions were met. The innocent landowner's defense required a new owner to undertake at the time of acquisition all appropriate inquiry into the previous ownership and uses of the property consistent with good commercial or customary practice. This became known as a "due diligence" investigation, which affected both the mom-and-pop gas station operators and their leaking underground storage tank as well as the giant petrochemical company flushing poorly treated chemicals into unlined lagoons.

In contrast to this apparent relaxation of the liability clauses in Superfund, the New Jersey Supreme Court expanded the scope of ECRA in 1992 to include the cleanup of land adjacent to industrial properties for sale if contamination had migrated offsite through windblown weathering of soils or groundwater plumes. This ruling significantly expanded the liability of property owners in New Jersey and heightened the potential costs involved with selling and cleaning up contaminated sites. Yet the ruling was in keeping with the legislative intent of the ECRA law and the government's philosophy that placed the cost of a cleanup on the polluter, thereby deflecting the cost from the taxpayer. Unfortunately, many of these ECRA transactions were caught up in time delays, loss of resale opportunities, or outright abandonment of contaminated properties that banks and mortgage companies then inherited. These abandoned or "orphaned" sites popped up all over New Jersey throughout the 1980s and 1990s, tying up urban renewal and inadvertently sending development to the suburbs. This accelerated the loss of green space outside the cities and exacerbated the negative aspects of suburban sprawl.

In reaction to these negative societal effects, the state legislature in the 1990s sought to fix this drain on the commercial resale of industrial properties by amending the law. In 1992, New Jersey established a Voluntary Cleanup Program and then in 1993 replaced ECRA with the Industrial Site Recovery Act (ISRA), which created two cleanup levels for contaminated sites, based on their intended future use.[4] Typically, this resulted in a less stringent and costly clean-up goal if the site was planned for continued industrial use. If residential properties were anticipated as part of the redevelopment, a much more aggressive and higher clean-up standard was used.

The business community was ecstatic about this development. Its members felt there should be different standards of cleanliness for industrial and residential sites, since kids cannot ride their bikes on fenced factory grounds. Hal Bozarth, a spokesman for the Chemical Industry Association, contended that there should be separate standards because a longtime industrial site is unlikely to be used for anything else. Sharpe James, the mayor of Newark at the time, agreed, saying: "if an industrial site near housing can be made safe for its neighbors, it need not be cleaned beyond that standard." Environmentalists said no to multiple cleanup standards. They felt it was backsliding, giving in to property developers and banks at the expense of public health. Their fear was that ISRA-remediated industrial properties that used these lax standards might be converted into residential properties later on. Edward Lloyd, the director of Rutgers Environmental Law Center at the time, said: "We shouldn't take the responsibility for future generations. New Jersey isn't big enough to leave a particular area contaminated. Do we want to have signs up all around that say

'Personal Risk—Do Not Enter?'" James W. Hughes, a professor in the Department of Urban Planning at Rutgers University, called the debate "a classic environmental and economic quandary." He compared the 1980s to the 1990s, contending that "every time we go through an explosive growth period we become complacent and standards start rising. We're so overwhelmed about managing new growth that the older cities' problems are put on the back burner. But when the economic down-cycle comes we hit a threshold change in attitude: 'Hey, we're desperate for economic change and planning!'"[5]

Ultimately, Governor James Florio agreed with the business community and signed ISRA into law, calling its predecessor (ECRA) "a symbol for regulations run amok!" and severely criticized the earlier law for creating a "bureaucratic nightmare, hindering both clean-up and further economic development at sites."[6] With ISRA, the aggressive "polluter pays" and "command and control" laws of the 1980s transitioned into something more business-friendly. Whether it was equally protective of the health of the citizenry and the environment continues to be debated. Some businesspeople and financiers claimed that both ECRA and ISRA expedited the decay of our inner cities to the point that empty factories and orphaned contaminated sites are the only legacy from that era. It is not surprising to them that within many New Jersey cities the more successful businesses are scrap metal shredders and concrete recycling facilities where demolition and the salvage of old factories is all that is left of our industrial heritage.

FACTORY TOWNS AND COLONIAL GENIUS

The legacy of abandoned hazardous waste sites in New Jersey at first glance can appear demented to most uninformed observers. Wondering aloud they might ask, "How on earth did they let it get that way?" (And who is they, anyway?) Unfortunately, you would need a time machine to ferret out the answer to such a simple question. Every abandoned factory sitting forlorn beside a riverfront carries a tale of American entrepreneurial spirit that thrived before it failed. It provided jobs to the community before its doors closed the day the company relocated or lost in competition to newer, more resilient start-up companies. The dilapidated buildings left behind belie the greatness of the American people who will take lemons and make lemonade, see a sand pit and turn it into a glass factory, divert a river to cool a steel mill or a blast furnace. Nations and mercantile empires can both rise and fall on the most inconceivable chances, whether the result of political tinkering or market forces that drive buyers offshore. This may leave America filled with vacant landscapes, without a clue as to what was manufactured there, what immigrant communities thrived there.

Yet if you look and listen, sometimes you can smell a whiff of brimstone and coke coming off an abandoned lot, or hear an anvil struck and the laughter of workingmen making an honest living, ghosts of New Jersey's once industrial might. I found one of these ghost towns not far from my office in Trenton. And the name of that town was Roebling.

The first time I heard the name John Augustus Roebling was in the 1960s on my first open-water scuba dive into the Hudson River at the Navy Yard in Bayonne, New Jersey. My instructor, a salvage diver, pointed at the Brooklyn Bridge across the bay and mentioned "caisson disease" as a warning not to come up too quickly or we would get the bends. He was referring to decompression sickness, a disease that crippled John Augustus's son, Washington Roebling, who had spent too much time in a pressurized caisson below the waterline as miners dug foundations for the stone piers of the bridge. The next time I heard the name, it was as an environmentalist in the 1980s when I visited the Roeblings' steel works in the village named after them along the Delaware River. By then the illustrious industrial history of the works had faded, leaving only a 220-acre abandoned factory filled with hazardous waste and a Superfund site surrounded by the faltering company town of four thousand people.

John Augustus Roebling was the quintessential American genius. Humble immigrant beginnings matched with an inquisitive nature and a wandering soul led him from one amazing engineering feat to another. He came to western Pennsylvania from Germany in the early nineteenth century when it was still a wilderness, no roads or railroads, just remnant Indian tracks and rivers to navigate. There he founded a plantation in Saxonburg where only tradesmen with the necessary skills to survive in the wilderness were allowed to live. Eventually he took a job surveying canal routes across the Appalachian Mountains for companies looking to move Pennsylvania coal to the blast furnaces in New Jersey and New York. The hills were too large and the valleys too deep for typical canal locks, so Roebling invented "inclined planes" using water wheels and sledges to pull barges up the hills. He also built aqueducts to extend the canal system across the valleys.

Like Buckminster Fuller, Roebling had an appreciation of tensile strength. He realized that trees stiffen as they grow upward, yet they are flexible enough along their entire length to sway but not break. The force of the wind is transmitted downward to the anchor of their roots. Using this observation, he devised a plan to weave steel ropes into cables, which eventually were used to build suspension bridges like the one across the Niagara Falls gorge between the United States and Canada. It was in New Jersey, however, that he built the iron works for processing steel into cables. Soon every great city in America wanted suspension bridges, aqueducts, and canals. This included New York

City, where he designed the bridge over the East River to Brooklyn. But John Augustus did not see this great project to its end, for in the first days of its construction his foot was crushed by a falling stone and he died of septicemia. It was his son, Washington Roebling and his indefatigable wife, Emily Warren, who carried the Brooklyn Bridge project to fruition. Roebling expanded the steel works and built a model factory town beside it with communal row houses, subsidized stores, and recreational facilities for the tradesmen and laborers he hired, just as his father had done at the Saxonburg plantation. As a young man Washington Roebling was an American legend. During the Civil War he joined the Union Army as a private and eventually rose to the rank of major in the fledgling Army Corp of Engineers. He constructed suspension bridges across southern rivers while dodging rebel bullets and was instrumental in the birth of the United States Air Force, acting as an artillery observer suspended over battlefields in hot-air reconnaissance balloons. In fact, from this aerie he was the first to telegraph General Meade that Robert E. Lee's Army of Northern Virginia was marching toward Pennsylvania. This led to an epic chase up the Shenandoah Valley that ended on the bloody fields of Gettysburg where his regiment pulled cannons onto "Little Round Top" at the last minute to save the Union Army from being flanked and annihilated.

The Roebling steel works went on to become the largest wire business in the world, providing telegraph wire, balling wire, electrical wire, bridge cable wire, and wire for ships. It was the exclusive provider of wire for the Panama Canal and the Otis Elevator Company. Washington Roebling and his descendents actively ran the business until 1952, when it was sold to a conglomerate that operated until 1988. Unfortunately, metals manufacturing generates a significant amount of toxic wastes, including chromium, lead, and asbestos. These materials were disposed of onsite into lagoons and landfills, wetlands and creeks. The site was added to the USEPA Superfund list in 1983, and the cleanup has gone on ever since, with the government taking control of the site in 1995, when the owners declared bankruptcy. Today much of the cleanup is completed, yet more remains to be done. Most of the seventy-four buildings are demolished and the wastes removed. The model factory town of Roebling still sits beside these ravaged fields and endures as a bedroom community to Trenton. Light rail trains now move past the site, shuffling workers to jobs north and south. Recently USEPA awarded a grant to Burlington County on how best to redevelop the former hazardous site. Plans include a marina for the nearby Delaware River and a shopping mall. But while these plans are debated, walking beside the leveled factory grounds seems a bit like visiting a ghost town.

I can't help but be impressed by the scale and scope of the Roeblings' dream and the vision they brought to their engineering feats. Their wire factory is gone, as are the canals and the aqueducts they built, most replaced by railroads. But it is their bridges that endure and lift the heart. Whenever I ride beneath the piers of the Brooklyn or the George Washington Bridges and see the wrapped cables rising into thin air, holding up the weight of a thousand trucks and cars, it seems as if the Roeblings had discovered the secret of weightlessness. Their dream saw majesty in technology, a soul for engineering beauty that combined the functional with the austere. Theirs was an American genius made rampant, filling our landscape with monumental structures that ancient Egyptians and Greeks might envy.

Yet we never see these fleeting images of greatness when we look at a crumbling chemical works or an abandoned factory today. It is the hazardous materials that lay just beneath the surface that we inherit. These toxic chemicals are the legacy of the Industrial Revolution, its haste and disregard for waste management as long as the product got out on time and a profit was made. And currently the only solution to making these sites productive again—in the face of costly cleanups—is to encourage development in a way that streamlines the process and supplies some limits on financial liability. This environmental policy jumpstart occurred in the late 1990s through federal and state legislative actions; it was called the brownfields initiative.

THE BROWNFIELDS INITIATIVE

In the broadest sense, brownfield land is land previously used for industrial purposes. In an environmental regulatory sense, it implies land contaminated by "low levels" of hazardous waste or pollution that has the potential to be reused once it is cleaned up. To a city planner, brownfield land offers opportunity for development and increased tax revenue by turning a burnt-out factory on the waterfront into condominiums or a minor league baseball stadium. Many brownfield sites are not so large, however. It might be a vacant lot or a dry cleaning establishment in a strip mall requiring minimal remediation of residual solvents before being converted into a shoe store. Land that is more severely contaminated with high concentrations of pollution, such as a Superfund site, is not considered a brownfield site. Those sites still carry all the requirements of strict and severable liability with constant regulatory oversight. A Superfund site is evaluated, ranked, and placed on the National Priorities List by USEPA, which qualifies it for federal cleanup money. It also allows the agency to put pressure on the responsible parties who own the site or the hazardous waste to pay for, or assist, in the cleanup.

In 1995, USEPA launched a federal brownfields program that empowered states, communities, and other stakeholders in economic redevelopment to work together in a timely manner to prevent, assess, safely clean up, and sustainably reuse brownfields. It defined brownfields as "real property where the expansion, redevelopment, or reuse of which may be complicated by the presence, or potential presence, of a hazardous substance, pollutant, or contaminant."[7] At the time, USEPA estimated that there were more than 450,000 brownfields in the United States and that cleaning up and reinvesting in those properties would increase local tax bases, facilitate job growth, utilize existing infrastructure, and take development pressure off undeveloped open land.

Initially, USEPA provided small amounts of grant money to local governments that launched hundreds of two-year pilot projects. These grants support revitalization efforts by funding environmental assessment, cleanup, and job training activities as well as planning and community outreach. USEPA claims that its investment in the brownfields program has leveraged more than $6.5 billion in cleanup and redevelopment, creating approximately twenty-five thousand new jobs. Subsequently, through the passage of the federal Small Business Liability Relief and Brownfields Revitalization Act of 2001, the brownfields initiative and policies were passed into federal law.[8]

The New Jersey brownfields program began in earnest in 1998 with the passage of the Brownfield and Contaminated Site Remediation Act.[9] This legislation was prompted by the fact that NJDEP typically oversees some twenty-three thousand contaminated sites, ten thousand of which are potential brownfield sites.[10] The act rewarded voluntary cleanups and offered developers and investors incentives to build on blighted areas. To encourage participation, NJDEP offered to consolidate and expedite permit reviews, allowed less costly remediation through the use of the two-tier cleanup criteria, and permitted less restrictive cleanup remedies called "institutional and engineering controls." These controls are used when a remedial action leaves some level of contamination behind after a clean-up. Institutional controls are not remedial measures but rather legal mechanisms intended to reduce exposure by controlling the behavior of the future owner of a brownfield site.[11] For example, an institutional control might be a deed notice alerting all future buyers that contamination lies beneath a building or a parking lot. Theoretically, this would preclude someone from converting a partially remediated hazardous waste site into a playground or a day care center. The intent is to restrict future risk through land use management. Institutional controls are generally used in conjunction with engineering controls such as capping and fencing an area, as was done at the Hudson County chromium sites.

Brownfield development is especially attractive in blighted urban areas where properties have trouble attracting adequate private funding for remediation or development. In these situations NJDEP offers to recoup real estate developers up to 75 percent of their cleanup costs and supplies liability protection with a written "covenant not to sue" after a successful cleanup. This covenant includes actions against any subsequent owners, lessees, or operators who come onto the site after the covenant is issued. As a result, speculators bought contaminated buildings and land at low prices, which they then remediated and replaced with condominiums, commercial space, or even a minor league baseball stadium. The resultant redevelopment and demolition activities in New Jersey were extraordinary, including major projects in every county in the state. Not surprisingly, many of these brownfields sites were in cities, and one of the most devastated municipalities in New Jersey was Camden.

CAMDEN, NEW JERSEY

I am a great believer in cities, especially the colonial cities that helped make America great but that now lie fallow and unaided after the twentieth century's downturn in manufacturing. Camden contributed significantly to the early rise of the Industrial Revolution; the old city was home to tradesmen's shops and entrepreneurial enterprises such as sawmills, candle factories, carriage and wagon makers, tanneries, blacksmith shops, and canneries. Later these specialists were replaced by large-scale industrial operations, including glass works, steel and iron forges, woolen mills, and chemical plants. A large jump in manufacturing occurred during the Civil War, when more than a hundred factories mass-produced material for the Union Army, including a shipyard for ironclads like the *Monitor*. There was also a nickel works, which served as the major supplier of coins for the U.S. Mint across the river in Philadelphia. A modest cannery opened up, called the Joseph Campbell Preserving Company. In 1899, John Thompson Dorrance, a chemical engineer and organic chemist at Campbell, successfully developed a method of canning condensed tomato soup. This innovation helped Campbell out-compete its rivals, who were still shipping heavy, uncondensed soup. Campbell shipped and sold his product at one-third the cost and still operates today in Camden as the Campbell Soup Company.

From 1899 to 1967, Camden was also the home of New York Shipbuilding Company, which employed thousands. My mother, Ethel Dewees, worked there as a "Rosy the Riveter" in the early days of World War II, when it became the most productive shipyard in the world. Notable naval vessels built at New York Shipbuilding included the ill-fated cruiser USS *Indianapolis*, which delivered the atomic bomb for Hiroshima in such secrecy that when it was sunk on the way home, its men were attacked by sharks for a week before anyone knew it had gone missing. The aircraft carrier USS *Kitty Hawk* was also built there, today the navy's oldest active warship, last used in 2003 for Operation Iraqi Freedom.

The first commercial nuclear-powered ship, the NS *Savannah*, was launched there in 1962. I visited this ship when it docked in Hoboken during my days working on the American Export piers in high school. The first commercial railroad in the United States opened in Camden as well, a beeline route between Camden and Amboy City on the banks of the Raritan River, where a ferryboat took riders to New York City. This was followed by another railroad, which perhaps had an even more impressive effect on development in southern Jersey, as it traveled through the deep Pine Barrens forest to terminate at a then sleepy coastal town called Atlantic City. Today Atlantic City is a premier tourist destination for gambling and recreation in the United States and can still be reached by this same rail bed that runs by my home in Haddonfield.

In 1840, Camden had a population of 3,371, about the same size as Chicago and three times larger that Saint Louis, Missouri. With rapid industrialization and the need for skilled and manual labor accelerating, immigration expanded the population throughout the nineteenth century, and by 1920 there were 116,000 people living in the city.[12] The ethnic nature of Camden changed radically as well during these years. Originally, colonial Camden was German, British, and Irish, but by the 1920s, Italians and eastern European immigrants became the majority ethnic groups. These groups formed insular communities surrounding churches and synagogues as the center of social life.

Today Camden is primarily black and Hispanic, with whites in the minority. Failing industries and hard economic times have reduced the population to about eighty thousand. The manufacturing and shipbuilding operations, which kept the city afloat throughout World War II, have gone dormant. What's left are moldering factories, the fallen-down industrial relics of nineteenth-century ingenuity, and vacant fields filled with ash and decaying structures, many of them targeted for urban renewal under the New Jersey Brownfields Act. Some of these brownfields sites are noteworthy for what they can teach us about the value of the brownfields law.

THE RCA VICTOR COMPANY

In 1901, the waterfront in Camden near the Benjamin Franklin Bridge was home to the Victor Talking Machine Company. The Victor Company originally produced recordings of the Philadelphia Orchestra as well pop artists like Fats Waller, who cut his famous vinyl disk "Sugar" in Camden, based on a style of swing he had learned while playing organ for silent movies in Harlem's

Lincoln Theater. Other artists who recorded at Victor included Enrico Caruso, Vladimir Horowitz, and Arturo Toscanini. Jelly Roll Morton, Duke Ellington, and the Carter Family also recorded there.[13] In 1929, the Radio Corporation of America (RCA) purchased the Victor Company, becoming "RCA Victor" and acquiring Victor's famous trademark—a Jack Russell terrier quizzically listening to a recording of "His Master's Voice!" in front of an old gramophone with a huge horn for amplification. Four huge stained-glass images of this dog called "Nipper" were built into all four sides of a fire tower atop the manufacturing building that could be seen for miles in any direction.

By the 1930s, the RCA Victor campus grew to fifty-four acres and hundreds of buildings, placing it on a par with Menlo Park, New Jersey, where Thomas Edison had invented and manufactured the first electric light bulbs only decades earlier. At its peak, ten thousand employees worked at RCA Victor, manufacturing electronic turntables and the first 33⅓ rpm records, and developing television as well as a new Radio Detection and Ranging system, which the engineers christened RADAR. By 1969, however, the Camden plant had lost many jobs, owing to highway construction, suburbanization, and racial tensions. Beginning in 1984, RCA Victor relocated all of its product lines away from Camden and began to sell off the property.

In 1986, the General Electric (GE) Company bought the RCA Victor site, triggering an Industrial Site Recovery Act, or ISRA, site investigation. I worked on this ISRA investigation and helped inspect every inch of the plant and its outlier buildings. My goal was to find spilled chemicals or areas where hazardous material might have been stored and that required some kind of remedial action. We found a report that RCA Victor demolished its original warehouse on the waterfront in the early 1960s by imploding it and then simply bulldozing the debris into the river. Yet when we went to look for the debris pile, all we found was a pier suspended over the river with an enormous 10,000-gallon oil tank on top of it. During our audit we walked every inch of the RCA campus, from the basements where the vinyl cutting vaults were located to the top of the boiler house where the twin smokestacks rose like fingers of stone into the sky. Over time we mapped the locations of all the hazardous materials and mandated their removal. In spite of all these efforts, GE eventually sold off the property and demolished most of the factory grounds save for a few of the original RCA Victor buildings. Building No. 17, the Nipper Building, with its iconic stained-glass images of the trademark dog was declared a national historical site and could not be demolished.

At this point the New Jersey brownfields law was in place, which acted as a template for the developers to remediate and refurbish the Nipper Building. The developer chose to perform, with state assistance, a voluntary cleanup and a redevelopment concurrently and in cooperation with key collaborative public sector financing partners such as the Camden Redevelopment Authority. During the remedial phase, NJDEP's Office of Brownfields Reuse supplied full-time technical coordinators and geologists to help the developer get the permit approvals for remediation and redevelopment before construction took place. They also identified technical problems and concerns during the remediation and created innovative final solutions that allowed the redevelopment to go forward on schedule.

The key contaminant of concern at the Nipper Building was PCB spilled from presses and electrical machinery used during manufacturing. The remedial measures that NJDEP approved included using industrial surfactants or soaps as well as scarification to remove the PCBs from contaminated concrete floors and walls. In areas where these technologies were impracticable (for example, the basement), case managers approved engineering controls. These included the entombment of residual PCBs by filling the basement with concrete and the establishment of deed restrictions not to excavate in the future. As an additional safety measure, NJDEP required pre- and post-indoor air monitoring within the basement area and in the shops on the first floor to address any human health concerns related to residential occupancy. Additionally, the developer received technical assistance from the New Jersey Department of Health, which reviewed technical documents and commented from a human health standpoint. NJDEP also required the removal of all sources of groundwater contamination from the site, the installation of an underground barrier wall, the injection of chemicals below ground to degrade residual soil contamination, and ongoing groundwater monitoring. Furthermore, we provided letters to interested parties and lending institutions to address any issues and/or questions they had concerning the remediation and funding for redevelopment.

Subsequently and after extensive remodeling and construction, the Nipper Building was renamed "The Victor" and is currently marketed as luxury apartments containing more than three hundred units, a restaurant, a spa, and a fantastic view of the Philadelphia skyline. The developers invested more than $60 million, including $7 million for environmental remediation to build Camden's first "market-rate" housing in over forty years. This acted as a seed for other nearby brownfields development in the area, including the siting of an aquarium, a minor league baseball stadium, an outdoor concert center, and the wharf for the battleship *New Jersey*. The success of The Victor and other brownfield sites along the waterfront in Camden is encouraging and emblematic of how economic, political, and environmental forces can come together to encourage and support urban renewal.

Figure 8. The Victor (RCA Nipper Building) in Camden, New Jersey, a former brownfield site. (Source: New Jersey Department of Environmental Protection.)

THE BROWNFIELDS LEGACY IN NEW JERSEY

Over the past thirty years we have seen New Jersey pilot some of the most innovative and stringent hazardous waste cleanup laws in the country. Originally driven by the lack of leadership, if not outright antipathy of the federal government to address this problem in the 1980s, New Jersey subsequently saw the initial "polluter pays" laws lead to stagnation and an abandonment of properties during the 1990s. This stimulated the state to new paradigms meant to jumpstart investment but also to impede suburban sprawl and the loss of open space—new piano tops to float upon for a while, as Buckminster Fuller would say. As part of these efforts, the state legislature relieved the pressure of the "strict, joint, and severable liability" provisions under ECRA, first by enacting ISRA and then the Brownfields Act to encourage banks to get back into the real estate business. The banks and developers responded with alacrity, and the reason for their optimism was apparent. However, there were some who felt this land rush might have unintended consequences.

Michael Greenberg, director of the National Center for Neighborhood and Brownfields Redevelopment in Rutgers University's Edward J. Bloustein

School of Planning and Public Policy, pointed out in a 2003 assessment of the initiative that "developing brownfields is a politically acceptable method of stimulating private enterprise, local government, and community groups into building new businesses, housing, and community facilities."[14] It is also worth noting that the biggest cheerleaders for brownfields development are typically the mayors, developers, and businesspeople who worked with the politicians to draft the legislation. To a certain extent they believe that the brownfields approach is mature enough to operate unimpeded and with little reassessment. Their overarching belief is that it is an unmitigated success. In contrast, Greenberg points out the ongoing challenges for health scientists who manage the process. The first he calls "time and financial pressure," because a stream-lined permitting process demands action in a matter weeks or months rather than months or years. This may result in a political and administrative push for action on a staff that is already depleted by major reductions in force. A second challenge Greenberg notes is dealing with developers and local officials who expect environmental scientists to agree with their redevelopment schemes even if the sites still pose measurable public health and ecologic risks. And lastly it has to do with trust. An opinion poll carried out by the National Center for Neighborhood and Brownfields Redevelopment showed that "the public do not necessarily trust local elected officials' and developers' characterizations of environmental risk. People are most likely to trust government scientists and academic environmental health scientists who they believe have a bias toward protecting them, not toward making money."[15]

In hindsight we can see that most of the regulatory changes meant to relax liability and allow less costly remedial measures on brownfields resulted in a booming inner-city real estate business in the past decade. Many of these trans-actions were actively encouraged by government as a means to get unsightly inner-city properties into more productive use. Yet in many instances people still reside near some of these brownfield factories and landfills, enduring the worst of the pollution without abandoning their homes. In other places new facilities have arisen on brownfield sites, which locals feel do not benefit their community and in fact may hurt them. The residents of the Waterfront South community in Camden argue that brownfields have been used to dump unwanted and unhealthy facilities on their neighborhood, such as a regional incinerator and a county wastewater treatment facility. They claim that the placement of these hazardous waste facilities amounts to an inequitable, if not downright discriminatory, practice of environmental injustice on both a racial and socioeconomic scale.

Yet environmental justice and brownfield initiatives are not necessarily mutually exclusive if handled in a considered fashion. To balance these concerns a redevelopment project must address both the public health fears of the residents and advances for urban renewal, recognizing that the needs of the impoverished may not be met if only a few jobs are offered in recompense for pollution exposures during a relaxed remediation. In the next chapter I shall explore this issue of trust as it affected a large and relatively stable community in the northern Camden community of Cramer Hill. There local and state politicians promised the removal of ugly brownfield sites in the neighborhood but did not include the affected community in their deliberations. The redevelopment plan to seize hundreds of uncontaminated homes along with the brownfield sites led to protests and lawsuits that serve as a textbook case on what not to do for redeveloping brownfields on inner-city property.

CHAPTER 8

Environmental Justice

In 1972, as part of a long line of unplanned career changes, I became a social worker at the Hudson County Welfare Department in Jersey City. And in some strange spiral of fate, my welfare district was in Lafayette, the same downtown neighborhood where my dad lived during the Great Depression of the 1930s. The neighborhood was named after the Marquis de Lafayette, that famous French nobleman and friend of George Washington whose military campaigns as a major general in the fledgling Continental Army helped win American independence from Britain. Yet the neighborhood's provenance went back even further—to the Hackensack Indians and the Dutch West India Company. The Dutch pushed the Indians off this prime real estate by the bay in 1612 and founded the village of Communipaw. This was only a few years after Henry Hudson had discovered the great river named after him and fifty years before my mother's ancestors, the Dewees, arrived from Holland in New Amsterdam.

In the 1600s, Communipaw was a fortified village surrounded by wooden palisades to protect the families from the indignant displaced Indians. There the Dutch farmed the bottomland, raised sheep and cattle, and sold their wares to the city across the harbor. By 1664, the English had thrown the Dutch out and were in turn shown the door by the colonial rebels. Meanwhile, Communipaw became Lafayette, and the shoreline was filled and extended a mile into the bay to create the foundations of the Central Railroad and the Long Dock Company. By the beginning of the twentieth century, when my dad lived in Lafayette, most residents worked on the railroad or at the port, each in turn harnessed to the hundreds of factories that consumed the raw materials carried in the boxcars or sold as products from the factories to the surrounding shops. My dad and grandfather were railroad men back then. Later, I spent summers working for the Port Authority, laying tracks under the Hudson River for the subway to New York City.

By the time I arrived in Lafayette as a social worker though, the sturdy brownstone tenements of my father's generation had deteriorated into slums.

With clipboard and welfare forms in hand, my job was to visit the indigent mothers who lived in the collapsing buildings and make sure their families did not starve. My clients were ecumenical: poor whites, blacks, Puerto Ricans, and Haitians mostly. They had moved into the same soot-stained houses that the Irish, Italians, Polish, and other European immigrants had used before them (at least until it was their turn to move up the hill). Unfortunately, many of the houses I visited did not fare so well, especially after the bustling docks and smoky railroads closed down, replaced by truck depots and container ports in Elizabeth on the other side of Newark Bay.

I remember home visits with the poor minorities in Jersey City. Sometimes faces come to me in fleeting vignettes, often spurred by random associations, like the wisps of steam rising from a sewer grate on a November morning. I remember one freezing winter's day walking into an apartment over a garage in Lafayette. The African American woman who lived there had six children but no heat. To address this dangerous situation, she had turned on all the burners of her kitchen stove and placed huge pots of water to boil, creating swirling miasmas of damp vapor that pooled through the rooms like a dank swamp. The fog was filled with dark shadows that I slowly resolved into the outlines of people milling about in their overcoats. I remember carefully stepping around little children in hats and gloves playing on the floor, warily watching my legs moving above them like redwood trees piercing the clouds. As I entered each room, everyone fell silent with a whisper: "Welfare Man's here!" And I must admit the silence made the swamp seem more sullen and spooky as I searched for my client in the gloom. Her home was more a cave than a habitation.

Another time I interviewed a Latino client in a house that had collapsed. At first I thought it was abandoned but then saw smoke coming out of the chimney and lights on the second floor. The building looked like a drunken sailor leaning against a lamp post for stability. One side had sunk onto its foundation while the other side slumped sideways into the void as if held up by marionette strings. Not sure if my client still lived there, but curious, I entered anyway. Looking up the stairwell, I saw that it tilted sideways like a funhouse at a carnival. Holding on to the railing, I pulled myself hand-over-hand until I reached the apartment door, sprung from its frame by the pressure of the tilted house around it. Peeking in I saw a family seated below me and across the room with all their furniture avalanche-piled against the far wall. The sloping floor had buckled in places, with broken floorboards sticking up like splintered teeth. Five pairs of eyes turned as I walked in and introduced myself, holding on to the doorframe so as not to lose my footing and slide across the floor into their coffee table. The mother I had come to see extricated herself from the sofa and carefully walked uphill like a mountain goat making its way along a precipice.

Surprisingly, the kitchen where I interviewed her had farm animals in it. There was a rooster that pecked at my shoelaces under the table, probably thinking they were worms. A billy goat wandered in from the living room and nuzzled my client, as she mindlessly scratched its little chin hairs, then pushed him away with a clucking sound as if it were the family cat.

"No one should live like this!" I remember thinking.

Yet I did my job. I sat down in the gloom and in the broken house to help these women manage their children's needs, hoping that the welfare money might get them out of the ghetto alive. But now, nearly forty years later, many of those houses I visited as a social worker are gone. In the late 1970s, through a fit of urban renewal, city politicians and administrators bid for federal housing and urban development dollars and tore down the waterfront slums and abandoned factories in order to rebuild. Notably, they revitalized Exchange Place, where the Goldman Sachs building now sits atop the ruins of the Colgate soap factory and the Newport Mall covers my clients' old tenements. Liberty State Park covers the unexploded ordnance of Black Toms and its old railyards, and Van Vorst and Hamilton Parks are now surrounded by gentrified townhouses. Like a phoenix reborn, the downtown area effected prosperity changes that spiraled outward into the surrounding communities, drawing light rail lines and waterfront gated communities to neighborhoods that were previously home to junk-yard dogs and homeless vagrants.

But where did the poor and the minorities go? In another twist of fate, I had a chance to find out, although in a different city on the other side of the state. I recently spent a lot of time on the streets of Camden, as part of a toxics trackdown study, looking for brownfield sites and abandoned factories that might be sources of contaminants to the surrounding neighborhoods. Camden is a city denounced by the federal government as the murder capital of America and one of most dangerous places in the country, owing to its high crime rate, drug dealers, and gang activity.

But moving through Camden's blighted neighborhoods, many denuded of homes or else left with abandoned factories riddled with gunshot holes and gang graffiti, I must admit I found life among the ruins. Parents still walk their kids to school each day in plaid uniforms, just as others do in the suburbs, and adults bus or bike their way to work in diverse mixed-use neighborhoods. Moving along the Camden waterfront with Philadelphia in the distance, it is not usual to find pickle factories and fruit processors, forges and canneries, all jumbled together with schools, day-care centers, and homes. The Beckett Street Terminal at the port still moves some bulk cargo the way it used to be done in Jersey City when I was a kid, with arm and brawn, hauling lumpy bags of cocoa off South American ships or moving plywood, machinery, and rolls of reprocessed steel.

Yet mixed in with this industry and humanity are chemical drum–cleaning operations that illegally wash solvents into the streets and concrete crushers that spew microparticles into the passing windows of antiquated buses. There are automobile shredders that run night and day, turning yesterday's model cars into piles of glass, steel, and fibrous plastic, with fugitive plumes of toxic "fluff" flying out over the sleeping neighborhoods. These industries and the abandoned hazardous waste sites that surround them have recently become the nexus of an interesting jousting match, a contest that pits the forces of brownfields redevelopment against crusaders for environmental justice.

THE CRAMER HILL BROWNFIELD DEVELOPMENT AREA

Like other industrial cites in America, Camden has numerous brownfield sites, many of them bundled into brownfield development areas (BDAs). Some of these brownfield sites, like the Nipper Building's resurrection as the upscale Victor, are considered success stories. Others are seen as huge weights we push uphill like Sisyphus, only to periodically lose our grip and watch as gravity overcomes our efforts and the rock of poorly considered redevelopment rolls over us and down the slope again. The machinations of municipal and state officials over the Cramer Hill Brownfield Development Area were just such a story of good intentions gone awry. In the case of Cramer Hill, it appears that the development did not go forward as expected, possibly because the developers and the politicians got too close and did not take into account the wishes and concerns of the residents.

The Cramer Hill neighborhood in northern Camden is bordered by water—the Delaware and Cooper rivers—and a large freight railyard on the other side. Cramer Hill was named for Alfred Cramer, a nineteenth-century developer who owned and laid out the original plots for a neighborhood rich in history that has seen its share of change and transition.[1] Cramer, the son of a farmer, began his career by selling books door to door across southern Jersey. He later opened a store and then moved to Camden, where he engaged in the coal business for a while. Then he turned to real estate, purchased some land with a view to laying out a town, and called it Cramer's Hill. Although primarily populated by Germans when founded in the early 1800s, Cramer's Hill was also home to one of Camden's earliest African American settlements. Cramer sold five hundred lots to families using a novel yet successful mechanism, homeowners paying in monthly installments, many houses bought by skilled mechanics and tradesmen doing business in Philadelphia. Today, according to the 2000 census, Cramer Hill's residents are primarily Latino, with a significant African American population, and although the City of Camden as a whole continues to lose people, Cramer Hill enjoys a stable population.

In 2003, the first year of the New Jersey brownfield development area initiative, NJDEP designated 140 acres across eight properties on Cramer Hill as a BDA. The municipal government sought the designation as part of its citywide redevelopment plan to successfully remediate and reuse the underutilized areas in the neighborhood. The Cramer Hill community initially went along with the idea, as the neighborhood has beautiful vistas of the Delaware River and the residents wanted to take full advantage of it by planning for open space along the water with parks and recreational uses as well as residential opportunities to take advantage of the waterfront environment. Cramer Hill, in contrast to the rest of Camden, has several assets that make renovation desirable, among them a housing vacancy rate of only 6 percent and housing stock that includes an attractive mixture of row, twin, and single-family structures, many with setbacks and side yards. In part because of these assets, the City of Camden's 2003 Strategic Revitalization Plan designated Cramer Hill as a key opportunity area, and it received priority for state Economic Recovery Act funding.[2]

When the Cramer Hill Redevelopment Plan was announced in January 2004, then Governor James E. McGreevey quoted the Bible at the unveiling, saying: "The stone the builders rejected has become the capstone. The Lord has done this, and it is marvelous in our eyes." McGreevey pledged on that day that "Camden is on the verge of an explosive, dynamic renewal."[3] What he did not realize was that the explosion would come from the outraged Cramer Hill residents, hearing for the first time that many of them would be forced to sell and leave their homes. The redevelopment plan called for the state to use its power of "eminent domain" to seize property and displace more than a thousand families.

A private sector redeveloper named Cherokee Investment Partners (an equity investor specializing in contaminated sites) was bankrolling most of the Camden project. It even created a new division called "Cherokee Camden" that would invest a billion dollars in private capital for the redevelopment.[4] As part of this package the Camden Redevelopment Authority and Cherokee wished to remediate the brownfields along the neighborhood's riverfront for replacement with upper- to middle-income housing, a golf course and a marina, as well as a new transportation linkage for commercial development. In the process many existing residents, a high number of whom were homeowners, would be displaced.

Governor McGreevey was there that day to make the announcement because the state had taken over the day-to-day operations of the ailing and mismanaged city in 2002 under the Municipal Rehabilitation and Economic Recovery Act.[5] This takeover was part of a comprehensive five-year plan to oversee Camden's complete municipal operations. Cherokee's motives no doubt were strongly influenced by the $175 million in New Jersey funds that the act gave the city. Based on the redevelopment plan, most of this would fund an elevated highway and bridge to strengthen Cramer Hill's access to Route 30 and the nearby Benjamin Franklin Bridge to Philadelphia. This highway would bypass the unsavory drug-infested streets of northern Camden surrounding Cramer Hill.

Yet by 2006, after the expenditure of $258,000 in legal fees to defend it, the Cramer Hill Redevelopment Plan was dead. The city abandoned the billion-dollar plan when the project became entangled in legal battles, first over environmental justice complaints and then when more than two hundred residents filed a lawsuit saying they did not want to surrender their homes. Ironically, the plan was decided by neither issue but voided by a State Superior Court Judge on a technicality as to the procedures used to develop the planning document. Perhaps exhausted by these deliberations and rounds of public meetings, on May 25, 2006, Camden's chief operating officer for the state announced: "The city will go back to the beginning, holding neighborhood meetings to ask residents what they want, and taking as few homes as possible." "We are not deaf," he added, "We have listened to our residents."[6]

The city decided eventually to adopt a new plan, and as recently as June 2008 sent officials into Cramer Hill to listen to the Cramer Hill Community Benefits Committee describe the results of a redevelopment survey it had commissioned. The survey revealed that the five highest priorities for the community (in anticipated redevelopment benefits) were job training and placement for residents, youth programs, funding for neighborhood safety and cleanup programs, dollars for the construction and operation of recreational facilities, and the construction of affordable housing for low- and moderate-income people.[7] The survey indicated that what the inhabitants liked best about Cramer Hill was the "diversity of neighbors" and a "sense of community."

Unfortunately, without the promise of a gentrified neighborhood and its golf course and marina, Cherokee Investment Partners dropped out of the planning process, leaving the community with little expectation of private redevelopment. Not that it was all that bad. One of the Cramer Hill brownfield sites went forward for redevelopment at the Harrison Avenue landfill along the river where Cherokee wanted to place a golf course. In 2008, the Camden chapter of the Salvation Army received a $54 million grant from the Ray and Joan Kroc Foundation (Ray Kroc was the founder of McDonald's hamburger restaurants) to build and operate a state-of-the-art, 132,000–square foot community center in Cramer Hill, which will feature an atrium-style town plaza, a family service center, indoor and outdoor recreational facilities, an aquatic center, a child-care center, and community enrichment, job-training, and antipoverty programs. Exactly what the Cramer Hill community wanted!

The Environmental Justice Initiative

Ironically, a month after Governor McGreevey formally launched the Cramer Hill Redevelopment Plan, he signed Executive Order No. 96 on February 19, 2004, that established an environmental justice policy initiative in New Jersey.[8] In hindsight the marriage of the brownfield and environmental justice initiatives, if rolled out in tandem and with overt linkages, might have produced a more positive outcome for redevelopment in Cramer Hill. The seeds for the state environmental justice program were planted by a number of national actions, one dating back as far as 1979. That was the first time the U.S. Civil Rights Act was used to challenge an environmental decision. It involved the siting of a waste facility in Houston, Texas (*Bean v. Southwestern Waste Management Corporation*), where residents filed a class-action lawsuit to block construction of a sanitary landfill in their suburban, middle-class neighborhood. The plaintiffs were subsequently defeated in court and the landfill was built, but the experience mobilized a number of other communities to use the same strategies.

Subsequently, more than five hundred people were arrested in protests over the construction and operation of a landfill for disposing of PCB wastes in Warren County, North Carolina.[9] The press coverage of the North Carolina protests stimulated Congress to ask the federal General Accounting Office (GAO) to conduct a study of eight southern states (Alabama, Florida, Georgia, Kentucky, Mississippi, North Carolina, South Carolina, and Tennessee) and to determine if there was a correlation between the location of hazardous waste landfills and the racial and economic status of the surrounding communities. The GAO report, addressed to Congressional Representative James Florio (later to become governor of New Jersey, years before McGreevey), showed a clear bias in landfill placement, with three out of every four landfills sited near predominantly minority communities, even though such communities made up only 20 percent of the region's population.[10]

It was not until 1991, however, that the idea of environmental justice would gain national attention, when the First National People of Color Environmental Leadership Summit met in Washington, D.C. The participants adopted seventeen principles of environmental justice as a means to challenge the existing environmental movement and its seeming lack of attention to the issues in communities of color. Notably these principles declared: "Environmental justice demands that public policy be based on mutual respect and justice for all peoples, free from any form of discrimination or bias."[11] Following this in 1992, William Reilly, the head of USEPA created a Work Group on Environmental Equity and later established the Office of Environmental Equity (renamed the Office of Environmental Justice in 1993). In 1994, President Bill Clinton formalized the initiative when he signed Executive Order No. 12898, titled Federal Actions to Address Environmental Justice in Minority Populations and Low-Income Populations.[12] This order was in response to his inability to compel a reluctant Congress to address the issue of environmental justice by way of legislation. President Clinton's order directed all federal agencies under the control of the executive branch to incorporate environmental justice as part of their mission by identifying and addressing disproportionately high and adverse human health or environmental effects on minority or low-income populations in their programs, policies, and activities.

Subsequently, in 2001, the USEPA under the direction of Christine Todd Whitman (former governor of New Jersey after Florio) mandated that all agency policies and programs be compliant with environmental justice standards. Each office was directed to develop and deploy an Environmental Justice Action Plan by 2003, making a commitment for implementation within the next five years. As part of this commitment, each USEPA office had to submit progress reports explaining how it met its goals for each fiscal year. Whitman's interest in environmental justice was not new, however. When she was the governor of New Jersey, she directed her environmental commissioner, Robert Shinn, in 1998 to create an Environmental Equity Task Force. This task force created state policies and guidance documents to develop a pollution permit process, which allowed early, expanded public participation for environmental justice communities. These policies were adopted as an administrative order by Commissioner Shinn, with regulations and screening procedures to determine if a community was suffering from disproportionate pollution burdens and whether racial discrimination played a role in those decisions. This regulation proved unwieldy, however, and Shinn's successor, Bradley Campbell, was directed by Governor McGreevey to withdraw it for replacement by an executive order.

McGreevey's order created an Environmental Justice Advisory Council consisting of fifteen members, with one-third in grassroots or faith-based community organizations. Additional members came from academia, civil rights and public health organizations, businesspeople, municipal and county officials, and organized labor. At the executive level, the order created an Environmental Justice Task Force to formalize the process as overseen by NJDEP and the Department of Health and Senior Services. This group created an ongoing comprehensive process in which "all executive branch departments, agencies, boards, commissions and other bodies involved in decisions that may affect environmental quality and public health shall provide meaningful opportunities for involvement to all people regardless of race, color, ethnicity, religion, income, or education level" (Executive Order No. 96). As a result, people of color, the poor, and other minorities could petition the state to have their community identified as an "environmental justice area," and have access to the fiscal and administrative resources necessary to challenge what they saw as racist or discriminatory business and regulatory policies. This might include the siting of hazardous waste sites, lax cleanup procedures, and the permitting of questionable industrial operations with a high probability of increasing health risks to their communities.

Shortly thereafter, in a strange turn of events, on August 12, 2004, Governor McGreevey resigned, announcing he was a "gay American."[13] Allegedly the governor was having an illicit affair with a man on his staff who had threatened a sexual harassment lawsuit. McGreevey's policy actions on brownfields and environmental justice in the waning moments of his governorship endured, however. McGreevey's environmental commissioner, Bradley Campbell, stayed on under the interim governor and took the executive order to heart. He hired Michelle DePass as a senior policy adviser to head up NJDEP's Environmental Justice Office. DePass was formerly the head of the Environmental Justice Alliance, an umbrella organization in New York City composed of member groups based in low-income communities whose mission was to empower its organizations to fight environmental injustice through the coordination of citywide campaigns. DePass had a law degree from Fordham University and was also an environmental compliance manager for the City of San Jose before becoming a William Kunstler Racial Justice Fellow at the Center for Constitutional Rights in New York. After a few years working to set up the program at NJDEP, she left to become a program officer at the Ford Foundation, managing its initiative on environmental justice and healthy communities. More recently, President Obama made Michelle DePass the assistant administrator for the Office of International Affairs at the USEPA. Many of her innovations and outreach initiatives to support communities of color can be found on NJDEP's environmental justice Web site.[14]

Commissioner Campbell also hired Lisa Jackson at this same time to run NJDEP's enforcement program. To some extent this made the two African American women the "Good Cop–Bad Cop" for many minority communities seeking help from NJDEP in dealing with environmental complaints in city neighborhoods. Upon departing state government for the Ford Foundation, DePass left behind a mature environmental justice program that Jackson inherited when she later became Commissioner of NJDEP under Governor Jon Corzine. In fact, Jackson and Depass's activities often went hand-in-hand, since lax environmental enforcement was the perennial complaint from most minority communities. Assistant Commissioner Jackson was best known for her inner-city enforcement sweeps while working for Campbell. For example, in October 2002, NJDEP's compliance and enforcement program conducted its first ever, week-long, multimedia enforcement sweep in Camden. Working with county officials, the State Police, and the USEPA, the department mobilized more than seventy inspectors and conducted 764 investigations. Inspectors found noncompliance with laws that regulated water quality, solid and hazardous waste, air pollution, and land use activities.[15] This enforcement sweep precipitated my first contact with DePass and Jackson, as I was then walking the streets of Camden looking for toxic sources that threatened the same neighborhoods, many of them in the Waterfront South environmental justice community.

THE WATERFRONT SOUTH ENVIRONMENTAL JUSTICE INITIATIVE

Right after Governor McGreevy signed his executive order, community representatives from the Waterfront South neighborhood of Camden petitioned to become a recognized environmental justice community. Their petition was approved, allowing the state to begin working with them to understand and address their issues. The primary goal was to develop a plan of intervention to alleviate the negative impacts of so many people living in close proximity to major waste treatment plants and hazardous waste sites as well as the industries still working along the waterfront. In support of this process NJDEP worked with community activists to help draft a stakeholder document called the Waterfront South Action Plan.[16] In many ways Waterfront South is a poster child for environmental justice complaints. Closeted into an area of one square mile are 531 households, 42 percent of which include families with children less than eighteen years of age. The neighborhood experiences a higher rate of cancer than expected based on a state health department study.[17] The poverty level is more than four times the rest of the state, with a population made up almost entirely of racial and ethnic minorities, many living in low-income rental units. Along with poverty come other social ills such as inadequate health care, poor nutrition, and a low education level. As a result of these inequities, there is a lack of understanding by the populace about how the risks from exposure to environmental contamination can affect public health.[18] To address this lack of knowledge, NJDEP performed an air toxics study managed by Joanne Held, formerly a bureau chief in the state's air program and now retired but recently appointed a member of New Jersey's Environmental Justice Action Council.

The objective of the air toxics study was to isolate the sources of air pollution in the Waterfront South neighborhood and to devise strategies to reduce them. The range of harmful air toxins found included arsenic, lead, and cadmium.[19]

Figure 9. Automobile shredder residue (fluff) stored for unconfined processing in Camden's Waterfront South neighborhood. (Source: Thomas Belton.)

Particulate matter was also investigated, which are tiny liquid or solid particles such as dust, smoke, mist, or fumes, which can cause a wide variety of health problems, including asthma and emphysema as well as learning disabilities and cancer. The project identified the contaminants that posed the greatest health risks, highlighted the sources of pollution, and recommended public health and regulatory strategies to reduce the danger. The study also identified major sources, including the Camden County sewage treatment plant, a municipal waste incinerator, and a cement manufacturing facility. It was the cement plant, however, that created the greatest ire, the largest challenge, and ironically the biggest success and failure in the nation's environmental justice movement.

In 1998, the South Jersey Port Corporation decided to lease space to the St. Lawrence Cement Company, which in 2009 became Holcim (Canada) Inc. St. Lawrence Cement produces cement, ready-mix concrete, asphalt, and aggregates (crushed stone, gravel, and sand). Internationally its operations include about thirty-five concrete plants, twenty quarries and sand and gravel pits, three asphalt plants, two cement plants, and about a dozen cement distribution terminals. The siting of the facility in Waterfront South precipitated a lawsuit by the Camden Regional Legal Service staff on behalf of South Camden

Citizens in Action. According to the lawsuit, the grinding process emitted 100 tons of pollutants a year, almost 60 tons as inhalable particulates and approximately 30 tons in the form of more dangerous, fine-size particulates. The cement company operations also generated up to seventy thousand diesel truck trips per year. This increased truck traffic, the group claimed, added a secondary health impact from diesel fuel emissions loaded with polyaromatic hydrocarbons, which are known carcinogens.

The legal service lawyer, Olga Polmer, charged that NJDEP had violated the 1964 Civil Rights Act in siting the plant in Waterfront South. Polmer argued that in issuing the air permits NJDEP had failed to take into account either the 90 percent concentration of minorities in Waterfront South or the environmentally hazardous activities already in place there. Her suit showed, via statistical analysis, that only 3 percent of the state's zip codes had more facilities with the potential to emit toxics than Waterfront South.[20] The lawsuit produced "friend of the court" briefs favoring the action from the ACLU, NAACP, and the Natural Resource Defense Council, all citing clear racial and class inequities. Other interested parties submitted briefs opposing the suit, including the National Association of Manufacturers, the American Chemical Council, the U.S. Chamber of Commerce, and the National Black Chamber of Commerce. These groups argued that closing the plant would stall urban development.

On April 19, 1999, the U.S. district judge in Camden ruled for the plaintiff, declaring that the approval of air emission permits constituted a Civil Rights Act violation and were thus invalid. This ruling prohibited the nearly completed $50 million plant from operating. The judge then directed NJDEP to evaluate the potential environmental and health impacts of air pollution on local residents. Two months after the federal district judge blocked the opening of the cement plant, Robert Bullard, a professor at Clark Atlanta University and director of its Environmental Justice Resource Center interviewed Phyllis Holmes, a member of South Camden Citizens in Action, the organization that won the precedent-setting lawsuit. In the interview Bullard asked Holmes if she thought race had anything to do with the way the neighborhood had been treated.[21] Holmes answered: "It's all about race. This is environmental racism in its purest form. We have a toxic overload and race played a major part in creating this environmental nightmare." When pressed as to whether she considered what was happening in her community to be a form of discrimination, she replied: "Yes, I do. We are a predominately black and Hispanic neighborhood. And of course I know that they have not put it in white neighborhoods. They tried and it wasn't accepted. If these facilities were so great for economic prosperity, then why did they give us more than our fair share? The truth is that these polluting industries destroy neighborhoods."

Bullard pointed out to Holmes that her group was small and did not have a lot of money and then asked: "What makes you think that you can challenge this big corporation?" Holmes said: "I believe that Jesus had twelve disciples and they were small and they did a mighty thing. You don't have to be big all the time. Just be true to what you believe and if you are going to give up your life, give up your life for the truth of living, not for dying, but for living." However, the celebration of the plaintiffs was short-lived. Shortly thereafter the U.S. Supreme Court ruled on another case, interpreting how discrimination under the Civil Rights Act could be demonstrated. Until that time, a "demonstrated discriminatory act" was enough proof to show that the law had been violated. But with this new ruling, the plaintiffs in such actions had to prove not only impact but "direct intent to discriminate."[22]

Appeals followed in New Jersey, resulting in a ruling in favor of the cement plant owners, who began operating their plant in June 2001. Yet the epic struggle in this tiny community still reverberates there and in other environmental justice communities around the country. And the South Camden Citizens in Action is still busy challenging any further attempts to dump on their neighborhood. Yet an important question remains unanswered: "How did so many major pollution-emitting industries become concentrated in such a small corner of the universe?"

REGIONALISM

Kathe Newman, a professor in Rutgers University's Program in Urban Planning and Policy Development, points out that "cities like Camden remain almost invisible outside of their borders. Camden residents and elected officials know the major storylines: job loss and its effects, suburbanization, a powerful regional political machine, a city government that lacks the capacity to perform basic city services, a jail that sits on prime waterfront property, and a structural deficit; but these stories have yet to reach a broader audience."[23] Similarly, Howard Gillette, from the Rutgers University Camden campus, believes that Camden fell prey to "regionalism," a post–World War II concept in urban planning.[24] Regionalism reached its zenith in New York City under the decrees of planners like Robert Moses who favored highways over public transportation and uprooted traditional neighborhoods by building expressways through them. Moses and his contemporaries gave little thought to the cultural integrity of the communities they demolished by seeking to bring a streamlined automobile culture out into the suburbs.[25]

This approach specifically affected Camden, bifurcating of the city with the construction of the Ben Franklin Bridge, along with its ramps and feeder highways

to Philadelphia. The bridge and roads created an impenetrable barrier that separated contiguous neighborhoods into gulags on either side. Regionalism was perceived by some as racist (if not intentionally, at least in effect) because it was the
more affluent middle-class whites who could afford cars and move out of the city.
This left only minorities behind and a decaying infrastructure to support the city's
tax base. In essence, all of the benefits of regionalism went to the suburbs, with few
reciprocal economic and cultural benefits bestowed on the city dwellers left
behind. Camden became a train stop on the way into Philadelphia. Today, some
academic planners argue that renewed calls for central city revitalization, such as
smart growth and brownfields revitalization, are a new form of regionalism,
which may result in similar negative outcomes by channeling investment into
already overdeveloped inner-city communities.[26]

In hindsight there were good reasons why such facilities were sited in
Camden, but in practice few opinions were sought from those they displaced.
Melvin "Randy" Primas, in 1981 the first black mayor of Camden, was among
the first generation of civil rights activists to become urban mayors, along with
Kenneth Gibson in Newark and Marion Barry in Washington, D.C. And
although Primas was determined to seek social justice, he was faced with a
dwindling tax base because of regionalism and needed to look toward county
and state government for solutions to bring money and jobs into Camden. The
first overture came from the State Department of Corrections, which wanted to
build a maximum security prison in northern Camden. Citizens protested but
Primas convinced them of its potential benefits. He said: "The prison was a
purely economic decision on my part. I saw the $40 million in construction,
the 4,000 jobs, and $450,000 spent annually among local businesses outside the
state bidding process, $1 million year in taxes, and I sold it to the city through a
public education program."[27] Ironically, in 2009, with local developers now
interested in extending the Camden waterfront development to the north of
the Ben Franklin Bridge, the prison was recently emptied, and there are ongoing discussions between the state and the city on tearing it down and building
luxury high-rise apartments in its place.

Governor Tom Kean also tinkered with urban renewal in Camden during
the early 1980s but in this case through redevelopment plans involving leisure
facilities for tourists, possibly hoping to mimic the success of Baltimore's Inner
Harbor and Boston's Waterfront Aquarium. Subsequently he sought and had
built an aquarium, an entertainment center, and a minor league ball park near
the Victor. Yet these attractions are isolated in a narrow corridor along the
waterfront facing Philadelphia, and few ancillary businesses and restaurants
have joined in the redevelopment plan. Local community activists complain
that the recreational opportunities cater to commuters and day-trippers from

the suburbs, not the impoverished citizens of the inner city who cannot afford the $20 fee to gaze at sharks and sea turtles. Regional environmental interests were also exploited by local politicians in Camden during the 1970s and 1980s, as city officials sought approval for the incinerator and county wastewater treatment plant in Waterfront South. City planners again offered income-generating reasons and tax relief for its citizens. Unfortunately, the residents of Waterfront South had little say in the days before the environmental justice initiatives took hold, which led to trucks, smoke stacks, and sewerage waste lagoons from such huge industrial facilities.

THE FUTURE OF ENVIRONMENTAL JUSTICE

Some social scientists argue that environmental racism is a distortion of perspective and that the problem is in fact a class issue (the poor, no matter what color, typically get dumped on). For example, the decision to place a high-level radioactive waste repository in Yucca, Nevada, was strongly pushed by the federal government in spite of objections from nonminority, yet poor and politically powerless, communities.[28] They argue that wealthy businesspeople or the government can situate pollution-emitting facilities in poor neighborhoods for economic reasons alone, which today just happens to be in places where people of color live. Some argue that if environmental justice concerns were evaluated a hundred years ago—when many slums were filled with poor, working-class whites—they would show similar inequitable outcomes, but without the taint of racism. Very few studies have been done to explicitly test this class-versus-race hypothesis, although some scientists have performed demographic census studies with environmental justice components. For example, a Massachusetts study analyzed the social and geographic distribution of ecological hazards across 368 communities by combining census data with a variety of environmental factors. The results showed both income-based and racial biases in the geographic distribution of seventeen different types of environmentally hazardous sites and industrial facilities.[29] The authors concluded that ecological racism and class-based environmental injustices appeared to be widespread in Massachusetts, yet they did not explicitly design their study to statistically compare race versus class, so they were unable to tease out which was more relevant.

In addition, there is a long-festering debate over the relative benefits of brownfield actions versus environmental justice initiatives. Balancing the scale between brownfield development and the environmental justice desires of those who live around these sites is often fraught with ambiguities. Sometimes things go asunder if the desires of those most affected by a brownfield redevelopment decision are ignored (as was the case in Cramer Hill). USEPA attempted to get a sense as to whether brownfield decisions exacerbate environmental justice concerns in a series of studies performed in 1998.[30] One of the more interesting findings was that most residents of environmental justice communities were not automatically opposed to redevelopment in their communities but emphasized two areas of concern for accepting a brownfield remediation. Their acceptance hinged on the positive economic opportunities from which they could benefit (such as jobs) and the function of the proposed facility once the site was remediated. For instance, if the proposed facility or use for the brownfield site was cleaner or more economically appealing than the former use, the community was more likely to support redevelopment.

A more recent study by the National Environmental Justice Advisory Council, a federal advisory committee to USEPA, did identify unintended impacts of redevelopment in five environmental justice communities.[31] Specifically, it concluded that USEPA may historically have unintentionally exacerbated gentrification and displacement in supporting development at the expense of low-income residents. This, the report added, was not the fault of any particular individual, program, or agency, nor were revitalization programs purposefully causing gentrification, displacement, and equity loss in environmental justice communities. It was simply that the implementation of these well-intentioned and otherwise beneficial programs were having a net effect, underscoring the power of market dynamics. The council also highlighted an opportunity for USEPA to exercise leadership in protecting these communities from unintended consequences by assigning USEPA staff to local redevelopment and revitalization projects and allowing *all* stakeholders to have *meaningful* involvement in redevelopment. It also strongly recommended that neighborhood demographic assessments regarding displacement be done at the earliest possible time in a brownfield project. This alone might have helped immensely in shepherding Camden's Cramer Hill Revitalization Plan through the public vetting phase. That plan failed for just such an oversight.

Disregarding public health concerns is another important omission, as noted by some social scientists. The question still remains as to how safe it is to live beside a brownfield site, especially while it is in the process of being revitalized. A recent study by Thomas Burke (former director of Science and Research) and two of his students at the Johns Hopkins Bloomberg School of Public Health warned that efforts to move brownfields to productive use may result in safety risks.[32] Their study of southeastern Baltimore showed excessive deaths from respiratory illness and cancers, as well as a spatial and statistical relationship between environmentally degraded brownfield areas and at-risk communities. They argued that incorporating public health programs into brownfield-related cleanups and land-use decisions would increase the odds for successful neighborhood redevelopment and long-term public health benefits. This same conclusion was more definitively illustrated in New Jersey at the Hudson County chromate sites (see chapter 5), where increased levels of indoor dust and chromium occurred during remedial excavation activities, as well as elevated levels of cancer in people living along the major roads connecting these sites. These facts argue for more public health education and aggressive regulatory oversight of brownfield sites under active remediation in order to protect poor minority populations living near them, recognizing that the sites may become profitable if removed but extremely more dangerous when exposed during redevelopment.

Thus each venture into brownfields must be carefully weighed against historical environmental inequity, which pleads for a lighter touch by municipal and state officials, plus lots of listening and involvement at the local level. But equally important is the need for a tangible response by regulatory agencies, such as more frequent inspections of targeted industries, perhaps stricter siting and permitting decisions, even free health screening. To redress the abandoned properties and health risks, we need to support developers and municipalities who seek to clean up brownfields, but we must also insist it be done in a safe manner that addresses the legitimate fears and frustrations of the poor and minorities. For admittedly there has been a long legacy of deep-pocket investors in New Jersey seeking waterfront property for condominiums and high-rise office buildings but who have no use for considering the concerns of the have-nots. Governors Whitman's and McGreevy's environmental justice initiatives have left behind a lasting legacy that other governors have respected, forcing all state regulators to be more introspective in making management decisions that are more equitable and, one hopes, free of racial bias.

New Jersey's environmental justice initiative is seen nationally as one of the most aggressive, with numerous cases where communities have petitioned the state for resources and recognition. Environmental justice programs at the state and federal level are intended to uphold the rights of those discriminated against by avaricious businesspeople who seek to place pollution-emitting factories in minority communities for profit. This is typically where residents are too uninformed and disorganized to coordinate a protest. Until recently, the odds favored the bankers and developers, allowing them to move forward without placing clean air and water, safe streets, and guaranteed jobs for the community into the balance. Until environmental justice polices were established in Washington and subsequently in New Jersey, the sad legacy of inner-city development was often surreptitiously dangerous and discriminatory toward those without the political muscle to protest what happened in their neighborhoods. Yet with these environmental justice initiatives in place, the playing field has been leveled. Because of these vociferous protests, the complaints are no longer a distant echo to those seeking land for their projects. The empowerment of the environmental justice activists is now of paramount concern for those who would build, and the banks, municipalities, and developers must finally take notice of those who live in the shadow of the factory's walls.

For me, participation in the environmental justice initiative through the source trackdown studies I performed in Camden was a panacea to a personal canker that gnawed at me for years. Although not a person of color or a minority, I too grew up in the inner city, surrounded by solvent-spewing laundries, incinerators, and coal-fired factories plopped down wherever a developer wanted them. And I too knew the impotent frustration of not being heard over the promises of powerful businesspeople and politicians when we complained. So, too, the memories of my father's, brother's, and mother's fates—who all died of cancer in the midst of so much industrial pollution—were finally assuaged in my belief that we had finally found a way for the disenfranchised to holler back and stop the injustice. I also realized that what I could do for my family had been done. I needed to look forward in my life to see the beauty and make a legacy for my own growing family based on the green things that surround us. And that's what I did. I found new interests and research studies that brought me up into the hills and forests of the state, where birds sang and animals moved oblivious to the city dweller's anguish.

CHAPTER 9

The Woodlands

Growing up as a housing project kid in the city, the trees in my early life were the junkyard dogs of the botanical world. Most were scraped clean of bark by hundreds of scuffed shoes, and their greenery was shorn by clutching fingers. It was up there in the branches, though, that we gained precious solitude amidst the cacophony that emanated from the brick buildings, the projects filled with the bedlam of five hundred people living like termites in a crowded colony. My own hopes were to get high enough into the sheltering leaves of the tree to become momentarily invisible in the greenery, to soar into silence with the wind, and perhaps fly over the distant spires like Peter Pan. The trees were not so much plants to me but ladders of imagination where I stretched my arms skyward and bathed in the rustling hum of that green oasis, swaying in the breeze like a caterpillar about to change into something more refined.

Later, as I grew older and wandered away from my island of humanity in Jersey City to the countryside, I discovered carefully nurtured orchards of apple and pear trees, fields of wheat and clover, the wild forests of oak and fir in the mountains. Trees, I discovered, could be covered in glory each spring, as seen in the light pink petals of the cherry blossom or the virginal whites of a dogwood heavy with blooms. It was in college, however, that I penetrated the mysteries of trees, learning that dogwood blossoms are not really true petals but specialized leaves called "bracts" that attract bees to pollinate. The true blossom is a minuscule green floret hidden deep within the white, starstruck face of the flower. These and other facts I was taught in my graduate school botany class at the City College of New York in Harlem, mostly on field trips through Central Park. For at City College we used our immediate environs to learn about nature, much as I would visit the aquarium on the boardwalk in Coney Island to study shark behavior.

My botany professor was a bearded hippie whose specialty was the life history of the southwestern ponderosa pine, *Pinus brachyptera*, which he studied every summer on the edge of the Grand Canyon in Arizona. For field trips he led us on exploratory escapades to all five boroughs of the city, all the while gesticulating excitedly and lecturing as he went. His field training was practical and mundane, meant to give us the forester's skills for studying trees as naturalists and not as aesthetes. We measured the length of willow tree limbs streaming down upon the tranquil waters of the boating pond in Central Park. To reach these trees we had to skirt Bethesda Fountain and carefully step around picnickers with their blankets strewn on the rocks. We went up to Shorakapok Preserve at Inwood Hill Park athwart the peninsula of the Harlem River as it poured into the Hudson. There we measured the girth of tulip trees, *Liriodendron tulipifera*, the tallest North American broad-leaved tree, whose flowers are tulip-shaped with brilliant orange florets. The Shorakapok Preserve is also filled with mature red oaks and the last coastal salt marsh left on the island of Manhattan.

We took a bus to New Jersey and visited Palisades Interstate Park on the far shore of the Hudson River. There we walked the footpaths of the Greenbrook Sanctuary atop the three hundred–foot bluffs where red oaks, hickory, and black birch dominated the forest. A small pond sat in the middle of this sanctuary, its outlet a 250-foot waterfall that cascaded down the cliff face, eroding it into broken basalt columns, with mists crawling across the spectacular diabase blocks covered with lichen and moss. Many of the trees along the palisade ridge presented their topmost crowns for our inspection, their gnarled roots clawed into the rock clefts below us to anchor them upright against the wind.

At Greenbrook I learned to use a "tree bore" and count the growth rings to gauge a tree's age. I remember my professor pointing at one dark ring close to the center of a bore from a northern red oak, *Quercus rubra*, and saying: "Around this time two hundred years ago and not far from here, Alexander Hamilton and Aaron Burr fought their famous pistol duel." Burr, the vice president of the United States under Thomas Jefferson, was subsequently arraigned for murder but later acquitted. The harsh criticism and animosity directed toward him, however, would eventually bring an end to his political career and forced him into a self-imposed exile.

And it was this remark of that stayed with me as one of those unintended life lessons, the conjunction of great age in the tree and the sudden death of a politician over an insult. I still remember vividly looking up into the towering crown of that colonial-era tree. "It still alive and thriving," I thought. And I wondered at human vanity and how ephemeral our actions may seem compared with the antiquity of a forest. Yet my jejune sentiment of admiration for the tree's longevity has been dampened by my life experience. I realize that today we mostly see trees of great age only where they are protected in publicly owned state and federal parks. The forests of New Jersey, as elsewhere in America, now appear precariously suspended above a chasm. A land grab and moral void seem to exist where developers and politicians seek to clear-cut anything that stands in the way of suburbanization and the utilization of open land. Yet one group is dedicated to thwarting the loss of this natural resource, the Forest Service.

THE NEW JERSEY FOREST SERVICE

For such an urbanized area, New Jersey has a surprisingly green ethic when it comes to preserving forests. We have conserved more open space than many other states, resulting in much less land to defend from rapacious development. I can only surmise that New Jerseyans are more sensitive to the loss of these forests because we are situated between Philadelphia and New York City, and have seen suburban sprawl overrun much of the state before we could react. As a result we will do anything to protect the acreage left to us. This includes an arsenal of weapons, such as underwriting bonds to buy open space, setting up land trusts, offering easements to landowners, and even the preservation of land through eminent domain as happened with the Pinelands on our coast. As a result, there are many huge forest tracts in New Jersey filled with more than ninety species of trees. Most of these are protected in parks or wildlife preserves purchased by prescient legislators to keep the state's uplands pristine and its lowland swamps shaded and covered with pine needles and cedar bark.

Surprisingly for such a densely populated state, New Jersey's woodlands are unique, because in no other state can you find so many species and differences in typography, soils, drainage, and vegetation. Three of the five major forest regions in the United States can be found in New Jersey, extending from the Appalachian Mountains to the Coastal Plain. But of course these are not the ancestral woodlands that European settlers first saw when they arrived here four hundred years ago. Back then, the coast was lined with impenetrable forests of pine and cedar, while the northern mountains were dominated by old-growth forests filled with hardwood oak and hemlock.

Native Americans used the bounty of these forests primarily for subsistence living as hunter-gatherers, leaving few marks on the land except where they burned the woodlands to flush out wildlife and to make travel easier. They did not use it as a commercial resource, as did the settlers who followed them, clear-cutting sections of the forest for farms and villages, building houses from the felled timber, and burning the wood for home heating and industry. The colonists even bled the trees for tar and turpentine, and hung pails to collect maple sap for syrup. Eventually the forests were culled and cut down many times over, especially in the nineteenth century to make charcoal and coke to fuel the iron industry. Surprisingly, the forests have shown regrowth since then. In a recent survey of the New Jersey woodlands, the United States Forest Service reported that forests now cover much of the state. This has probably occurred for two reasons: a sharp decrease in wood harvests after the Civil War in 1865 as the iron industry faltered and a subsequent steady loss of farmland in the twentieth century.[1] The Forest Service survey carried out in 1999 showed that forests now constitute 45 percent of the state, covering more than two million acres. This is quite remarkable for a state showing such high population growth and economic development in the past few decades.

The New Jersey Forest Service believes that much of the forestland has remained stable because population growth in the state has historically concentrated only in the areas adjacent to New York City and Philadelphia. Even today, forested areas are unevenly distributed on either side of the Route 1 corridor, with flowering deciduous forests to the northeast and pine-dominated stands clustered in the barrens of the southwest. But more important to this increase in forest is the net decrease in the amount of agricultural land. Although officially named the "Garden State," the amount of land currently farmed in New Jersey is less than half of what it was in 1956, a loss of more than a million acres. Much of this former farmland was developed into housing tracts, although a substantial portion was left untended. These feral farm tracts reverted back to forest through natural ecological succession and regeneration. As a result, the newly forested areas have negated any gross loss attributable to suburbanization and development. However, there are still economic pressures to cut down these regenerated woodlands.

Yet despite regeneration, there remain ecological risks to overall forest health, even in the preserved tracts. For example, regenerated forests mature at a uniform pace, and as they age their species composition undergoes what ecologists call "forest succession." During this process long-lived plants that can tolerate shaded conditions replace short-lived plants that need full sunlight to thrive. This process is also influenced by disturbances from natural as well as human sources such as drought, fires, outbreaks of insect pests, and pollution from contaminated water and air deposition of industrial chemicals. This natural process of succession and disturbance created a mosaic of different aged tree stands in forests. To some degree New Jersey's regenerated forests mimic tree farms or cultivated crops. For example, two-thirds of the state's forests are younger than sixty years old. And since there is no economic use for this timber within the state, as they mature the stands are not replaced. This is not good ecologically. Maintaining forests that are well distributed across age-classes enhances the biodiversity of the landscape and reduces their susceptibility to catastrophic damage, such as one invasive insect, or one uniformly damaging pollutant, like nitrous oxide in acid rain.

The New Jersey Forest Service routinely measures forest health in the state as a means to maintain biologically diverse ecosystems, to sustain wildlife that depends on the forests, and to protect threatened and endangered plant and animal species. Healthy forests also protect water quality, supply recreation activities, and protect historical, aesthetic, and cultural resources present within the forests. To monitor forest health the Forest Service runs thirty monitoring plots, collecting data on indicators that reflect the influence of climate change, insect infestation, disease, and the effects of air pollution from ozone and acid rain. This is a difficult task owing to the great number of tree species found here in such a variety of ecoregions. The oak/hickory forest grouping is the most common type, covering almost two-thirds of the state. This includes red maple, pitch pine, and oaks as the most numerous and dominant tree species. In the south, where the Pine Barrens ecoregion dominates the landscape, distinctive loblolly/shortleaf pine and the oak/pine groups are important stands of trees, which have a long history of wildfire that promotes their growth.

The types and number of wildlife species that inhabit them also change as these forests mature. In the seedling/sapling stage that follows a major disturbance such as fire or land abandonment, there are typically many animals that use low-growing herbaceous and shrub vegetation. These typically include small songbirds, rabbits, and voles. As larger trees become more established through forest succession, shading occurs and kills the low-growing vegetation and shrubbery. This brings other animals into that patch of forest until the number of species rises and reaches a maximum found only in mature stands of trees. These include beaver, black bear, white-tailed deer, and wild turkeys. It is a unique challenge to the Forest Service to make sure that these climax forests remain healthy and do not succumb to wasting diseases such as chestnut blight or Dutch elm disease, or else are burned by acid rain or weakened by insect invasions. There is one area of the state, however, where the job has been made easier through an exercise in land-use preservation on a mammoth scale—the New Jersey Pinelands. The state and federal laws passed to protect it have become models for ecosystem and forestry management throughout the United States.

THE PINELANDS BIOSPHERE

The Pinelands International Biosphere Reserve is an internationally protected and important ecological region that spans more than a million acres in New Jersey and occupies 22 percent of the state's landmass. Pine barren ecology is one of stark, sandy soils interlaced with brown, acidic, "cedar" waters and wild-fire-sculpted pygmy forests. Its pitch pine–dominated landscape can change in a few miles at sharp ecotones from sand-blasted heaths to dwarf forests to fragrant cedar swamps. Its stark environment is the product of a million years of ecological succession, alternate glaciations, and serial inundations through sea level rise and fall. At various stages the barrens have been underwater and filled with oyster beds, lowland swamps traversed by Leni Lenape Indians, and wild-fire-prone forests, much as we see it today.

As early as 1876, there were grandiose plans to harness the Pinelands' natural resources. At that time an entrepreneur named Joseph Wharton purchased thousands of acres with the idea of damming up the rivers to send fresh, potable water hundreds of miles to New York City and Philadelphia. These cities had water supply and pollution problems associated with their burgeoning populations. Initially the New Jersey Legislature liked the idea, but when it came time for a vote, the plan was scrapped. In the twentieth century, similar plans were concocted to make use of this seemingly useless land.

In the 1960s, a plan was afoot to construct a massive jetport in the Pine Barrens, with a new city around it to alleviate congestion in other nearby major airports. This facility would have been four times larger than Newark, LaGuardia, and JFK airports combined. Then in 1976, casino gambling was approved for the first time in the state but only within the city limits of Atlantic City, which borders the Pinelands. Within two years the first resorts opened up, bringing in more than forty-seven thousand new employees, all of whom needed a place to live. Many casinos sought the development rights to pristine lakefront property in the Pinelands to support this large workforce. Environmentalists and small-town politicians resisted, fearing pollution and the loss of their small-town lifestyles.

What followed was a tumultuous political and social debate, which culminated in the passage of laws and protective statutes that succeed to this day in protecting this unique ecosystem. Stories by John McPhee in the *New Yorker* and sales of his book *The Pine Barrens* helped by describing the seemingly bucolic lives of the Pineys (as they called themselves), which helped win over public opinion. Ralph Good, a botany professor from the Rutgers Camden campus supplied volumes of his research to the activists seeking to preserve the Pinelands. Good believed that the uniqueness and fragility of the barrens required extraordinary amounts of protection, and his efforts culminated in the scientific information necessary to persuade legislators to act.

Governor Brendan Byrne, convinced by these environmental advocates, set into motion a series of initiatives in the late 1970s, including an executive order that created the Pinelands Planning Commission. This body was tasked with overseeing development while mandating a construction moratorium in a 576-square-mile core of Atlantic, Burlington, Camden, and Ocean counties. Governor Byrne, working with an increasingly sympathetic legislature, subsequently signed into law the Pinelands Protection Act amid great debate and controversy.

At the time of the act's passage in 1979, New Jersey's highest population density was forty thousand people per square mile. In contrast, the Pinelands' highest density was fifteen people per square mile—a political vacuum that developers hoped to exploit in order to fill it in with tract housing and shopping malls. Byrne's environmental protection commissioner, Daniel J. O'Hern, immediately used $30 million in Green Acres bond money to buy seven hundred thousand acres surrounding the reserve's four existing forests. Some felt this was a taking of private lands and an early form of eminent domain. Other parties praised the move because local planning boards did not have the expertise and ability to stand up to big developers.

Federal legislation followed, establishing the million-acre Pinelands National Reserve. This was the first national reserve created by Congress under the National Parks and Recreation Act of 1978. It is managed by a governing body called the New Jersey Pinelands Commission that uses a stakeholder-drafted Comprehensive Management Plan to govern land-use decisions, the issuing of permits, and resource management decisions.[2] Subsequently, the Pinelands was given added protection when designated an International Biosphere Reserve in 1983 by the United Nations Educational, Scientific and Cultural Organization (UNESCO). In declaring it a biosphere reserve, UNESCO noted that it was "the first formal attempt at large-scale regional ecosystem management in the United States and represents a successful test case on whether multiple jurisdictions could come together and achieve an agreement to mitigate development impacts on regional ecosystems crossing jurisdictional boundaries."[3]

The commission that manages the preserve consists of fifteen members, seven appointed by the governor and another seven appointed by each of the seven counties affected by the Pinelands Protection Act. The fifteenth commissioner is appointed by the U.S. secretary of the Interior. Upon establishing the law, the legislature also felt that certain portions of the Pinelands were especially vulnerable to environmental degradation and as a result designated certain tracts as "preservation areas," where more stringent regulations and restrictions on development are applied. Later, the Pinelands Commission formulated two sets of regulations, one for the development area and another for the preservation area.[4] For example, in 1989 NJDEP designated 3,800 acres of stunted trees in the Pine Barrens, only four to six feet in height, as a natural preservation area. That meant that the pygmy forest would remain forever wild.

Scientists from all over the world have studied these trees, yet there is still no consensus on what causes their stunted growth. A century ago scientists believed that it was the poorly fertilized and sandy soils that did not provide sufficient nutrition. This hypothesis was rejected, however, when researchers found pitch pine trees in essentially the same soil growing to heights of thirty to sixty feet a few miles away. Robert Cartica, a plant ecologist with the Office of Natural Lands Management, observed that more recent theories have focused on the cycle of natural wildfires that routinely sweep through the Pinelands region but that occur in the pygmy forest about twice as often as in other areas. He felt that the pitch pines "seem to have adapted to the fires: their seed cones only open under tremendous heat, and the trees themselves send up new shoots from the base of their trunks even if the rest of the tree has been killed in a fire."[5]

THE NEW JERSEY FOREST FIRE SERVICE

The Pinelands upland forest is dominated by pitch pine (*Pinus rigida*) and scrub oaks (*Quercus ilicifolia*). This stark, sandy habitat is uniquely populated by trees of a low height, a paucity of seedling regeneration, and the "serotinous" habit of the cones. Serotinous pinecones remain closed for an indefinite number of years after they mature, and only open in response to intense heat generated from a wildfire. This trait ensures that seeds are shed at the most opportune moment for regeneration, when the competing vegetation has been eliminated and the fertilizing mineral bed exposed.

Yet preserving tinder-dry forests and protecting the thousands of people who live around them has proven more complex than originally anticipated. This unenviable task falls to NJDEP's Forest Fire Service, which fights wildfires. The potential for a wildfire disaster in New Jersey has been realized many times. Large conflagrations occurred between 1930 and 1977, and most recently in 1995. The most notable of these fires was on the weekend of April 20–21, 1963, when wildfires destroyed 183,000 acres of land, consumed 186 homes and 197 buildings, and were responsible for seven deaths.[6] The New Jersey Forest Fire Service describes residential communities located within forested areas as the "wildland urban interface." It is in these communities that the service teaches forest fire prevention to local municipalities and landowner associations, recruiting them to educate their residents of wooded areas to take the threat seriously and implement precautions to prevent wildfires.

Native Americans were the first to introduce prescribed burning in New Jersey's woodlands, primarily to facilitate travel through the dense underbrush, improve hunting, drive away insects, and to increase the shrub cover, which was filled with nuts and berries. European settlers used fire to clear lands for

Figure 10. Wildfire in the New Jersey Pinelands. (Source: New Jersey Forest Fire Service.)

towns, homes, and agriculture until these practices caused huge, uncontrollable fires that threatened lives and property. In the 1920s, cranberry and blueberry growers in New Jersey protected their property by using prescribed fire to remove heavy accumulations of forest fuels from around their fields and buildings. From the 1930s to the 1960s, Silas Little of the U.S. Forest Service, in association with other forestry professionals, conducted research on the practice and effects of prescribed burning. In 1948, the practice of prescribed burning as a fire management tool was introduced to the public; soon after, it expanded to involve both private and public lands.

Prescribed burns are only done by the New Jersey Forest Service in the state, and only between October 1 and March 31, to prevent runaway wildfires. Technically, a prescribed burn is defined as a "the skillful application of fire under exacting conditions of weather and fuel in a predetermined area, for a specific purpose to achieve specific results."[7] The use of fire in this way requires a level of skill and competence developed through extensive and ongoing training. Planning is a critical component in a prescribed burn, to keep it from getting out of hand. Any individual burn requires a specific knowledge of forest fuels, fire behavior, suppression techniques, local weather conditions, and fire effects.

This strategy is primarily meant to protect the people in dwellings that each year creep ever farther into the wildland urban interface but also to maintain the Pine Barrens in the closest proximity to a natural condition. This danger becomes all too apparent as uncontrolled wildfires flame up every few years, some redolent with controversy, and often the Warren Grove Gunnery Range in the midst of the pygmy forest is at the heart of the dispute. This section of the reserve is owned by the United States Air Force as a bombing run for warplanes and helicopters flying from air bases stretched all along the eastern seaboard.

On May 15, 2007, a flare dropped from an F-16 fighter jet on a bombing run at the Warren Grove Gunnery Range set off a huge wildfire that engulfed almost fourteen thousand acres of parched forest in a matter of hours.[8] More than twenty-five hundred senior citizens were ordered to flee surrounding gated communities or else were evacuated from nearby nursing homes. Previously, in 2002, bombs touched off a fire that burned eleven thousand acres, and in 1999 a fire at the range destroyed about sixteen hundred acres of the Pinelands. Despite these risks, however, the military said that the accidental fires would not deter it from conducting future training missions. It has no plans to move the firing range, which has been used by the military for more than forty years. A spokesman for the range pointed out that the area near the range—about twenty-five miles north of Atlantic City—is far more developed now than it was when the military began conducting missions there in the 1960s. This hardly detracts from the danger, however. It took one thousand firefighters and emergency response workers to fight the 2007 blaze, which was only quenched by ninety minutes of heavy rain that doused the flames. No one was hurt in that conflagration, but a dozen homes were damaged or destroyed. And although annoyed by the evacuations, some in the area accepted the threat of fire stoically, as just another part of life in their rural swatch of southern Jersey. Yet the complacency of these Pineys is offset by the watchfulness and the dedication of thousands of NJDEP fire wardens and firefighters who drop everything at the klaxon's call to extinguish wildfires and, ironically, also set fires to protect the public.

In March 2008, almost a year after the runaway wildfire at the Warren Grove Gunnery Range, the New Jersey Forest Fire Service planned a controlled burn for what it called a "fuel island" in the Stafford Forge wildlife management area adjacent to the range. Interested in how these burns were carried out and how fires might regenerate forests, I accompanied a crew from the Forest Fire Service to observe this strange phenomenon of setting forests alight instead of putting them out. We met at a staging area filled with equipment and fireman near a beautiful lake in the midst of the woods. There were ten fire engines, plus some tractors and backhoes, surrounded by about fifty men. Behind them was a specially designed helicopter called a "Heli-Torch," equipped to drag a lighted flame on a long leash across inaccessible swampland beside the Pinelands streams.

I was introduced by the fire warden as the "the science dude" who was there to study the nutrient cycling and forest fertilization effects of the fire, such as the nitrogen, phosphorus, and carbon returned to the soil. Most of the men were local volunteer firemen, Pineys who knew the terrain. There were grizzled old-timers and some younger guys with beards down to their belts who looked like members of the band ZZ Top. Some were schoolteachers, local business-men, and laborers. They all shared bonhomie and a joviality that contrasted with the bizarre nature of our gathering, a destructive visit to the forest on a thoroughly human scale. Many of the men were forest lovers—woodsmen and hunters—who talked about retriever dogs, bow hunting, and the biggest buck they'd ever taken down. There were many fire jokes and wisecracks about other firefighters not present. One fellow told a story about his brother-in-law. He said he had set a road flare attached to a timer in his brother-in-law's suitcase as he was going to the airport back in the 1970s. A number of men shook their heads smiling, admitting jovially you could not get away with that today in our post-9/11 mentality. But nonetheless the crowd was in stitches as the fellow described how his brother-in-law came back from the airport furious and carrying a blackened suitcase filled with scorched shorts and charred socks.

I found the first moments of the prescribed "set fire" sensuous, as the fire-men's drip torches lit the dead grass, and the low-lying yellow flames moved with the wind along the forest floor. There was a soft pall of white smoke that crept along the ground and sudden red explosions as the fire undulated like a snake through the underbrush, leaving curved tracks of burnt ashes. Dry tinder pushed beneath bracken by winter storms ignited with little woofing sounds, as if tiny dogs where shepherding the flames forward, running about and barking amid the blaze. The shrubbery had not leafed out yet, so the woods were open to the eye for hundreds of yards beneath the canopy. The firemen walked behind their sets in a line, like beaters ushering it forward or goading a child to crawl for the first time. Then the wind suddenly caught the rising flames, turn-ing them blue at the base and cherry red at the tip, until, like a race horse released by its handler, they took off at a sprinter's clip, the bushes exploding as the equine creature reached a canter. The fire then sped off with a great whoosh and took on its own shape, no longer the crawling child set free but a galloping dragon devouring everything in its path. Even the smoke changed character, turning black and sweetly resinous, the bark and sap of the pine saplings caught fire, and the black conflagration rose above the canopy, mixing with the white traces from the smoldering grass. The roar of the fire became a palpable being that drove the deer and all larger aboveground creatures before it with great urgency. Even the complexion of the men around me changed, from pale, studied concentration to red-faced determination mixed with fear as the thing they created was set free.

Most of the small forest critters were still below ground in March, and I imagined them huddling down in their burrows as the earth grew warm around them and tendrils of smoke crept down their tunnels, the young pups of field mice, badgers, and raccoons, snuggling closer into their mothers until the conflagration moved on and the earth settled back into its cool, even stillness, the aboveground surface charred but fertilized by the earth-replenishing fires, ready to raise new shoots and berries that wild things could feed on. At the other end of the forest there were fire receivers. Teams of firemen, police, and emergency response crews stationed on back roads and across major highways where the controlled burns were designed to flame out at firebreaks, streams, and previously burned tracts. These men whom I caught up to later had a more determined look on their faces, for their job was to stop the powerful conflagration. Theirs was to watch beside pumper trucks with hoses in hand at firebreaks as the raging fire approached them, igniting whole pitch pine trees some fifty feet high, sparks racing ahead of the smoke to ignite other stands, creating a blackened forest both acres deep and miles wide.

By then the fire cloud was a huge mushroom that drifted across the woodlands and could be seen from Atlantic City. The Forest Service had published in advance the location it planned to burn so as not to scare the residents or cause a panic on the roadways, many only slightly better than the sand tracks set down by their ancestors who pushed into the impenetrable marsh bottoms a generation ago. Some of the flames reached to the tops of the canopy, and the heat from the fires warmed the late March day to August intensity.

As I looked deep into the burning woods that day, I thought about their provenance. The woods were called the Barrens because up until the twentieth century they served no apparent economic purpose. This was true at least until the Civil War exploded and bog iron from swamp peat was needed to cast cannons, and then again in the early twentieth century, when careful botanical experimentation refined cranberry cultivation and created high-bush blueberry agriculture. This inventiveness proved such a worthwhile endeavor that the cranberry and blueberry industry in New Jersey is now our number one agricultural commodity. But before people moved into the Barrens to follow these endeavors, if the woods went ablaze, they were allowed to burn. In past centuries, if wildfires swept through acres of forest, the blackened ground went unobserved, the raging infernos extinguished only when their flames met uncrossable rivers or were doused in drenching rainfalls. Today, with suburban sprawl impinging on the Barrens, the Forest Fire Service is all that stands between people and a devastating blaze.

The typical prescribed burn plan is to create a catcher's mitt–shaped area of burned dead ground in a forest. If a wildfire then occurs in the future, the service's tactic is to set backfires and push it into the "catcher's mitt" of the prescribed area to snuff it out by loss of fuel and energy. My companion explained to me that almost all the towns in the Pinelands that have survived since colonial days have significant wetlands to the west and the northwest. This protects them from natural fire corridors. He told me that all the ghost towns in the Pine Barrens, like Hongs Hat, were repeatedly burned out and abandoned owing to their unfortunate placement in these fire corridors. As I sat in one of the Fire Service red brush trucks within a caged cab to keep out errant tree limbs on backwoods tracks, I looked into the woods burning so intensely and thought of them as one fragment of a coastal forest that once extended from Long Island Sound in New York through New Jersey's coastal areas and along the Delmarva Peninsula past Chesapeake Bay into the Carolinas. Each state holds a piece of this ancestral forest, but New Jersey's Pinelands are the largest. My Forest Fire Service guide asked that day what I planned on doing after viewing the prescribed burn. I told him I was interested in how the trees might react to air pollution.

AIR POLLUTION AND FORESTS

Air pollution and climate change can be long-term threats to forest health. Air pollutants such as ozone can burn foliage, while acid rain and its deposition products can alter soil chemistry. To assess these effects, the Forest Service historically has measured crown dieback, ozone foliar injury, the die-off of lichen communities, and changes in soil chemistry. It was just such a concern in the late 1990s that led me to devise an air pollution study designed to quantify the potential impacts from the millions of tons of nitrous oxide and sulfuric acid released by coal-fired power plants every year. I was encouraged to initiate this endeavor when asked to be the state's witness for a New Jersey Department of Law suit against a number of coal-fired power companies upwind of us in the Ohio River Valley. The lawsuit contended that pollution from these power plants drifted over Pennsylvania and wafted down onto New Jersey forests and cities, causing both human and ecological damage. This exacerbated our own attempts to control emissions from New Jersey power plants.

John Dighton, the director of Rutgers University's Pinelands Field Station, started his career in the late 1970s, studying "lime aphid honeydew" effects on soil organisms.[9] Aphids are tiny sap-sucking insects that feed on plants and trees, and honeydew is the carbon-rich waste product they excrete, which accumulates in the soils and on roots. He subsequently specialized in the population dynamics and ecology of a specialized group of organisms involved in "mycorrhiza," a symbiotic association between a fungus and the roots of a plant. Symbiosis occurs in various ways, such as "parasitism," where one organism gains at the other's expense. Examples of parasites include tapeworms and the malarial protozoan that both use humans as host. Mycorrhizal fungi, in contrast, have a positive symbiotic relationship with trees and are "mutualistic," meaning that both organisms benefit. In fact, mycorrhizal fungi are a crucial part of the health of almost all plants growing throughout the world. They attach to the roots and help plants to absorb water and organic nutrients from the soil, such as nitrogen. In exchange, the fungi receive from the plants carbohydrates produced as part of photosynthesis. Typically, mycorrhizal fungi form very thin filaments around a plant's roots, adding to their length so that they can absorb more nutrients from the soil and add to their efficiency so that they are better at surviving droughts. Mycorrhizal fungi also boost plants' immune systems, making them resistant to soil-borne pathogens, and help to keep parasitic nematodes away.

In the 1980s, like many other scientists at the time, John studied the effects of air pollution and acid rain on forests, especially through the sulfuric acid deposition effects on the roots and mycorrhizal fungi of pine trees.[10] By the time I met John in the 1990s, though, his graduate students primarily investigated nutrient dynamics in soils impacted by forest fires. Amy Tuininga was one of these talented scientists. Her research studied the effects of fires on the Pine Barrens forest and specifically how it responded to "prescribed burns" carried out by the New Jersey Forest Fire Service to reduce fuel loads and the risk of wildfire. To do this, she undertook field studies in two upland pine/oak forests subjected to different burn regimes. Amy took soil cores around the roots of pine trees, separated out the fungi she found, and identified them by genus according to morphological or physical characteristics. She then measured nitrogen and phosphorus availability using root bioassays and showed that plots exposed to more frequent fires decreased in the total abundance of fungi and that the availability of nutrients to roots was higher in the burned plots. This showed a fertilization effect of the fire, allowing rapid regrowth and recolonization of the blackened forest floor.[11]

John, Amy, and I devised a different kind of study, however, to measure the potential effects from atmospheric deposition of air pollutants on the extremely fragile Pinelands forests. Nitrogen oxides, or NOx (pronounced "knocks"), is the generic term for a group of highly reactive gases, all of which contain nitrogen and oxygen in varying amounts. This pollutant is of national concern, and the state monitors it on a regular basis. There are National Health Standards for only six air pollutants: carbon monoxide, lead, nitrogen dioxide, ozone, particulates, and sulfur dioxide. The major sources of NOx are power plants, large industrial facilities, and motor vehicles. Nitrogen dioxide irritates the nose and throat, especially in people with asthma, and appears to increase susceptibility to respiratory infections. When nitrogen dioxide reaches unhealthy levels, children and people with respiratory disease are most at risk. NOx also combine with volatile organic compounds to form ozone.[12] Additionally, NOx contribute to the formation of acid rain, and they react to form toxic chemicals that contribute to global warming. These compounds can be transported over long distances on prevailing wind patterns, which means NOx effects are not always confined to areas where NOx are emitted.

Our goal was to map ecological differences in three New Jersey forests using tree-root fungi and their relative responses to NOx deposition. These forests were selected along a north-south transect through the Pine Barrens and along a NOx deposition gradient recorded by the National Atmospheric Deposition Program.[13] The federal data showed higher levels of NOx deposition as one moved northward across the state. We collected soil and root samples and set up samplers to collect rainfall for nutrient chemical analysis of nitrogen from NOx air deposition. We also designed greenhouse studies to mimic what we were doing in the field by growing seedlings under more controlled conditions. Two seasons of sampling later, our results showed that a distinct gradient of increasing nitrogen deposition did exist through the Pine Barren forests. We showed that the mycorrhizal fungal community changed in response to this gradient. The field transect showed a small but significant increase in nitrogen deposition from south to north, with mycorrhizal abundance and richness declining under the pitch pines. This decline in richness was significantly correlated with the nitrogen deposition rates.[14]

Our greenhouse study showed that as nitrogen supply increased, the species richness, or biodiversity, of the fungi attached to the tree roots was diminished. A reduction in biodiversity is recognized as a potential impairment of an ecosystem, because the more biodiverse a biome is, the more likely it can rebound from disturbances such as drought, fire, or pollution. These shifts in the community structure like any other delicate symbiotic ecosystem could result in the loss of the trees if the fungi they depend on for fertilization suddenly die off. Importantly, we found that New Jersey pitch pines responded to extremely small increases in the deposition of nitrogen compared with similar forests in Europe. From a forestry perspective, these fungal indicators could prove invaluable to natural resource managers and foresters in the coming years, allowing them to track hitherto unforeseen biological changes to the forest ecosystem that result from air pollution.

STATE PARKS AND CEDAR SWAMPS

The Pinelands International Biosphere Reserve contains a unique ecosystem of oak/pine forests intermixed with historic villages, bog-agriculture cranberry and blueberry farms, as well as extensive freshwater and salt marsh wetlands. Two Pinelands rivers that traverse the reserve, the Great Egg Harbor River and the Maurice River, also receive additional protection as part of the federal National Wild and Scenic River System. In addition, the Barnegat Bay estuary, located along the extreme eastern portion of the reserve, was accepted into the National Estuary Program by the USEPA in 1995, and the estuarine portion of the Mullica River was designated the Jacques Cousteau National Estuary Research Reserve in 1998. The Pinelands Reserve also contains a number of large state parks, including Wharton State Forest, the Brendan T. Byrne State Forest, and the Bass River State Forest, all of which supply public recreation facilities and wildlife management areas. In spite of this, the reserve is surrounded by dense suburban tracts, which exert continuing pressure for development. This is allowed primarily on the periphery, although restricted by aggressive regulations that seek to preserve the Pinelands' natural character.

I remember the first time I ventured into the low-lying cedar swamps of the Pine Barrens. Pine shrubs and thick underbrush crossed by thin tunnels of deer tracks led down to the slow-creeping waters of the woods, where sphagnum moss and hummocks of saplings pushed up through the oozing mud. The sphagnum moss have strong ion pumps that push out hydrogen into the surrounding waters, creating an acid broth in which the tannins and humus of the fallen pine needles are leached out, turning the water into the color of blood, and the iron so common to these soils is precipitated too, creating crusty coverings on the quiet pools and dark channels.

At the edge of these silent waters, miniature carnivorous plants splay their sticky tendrils into the air, waiting for some unfortunate insect to stumble onto their outstretched palms—like the sundew, which rolls down and sucks the animal dry, or the pitcher plant, which is filled with invitingly sweet water and deadly hairs that project downward for drowning its prey in the liquid. A third carnivore, the bladderwort, has pretty yellow flowers and a massive underwater root system, where tiny bladders with trap doors wait for aquatic insects to stumble in and then close without warning.

Yet is spite of this macabre bestiary, there is a stillness and a beautiful isolation too. The trees rise to a towering height above the wetlands floor, loosely spaced and empty of leaves save for their upper stories. Down below, the undergrowth is sparse except for a number of low huckleberry bushes, the moss, and the muddy pools interspersed by the hummocks of saplings, which reach up for sunlight in the dense shade. The blueberry bushes are filled with fruit as blue as deep water, and their pink, purple, and green flowers spread across the path along with their broad, waxy leaves. The earth is mindless here. It revolves on an ancient axis; it spills, recedes, then spills again—no mother, no antecedents, the logic of this wet fecundity perpetuates itself with an ease that predates wisdom.

And of course most people can gaze on these spectacles in the Pine Barrens because of the numerous state parks that criss-cross its woodlands. State parks in New Jersey have their own ambience. Of course they don't offer the long-distance awe of the Grand Tetons in Yellowstone or the lofty ocean views on the Olympic Peninsula in Washington State. But New Jersey can boast a more diversified park system, with rocky outcroppings and breathtaking views along the Appalachian Trail, bright barrier island beaches near the green Atlantic Ocean, and deep-forested woodlands filled with dwarf pine trees and carnivorous plants in our southern Pine Barrens. And I have spent many vacations in these parks, as have many of my family, friends, and coworkers, because as a uniquely urban state, caught between the spreading megalopolises of New York City and Philadelphia, we have learned to appreciate what open space we possess within our borders. And because we are such a small state, with family members and friends living only a short distance away, I have found that we often visit our parks in tribes.

When I first moved to colonial Haddonfield, New Jersey, when my son was only four years old, I discovered a group of friends who loved to go camping in the nearby Pinelands. The campsite we usually chose was in Wharton State Forest along the Batsto River just above creaky Godfrey's Bridge. I owned a big, red canoe at the time, as did a few other dads, which we would load onto the bed of a pickup truck filled with kids. We would then drive off in a cloud of dust through the forest a dozen miles upstream to a canoe launch. There we would pile out, drag the canoes into the water, and set off downriver. We paddled through ancient tracts of oak and pine, towering swamp maples and prickly cedars, and lowland swamps whose blue breaks in the canopy were filled with hovering red-tailed hawks, spying on us suspiciously as they soared. And on we paddled, through long meadows of grassy wetlands and deep green forests until finally we arrived right back where we'd started. Then another crew of dads and kids would do it all over again.

The most memorable of these trips came, however, in what would normally be the most inauspicious of circumstances. It was the weekend that it rained, poured, deluged our campsite until the kids and adults could no more stay dry than the river subside from its banks. The kids, being young, had no real qualms about the weather and did what they would do anyway. They went swimming as the clouds poured cataracts; held on to branches against the current, laughing aloud at the raging river; and somehow kept a campfire going for hours in the midst of a downpour that would have made Noah weep.

But one of the most wondrous things about this one wet weekend was how it changed the way I viewed my children. My son, Dan, was in high school by then, and it was his younger sister, Laura, that I'd taken camping that year. Dan was working that summer for the New Jersey Park Service just downriver in historic Batsto Village. He was a docent, or historical interpreter, responsible for taking visitors on tours through the reconstructed nineteenth-century living history museum. The town was frozen in time and populated by reenactors who re-created life as it existed in the Pine Barrens during the 1800s. The reconstructed village had an operating sawmill and blacksmith shop, barns filled with animals, a piggery, an ice house, and a horse stable. Dan started his day by sweeping water snakes off the road that traversed the lake's dam, which led to the village. He then fed sheep, pigs, and cows that were kept as part of the living history farm. He even ran the sawmill on the spillway of the lake's earthen impoundment.

So it was on that wet day in June when I'd gone camping with his sister in a downpour that Dan came into our campground driving a park ranger's truck to warn us that we might have to evacuate the park if things got any worse. Dan and all the other park employees had been sandbagging the Batsto Lake dam to keep it from failing. And my emotions were in serious disorder as I watched him drive away through the downpour among those towering pitch pines with a dozen kids running about oblivious to the dangers of the real world and its imminent tragedies. That a simple thing like heavy rainfall could breach an earthen dam and wash away all that lay in its path downstream, people's homes, bridges, and livestock, tearing up their lives and livelihoods all the way to the sea was hard to digest.

Yet I had another child to keep happy that day, my daughter, Laura. And she was happy even in her soaked state as long as she had friends to hang with. But she wanted to go for a canoe trip in the rain. And in hindsight perhaps I should have thought twice about it, based on what my son had just told me. But we were miles above the lake and the Pine Barren rivers are normally shallow and not too dangerous. So seeing little real danger in her request, I agreed. I had one of the other men drive us upstream, where we launched our canoe into the ripping current, the red cedar waters now deep brown with silt and angry with foam. We ran the current as best we could, although the old riffles were now full of white water, and the pools we had previously visited for leisurely swims were now lost beneath the raging torrent that pushed us forward in a monstrous rush of water. It was in these circumstances that the effort of paddling became a chore; a backbreaking effort was required to turn the canoe against the foreshortened runs; stream reaches that used to take a half-hour to traverse now we crossed in minutes. Overarching trees that we passed under on more placid days had become treacherous gates that blocked our way and dragged the water to tumultuous breaks dangerously close to the shore, where sticker brambles reached for our clothes.

It was then we came to a part of the river that flowed through a cedar swamp and its moss-covered trunks that crept right down to the shoreline. I could see that the floodplain within was completely underwater. I marveled at the wide buttressed trunks of the towering red trees and their tickly needles awash in floodwater, the rising columns like pillars in a beautiful Gothic cathedral, ceilings and apses made of bending branches and marbled floors the gurgling rivulets below. I was so moved by this beautiful vision that with a deft turn of my paddle I maneuvered us into the drowned woods between two broad trucks, entering the swamp with Laura in the bow. And I felt the tug of the river subside, the canoe gently toeing its way forward as my daughter reached slowly out and pressed her fingertips to a moss covered limb, pushed a hanging Virginia creeper out of her face, directing us gently forward from limb to limb.

She looked over her shoulder and at me and said, "Wow, daddy!"

And I smiled, "Wow indeed!"

The roar from the river had diminished to a muted grumble among the downward-hanging cedar branches, and as I turned in my seat, I felt the tug of the broad sheet of water moving us across the floodplain, our canoe moving in synchrony with the deep-channeled water out on the open river. I marveled at God's creation of such a wonder as a cedar swamp in flood. I felt a hush fall upon the world, the soft green sphagnum moss that lined the base of the trees but bumpers as we drifted down-current. And I sensed the animals about us, huddled against the flood in burrows or up in the trees, the sheeted flow beside us filled with tiny fish that sought to hide in the leeward eddies of giant tree trunks.

And of course there was Laura in front of me. Tiny and not yet a teenager, a girl still in wonder, marveling at this water world. Yet what we shared that day was a world I'd never seen before either; the two of us travelers in a strange, flooded land. And when I think about that weekend—the flood and the moments with my son and daughter, the terror of my son scrambling at the foot of an overreached dam, the splendor of a water-filled forest—I marvel at how easy it is to miss the dangers and wonders before us. And how important it is for us to share life and nature with those you love. My family and I have

traveled since then through Rocky Mountain National Park and to the edge of
the Grand Canyon, and we have swum in the crystal blue water of the
American Virgin Islands, yet to me those wondrous intimate moments under
the flooded cedars of Wharton State Forest are more precious and more meaningful than all the magnificent vistas of lost Babylon.

THE FUTURE OF NEW JERSEY'S FORESTS

New Jersey is a national leader in protecting land by regulatory legislation, as is
epitomized by its passage of the prescient Pinelands Act. Conservation efforts
continue statewide to keep forests, farms, and other green space open, including both the purchases of land and easements by state and nongovernmental
organizations. Still, despite these conservation efforts, a steady decline in forest
land area is likely throughout the state owing to continued pressure placed on
forests and farmland from development. A major problem when large portions
of a forest are lost to development is that the remaining forest becomes broken
into smaller tracts. This phenomenon, known as "forest fragmentation," creates many ecologic problems because it degrades watersheds, reduces wildlife
habitat, increases site disturbances, and favors invasion by exotic plant species.
Many wildlife biologists believe that fragmentation is a contributing factor
in the decline of some bird and wildlife species, though fragmentation
favors species such as raccoons, squirrels, and white-tailed deer. These species
are habitat generalists that have become acclimated to living near humans.
Fragmentation also changes the character of rural areas, because unlike owners
of large tracts, owners of small parcels are less likely to manage their forests
and/or allow access to their land for activities such as fishing and hunting.

In general, New Jersey's forests are healthy and resilient, and they will continue to mature. Current trends indicate that the state's future forests will have
larger trees, higher volumes per acre, and more old-growth characteristics. But
these forests will be vastly different from the original forests that confronted
the early settlers. As the Garden State's economy and population grow, the
impact on the forest resource will only increase. Land cleared for development
will remain in this condition permanently, even as more land is cleared.
Fragmentation of forests into ever-smaller patches will continue, rural areas
will become more urbanized, and the introduction of unwanted invasive
insect, disease, and exotic plant species will continue to threaten native species.
Once established, many nonnative species become a permanent part of the
ecosystem they inhabit. The adverse effects of these changes may not be immediately evident, and the overall impact may be difficult to assess, because forests
change slowly. High deer populations are causing changes in species composition

and hindering the ability of forests to regenerate. Natural processes within the forest are disrupted by interference from humans—for example, increased efforts to control wildfires, as homes and new developments encroach on forests, thereby breaking the natural fire cycle to which the state's Pinelands are adapted. As a result, in the Pine Barrens, pine eventually could lose its dominance to hardwood species.

Threats to New Jersey's forest from beyond its borders include pollutants carried into the state by wind, as well as possible changes in climate. These and other factors will make it increasingly difficult to manage the Garden State's forests. As hazards to forest health increase, the monitoring and tending of forest land will become more important. It may be that the amount of forest in the state has peaked, as the area of new forests being created from abandoned agricultural lands now is being outpaced by development. In reaction to this, public ownership of forests probably will continue to expand. Land trusts, nonprofit organizations, and the public will need to participate in conservation. And I am sure we will rise to the occasion as we did once before with the Pinelands. In fact, comparable legislation, called the Highlands Act, has recently passed. It affords similar protections and the creation of a preservation area encompassing thousands of acres in the Appalachian Mountain ecoregion of northern New Jersey.

I have found in my travels across the state that it is the wild places that better define us and not the baseball stadiums that pop up like mushrooms in every brownfield community or the light rail lines that funnel us into those tiny little boxes we call houses. And as the forests go, so goes the wildlife that survives under their protective limbs. This includes humans, the so-called top predators. For without biodiversity in our natural lands, our environs will be diminished to point that the adage I learned as an uninformed city kid becomes true: that all birds are pigeons and all insect either flies or ants. Now I know better, for without biological integrity, without protection against invasive species that choke our woodlands, without a biological mosaic of preserved habitats to match our state's natural needs, we will all live in a concrete jungle of our own design, devoid of wildlife and trees.

Fortunately, there are wildlife biologists at NJDEP who work indefatigably to protect the creatures that live within our parks, just as diligently as the state's Forest Service and Forest Fire Service labor to protect its trees. These include ornithologists who transplant Bald Eagles to nest on our waterways, entomologists who hike up forbidding headwaters in search of endangered dragonflies, and herpetologists who track rattlesnakes through housing developments, seeking to understand and protect the biotic mosaic of animal habitats that surrounds our cities and villages.

CHAPTER 10

The Biotic Mosaic

As a boy scout I was nominated to join an honor society called the Order of the Arrow. This distinction was predicated on initiation rites that involved months of public service, culminating in a camping trip to the mountains of northern New Jersey. On this expedition we were challenged to remain silent for two days and to perform backbreaking physical labor. As a fetish to our initiation, we each also whittled a small wooden arrow that hung from our necks by leather thongs. But here was the rub: if we spoke while on this trip, one of the members of the Order could notch our arrow, and if we received five notches, we were out.

The first night of the trip we were feted at a bonfire and then blindfolded and guided into the woods, our companions leading us in circuitous paths before leaving each of us alone to sleep with nothing but the clothes on our backs. In the morning we were expected to use our orienteering skills to find our way to the lodge for breakfast. Most of us did this, although some had to be rescued from aimless wandering the next day. But I must say that an irrational fear swept over me as I removed my blindfold and saw nothing on that moonless night. I was as close to panic as I had ever felt in my short life. It took great control to sit still and wait until my night vision adjusted and I could make out the shapes of trees and boulders around me. But it was the rustling of the night creatures in the surrounding underbrush that proved more unnerving. That is, until I decided they were avoiding me, moving on the periphery of my silent vigil, and just going about their nightly chores.

The next day we were all trucked to the entrance of the camp, where a bull-dozer and a dump truck awaited us. There we worked moving boulders and digging holes in preparation for a set of Indian totem poles that were to be ele-vated as the pillars of a new gateway. Like industrious ants, we descended upon the site and all day long pulled huge rocks out of the ground or pushed earthen piles up against the poles, which were decorated with upwardly spiraling carvings of eagles, foxes, and bears. That night we were told to lie down where we had worked, and sleeping bags and a hot dinner were brought down to our bivouac. Totally exhausted, we ate as the sun set, then fell asleep among the rocks. It was not long after that I awoke and felt a weight on my chest, as if someone had placed a heavy rope across my torso. I had fallen asleep on my back looking at the Milky Way in all its majesty above the chilly mountain, so leaning forward I peeped my exhausted eyes open to notice a shape slither along my bag onto the ground. My heart hammered as my mouth gathered into an "O," and I jumped up with my sleeping bag still wrapped around my legs, almost spilling me atop the writhing animal. And as I looked around me, I saw dozens of the creatures moving among the sleeping figures on the ground. I screamed, "Snakes!" which led to beldam as my companions rose as one and scrambled out of the rocks and onto the roadway.

Shining our flashlights into the abandoned campsite, we saw dozens of timber rattlesnakes creeping back into the hollows beneath the boulders we had overturned. It seems we had constructed out bivouac atop a "hibernaculum," or overwintering cave where the snakes hibernated in the hundreds until the warming days of spring revived and brought them to the surface. There they would bask in the spring sunlight, molt, and then grow, gathering their strength for the annual pursuit of food and a mate.

Inadvertently on our spring foray into the woods we had interrupted their sleep and accelerated their awakening with the proximity of our warm mammalian bodies. So in a strange conjunction of fates we humans and our reptilian brothers shared a momentary lapse of reason and slept together; vipers and country greenhorns snoozing on the same rocky ground. And in spite of my timely warning, and the lucky fact that no one was bitten by the sleepy rattlers, I received another notch in my arrow for shouting "snakes." I was not excluded from the final initiation rite the next day, however, as it seemed fitting that I was brother to the snake.

Snakes under the House

Dropping a campsite on top of a snake den is just as illogical as dropping a house on one. Yet suburban sprawl does exactly that. Inadvertently and thoughtlessly, as we place roots down on apparently virgin ground, we ignore those that were there first. As a result, the animals that live in these degraded habitats are driven out, or else, if sufficient pressure is applied, become extinct. New Jersey has a special section within our Division of Fish and Wildlife to deal with such contingencies called the Endangered and Nongame Species Program. Through enabling legislation, its mission is to actively conserve New

Figure 11. Pinelands timber rattlesnake, *Crotalus horridus*. (Source: John F. Bunnell, New Jersey Pinelands Commission.)

Jersey's biological diversity by maintaining and enhancing endangered, threatened, and nongame wildlife populations within healthy, functioning ecosystems. The program is daunting when one considers that it is responsible for the protection and management of nearly five hundred wildlife species, seventy-three of which are listed as endangered or threatened. The timber rattlesnake, *Crotalus horridus*, is one of these species. And what makes the program's efforts so much more heroic is the fact that it is funded primarily by donations from the sale of "Conserve Wildlife" license plates. Without the support of the public, competitive grants, and the state income tax check-off, the program would be unable to accomplish its many achievements.

The New Jersey Endangered and Nongame Species Program probably has the most passionate and esoteric scientists in the department. The legislation creating their group was the Endangered Species Conservation Act, signed into law on December 14, 1973. This was two weeks *before* President Nixon signed the federal Endangered Species Act, which shows how passionate and forward-looking New Jersey residents can be when confronted with prioritizing natural resources over property development. The law gave NJDEP the power to protect species whose survival continues to be imperiled by the loss of habitat, overexploitation, and pollution. This is accomplished by regulations that force developers to avoid habitats where threatened and endangered species are typically found. Yet the protection of endangered species is often fraught with ambiguity, as habitats become fragmented during development, resulting in a mosaic of biotic integrity and unclear boundaries as to where an animal's habitat begins and where the human interface ends. A good example of this imbroglio comes from the recent siting of a housing development in the Pine Barrens. At the heart of this confrontation between developers and regulators was a nest of timber rattlesnakes and the Pinelands Commission science office.

The Pinelands science office manages one of the most exciting natural science research programs in the United States, as it is restricted to the ecoregion of the Pinelands Biosphere Reserve. The staff is small but composed of wide-ranging expertise in ecology, hydrology, botany, and environmental science. Their mission is to provide the fifteen members of the Pinelands Commission with the technical information necessary to formulate and evaluate environmental policies and programs. Studies completed by the science office address a wide range of terrestrial, aquatic, and wildlife topics. These studies are often driven by the unique Pinelands soil and water quality, which is highly acidic, owing to the waxy coats of the falling pine needles. Most botanical and animal species are adapted to thrive only in these low pH conditions. The office also performs comprehensive studies of river hydrology, aquatic and wetland ecology, wetland identification and delineation, resource management, and wastewater technology.[1]

In 2004, Kim Ladig, from the Pinelands science office, and Dave Golden, from NJDEP's Endangered and Nongame Species Program, completed a three-year study monitoring the movements of timber rattlesnakes in the vicinity of a partially constructed residential development in Evesham Township, New Jersey. Ironically, the high-end development is named the Sanctuary. The Sanctuary was about one-third built when rattlesnakes were found and lawsuits filed, bringing construction to a halt. Initially, the Pinelands Commission allowed the construction of 144 of the 300 homes originally planned for the development but also directed the owners to set aside 1,200 acres to be permanent protection for the snakes, the funding of a rattlesnake research project, and the construction of fences and under-road culverts designed to redirect the snakes away from residential properties.

The settlement was not met with universal approval, however, and many environmentalists rallied for more stringent protection for the rattlesnakes. The New Jersey Audubon Society and the Pinelands Preservation Alliance felt that the "deal" worked out by the Pinelands Commission was "unnecessary." They felt the Pinelands Commission could and should apply its regulations more conservatively, as "that course of action would protect the rattlesnakes and the Pinelands Plan."[2] The Audubon Society and the Pinelands Preservation Alliance went to court and sued the state to intervene on its side, arguing that under state law, as well as the terms of the Pinelands Management Plan, the presence of the threatened rattlesnakes should have halted the building *completely*.

At the time of the initial compromise by the commission, Janet Jackson-Gould, executive director of the Cedar Run Wildlife Refuge in Medford, a few miles from the Sanctuary, said: "Unlike most suburbanites (or perhaps like them), snakes don't have the reasoning ability to adapt to a local traffic pattern. Last spring, when the snakes came out of hibernation, they got lost on the development's streets, named for artists, and some were squashed on John Singer Sargent Way." Carleton Montgomery, executive director of the Pinelands Preservation Alliance, another conservation group, felt that the timber rattlesnake had image problems. He said: "Like with coyotes, there's a traditional long-standing cultural bias against this animal. The public would be much more supportive of an endangered animal that was cuter."[3]

The major focus of Ladig and Golden's rattlesnake study, mandated by the settlement, was to evaluate the effectiveness of a two-mile fence and culvert system intended to direct the movements of the reptiles away from the development and toward a forested area. The researchers carefully caught the animals and placed minute radio-tracking tags on their scales after they molted. Snakes periodically shed their outer skin in one piece during a molt. When the snake is ready to shed its skin, it scrapes the edge of its mouth against a hard surface. It then continues scraping and crawling forward until it is completely free of the dead skin.

In the study five males and four female timber rattlesnakes were radio-tracked at various times of the day and night over a three-year study period. Using a global positioning system, the location of each snake was recorded every other day until it reentered a wintering den, or hibernaculum, in the fall. The radio-telemetry indicated that the rattlesnakes used extensive areas of the forested uplands and wetlands within a six-square-mile area around the development. Two large males had the largest activity range, showing round-trip travel distances of almost seven miles. More important, the study indicated that several timber rattlesnakes heavily utilized areas that were to be developed in the future. The data also showed that fences did not prevent any of the transmitter-equipped snakes from entering constructed portions of the development. The culverts, however, were used by two of them to move beneath a street to forested lands east of the development.[4]

Using this information, the Pinelands Commission authorized a new settlement, requiring the developers to add protection for the endangered pine snake, *Pituophis melanoleucas*, which was discovered in the Sanctuary during the timber rattler study. This agreement allowed the completion of an unfinished portion of Georgia O'Keefe Way by directing the developer to build twelve-foot-wide box-type culverts under the road, which allowed both of the endangered snake species to pass through, minimizing mortalities by motor vehicles.[5] Under this agreement, building lots with snake nesting areas in them were permanently protected through deed restrictions. These protected lots were also contiguous to a 350-acre conservation area set-aside that served as a wildlife corridor to the undisturbed forests to the east of the subdivision.

THE BALD EAGLE: LESSONS IN BIOTIC RECOVERY

Sometimes the source of the stressor that impairs an animal's livelihood is not losing its home range but pollution, which taints its food, water, or even the ground that it burrows through. As developers cover wildlife habitats with houses and manicured lawns, they also spray to keep bugs off the grass, not realizing or caring that the breeze may carry their insect poisons downwind to lakes and forests where wild things live. There are not many stories of endangered species crawling back from the edge of extinction. But when they are told, they usually reflect near-heroic endeavors that are both dramatic and labor-intensive. The story of the near extirpation from the North American continent of the Bald Eagle (*Haliaeetus leucocephalus*), owing to the indiscriminant use of the pesticide DDT was trumpeted by Rachel Carson's book *Silent Spring*.[6] Carson pointed out that DDT caused thinner eggshells, resulting in reproductive problems and death for many bird species. The chemical toxins affected Bald Eagles more drastically than some other animals because of biomagnification of the contaminant through the food web ending in their primary food, fish. The Bald Eagle is the only eagle unique to North America. It ranges over most of the continent from Alaska and Canada down to northern Mexico. Male Bald Eagles generally measure three feet from head to tail and weigh seven to ten pounds with a wingspan of about six feet. Females are larger, with some having a wingspan of eight feet. The raptor has large eyes and a powerful yellow beak with great, black talons that its uses to snatch fish from open water. The distinctive white head and tail feathers appear only after the bird is four or five years old.

New Jersey's Bald Eagle population was hit especially hard by eggshell thinning and loss of habitat, to the point that by the late 1980s there was just one active nest remaining in the state. We gained a second nest in 1988, however, and the population has been growing ever since thanks to the bird's reintroduction to the state by NJDEP's Endangered Species and Nongame Program. Larry Niles, the lead ornithologist in this effort, initially removed eggs for artificial incubation and then fostered the young eagles back to the nest.[7] However, the mortality rates were high in these young eagles, as high as 80 percent, and since the species did not reproduce until about five years of age, it took too long to establish a viable population. Niles then instituted a "hacking program" in 1983, which was more successful. Bird hacking involves the hand-rearing and release of captive-bred and captive-reared birds. This resulted in the release of sixty young eagles in New Jersey over an eight-year period, which contributed to a significant increase in nesting pairs since 1990.

In fact, the latest 2008 survey of Bald Eagles in New Jersey showed a record high of sixty-nine mating pairs during the nesting season, with sixty-three of these nests active (with eggs). The Delaware Bay region showed the strongest recovery, with forty-six percent of the successful nests. Overall there were 264 Bald Eagles reported in the state, a new record high count.[8] The biologists who perform the hacking and surveys do not stop there in their labors to nurture these magnificent birds. They climb to dangerously high nests and leg-band the juveniles, take blood samples for pesticide analysis, and sometimes place little backpacks on the fledglings with radio-telemeters attached to track their foraging behavior. These backpacks are designed to fall off as the bird grows. I joined one of these volunteer trackers once, and it proved a harrowing experience.

He held what looked like an old TV antennae out the window of his moving car, steering with one hand while periodically looking at a dashboard monitor and then a map to keep aligned with the swooping eaglet as it flew in and out of sight, leading us on a wild chase over back roads from one feeding ground to another. The back of the tracker's car was stuffed with clothes and a cooler filled with food, as he often slept in the car to catch the early-rising eaglets. I learned on that harrowing ride that it takes dedication and a bit of manic energy to be a bird tracker for the Endangered and Nongame Species Program. But its staff are quick to point out that the state's eagle population would not be thriving without the efforts of hundreds of dedicated volunteers who live nearby and observe the nests twenty-four hours a day, report sightings, and help protect the surrounding habitat from human encroachment.

Yet in spite of this success story for reestablishing breeding populations of Bald Eagles in New Jersey, we should be cautioned by our inability to protect other wildlife species. For there are equally egregious stories of near-extinction in the state, whose solutions may still evade us and whose causes are more tenuous and complex. For example, some endangered bird species land in New Jersey only on their way to somewhere else and may face threats that are local in origin but whose impacts are global in nature.

THE RED KNOT AND THE HORSESHOE CRAB

Animal migrations are one of the most wondrous and mysterious phenomena in the world. The basic explanations of why they evolved typically involve temporal or seasonal movements to coincide with optimal feeding or mating conditions. The triggers for these movements are less precise, however, and might entail the seasonal height of the sun, temperature changes, or the length of the day. This might cause a herd, a school of fish, or a flock of birds to move to a milder or more productive habitat. Some of these movements may be daily actions representing phototaxis to the light of the sun. For example, the nightly migration of trillions of tiny shrimplike copepods from the ocean depths to the surface for feeding, and then a return to the abyssal depths with sunrise, may have evolved as an antipredation strategy for feeding in the more productive waters at the surface under the shade of darkness.

And sometimes there is a fascinating overlap between terrestrial and aquatic migrations that elicits awe at the parsimonious complexity of our world and the ineffable beauty of it biological synergisms. Bird migrations are typically triggered by seasonal changes in the length of the day and the angle of the sun. As the earth moves on its axis, the seasons shift from summer to winter leaving in their wakes fields of plenty and then scarcity. Many animals will survive the long winter through fastidious stocking of larders in burrows, or they will estivate or hibernate until the season of abundance returns. Birds, on the other hand, with their incredible mobility, can keep pace with the planet's seasonal precession and move to areas where it is perennially summer, or at least to more benign locations to wait out the winter's cold. Some birds can travel even greater, intercontinental distances, taking advantage of the planet's elliptical orbit. These species use the earth's hemispherical seasonality to follow the dipping sun below the equator to winter at the far end of South America while we shiver in New Jersey.

One of these transcontinental travelers is the Red Knot (*Calidris canutus*), a shorebird that visits New Jersey annually during its migration. Carefully observed for years by the Endangered and Nongame Species Program, the Red Knot was listed in New Jersey as a threatened species in 1999 because of its population decline. In a more recent U.S. Fish and Wildlife study involving eighteen ornithologists from both North and South America, the Red Knot, which breeds in the central Canadian arctic and mainly winters in Tierra del Fuego at the other end of South America, was shown to be in dramatic decline over the past twenty years. Previously estimated at 100,000 to 150,000 birds, the population now numbers only 18,000 to 33,000. The Fish and Wildlife study estimates that if adult survival remains low, Red Knots could go extinct in about ten years.[9] Larry Niles, former chief of NJDEP's Endangered and Nongame Species Program, was the head of this team.

Yet despite intensive studies by Niles and others, the reasons for this population decline and reduced adult survivability are imperfectly known. However, one of the suggested stressors is a reduction in the birds' critical food supply, crab eggs. During their northward migration to nest in the arctic, most Red Knots stop over in the tristate waters of Delaware Bay, where they mainly feed on the eggs of the horseshoe crab.

The horseshoe crab, *Limulus polyphemus*, is sometimes called a living fossil because it has changed little from the earliest specimens imprinted on rocks from approximately 450 million years ago. The crab has little human food value but has been a valuable commercial resource; it is used as fertilizer, as calcium enrichment for fowl grains, as bait for fish traps, and more recently, medicinally, to identify human blood endotoxins. Frederick Bang in the early 1950s discovered that the blood cells of the horseshoe crab, called amoebocytes, contain a clotting agent that attaches to dangerous endotoxins produced by disease-causing, gram-negative bacteria. In 1977, the Food and Drug Administration approved a new procedure for identifying these endotoxins using the Limulus Amoebocyte Lysate (LAL) test, which is derived from horseshoe crab blood.

The bulky crab is ungainly and has been described as an armored box that moves; its appearance similar to the prehistoric, extinct trilobite. The animal looks like a horseshoe when viewed from above. But the biologist who named the species *polyphemus* was probably thinking of its resemblance to the one-eyed cannibal and giant that confronted Homer's Odysseus in his epic poem *The Odyssey*, when the Greek hero famously bested the monster in a drinking match and blinded him to escape his cave. Ironically. the crab possesses ten eyes, each sensitive to light and capable of detecting ultraviolet light from the sun as well as the diffuse light reflected from the moon. Horseshoe crab spawning occurs in May and June, reaching its peak at an evening high tide during a full or new moon. The adults scrabble ashore onto beaches in Delaware Bay that are protected from the surf.

The sight of these boxy creatures pulling themselves out of the water by the thousands at midnight to gain higher ground, and the pile-up as males seek to mount nesting females is eerie and unsettling. Typically, the males arrive first to patrol the beach and wait. The females arrive later, giving off a chemical pheromone that attracts the males, who follow. The males, which are much smaller than the females, use a specially developed claw to latch onto the back of the female. So during spawning the crabs form dense huddles, with numerous males draped atop a crawling female. Each female can lay about eighty thousand eggs in the sand, which are fertilized by the attached males. There they sit buried, until the next lunar spring tide brings high water and a signal for hatching. And it is this cornucopia of eggs that attracts the flocks of migratory Red Knots who are entrained to arrive on the shore at the midpoint of their annual migration across North and South America.

The Red Knots need to lay down fat and protein reserves to fuel the last leg of their two thousand–mile flight to the arctic breeding grounds, and to ensure their survival once they arrive, since as food availability is initially low. The Fish and Wildlife study proposed that the main identified threat to the Red Knot population was the reduced availability of horseshoe crab eggs at this layover. This, it argued, could be attributed primarily to overfishing by humans. Adult crabs are harvested locally for bait by the conch- and eel-fishing industries common in Delaware Bay. In the past, NJDEP has taken actions to improve feeding conditions for Red Knots in Delaware Bay, including beach closures to prevent disturbance, building exclosures to reduce competition from gulls, and establishing harvesting quotas as well as the designation of a marine sanctuary for the crabs off the mouth of the bay.

Yet the issue is as not as clear-cut as this one study might indicate. Virginia Tech's Horseshoe Crab Research Center was tasked by the Atlantic States Marine Fisheries Commission in 2006 to perform a study to assess crab population viability in the Delaware Bay fishery. The results of this study showed "positive" population growth for horseshoe crabs. The fishery seemed to grow-ing and not declining.[10]

In spite of these conflicting studies, New Jersey was faced with the conse-quences of doing nothing: the possible extinction of the Red Knots. Therefore, more aggressive steps were taken to protect the endangered bird. New Jersey imposed a two-year moratorium from 2006 to 2007 on horseshoe crab har-vesting to give the population a chance to recover. Unfortunately, crab har-vesting continued in the state of Delaware on the other side of the bay. Delaware had attempted to institute a moratorium, but its efforts had failed, and harvests in Delaware continued. Subsequently, in 2008, the New Jersey Legislature acted more demonstrably. Representative Douglas H. Fisher, chair-man of the New Jersey State Assembly's Agricultural and Natural Resources Committee, helped draft legislation to completely stop the horseshoe crab har-vest in the state. He said at its passage: "Though I represent commercial fisher-men, to decimate a species, in this case maybe both red knots and horseshoe crabs, for a buck apiece for bait for less than 40 licensees seems senseless." Greg DiDomenico, the executive director of the Garden State Seafood Association countered: "You might say, 'Well, this is only 39 fishermen,' but then what minority will be next? It's an industry that deserves to survive, and it hasn't been absolutely proven that the moratorium is a benefit to the overall red knot population."[11]

On March 25, 2008, Governor Jon Corzine, in spite of this disagreement and the scientific uncertainties, signed the bill establishing a moratorium on har-vesting horseshoe crabs in New Jersey. At the signing, Governor Corzine said: "The effects of human behavior often have widespread, unintended conse-quences that reverberate across the animal kingdom for generations, like the ripple effect in a pond that started out as one small disturbance. It is with that in mind that we are here today to extend the moratorium on horseshoe crab harvesting, so as to reverse the endangerment and prevent the extinction of the red knot species and other shorebirds."[12] The bill stipulates that the moratorium will be in place until the populations of both horseshoe crabs and Red Knots have returned to a level where they will be self-sustaining as determined by the U.S. Fish and Wildlife Service. Fines for the continued harvesting of horseshoe crabs were set at $10,000 for the first offense and $25,000 for each subsequent offense.

Biological Integrity

And yet while the actions of the Endangered and Nongame Species Program are laudable (and pitifully underfunded), we should not lose sight of the fact that the state has many other animals and plant species with problems that are not yet dire but still require careful management. NJDEP's Division of Fish and Wildlife houses many such programs that monitor and protect freshwater fish, marine and shellfisheries, fur-bearing animals, and even insects. Its goal is to maintain the state's rich variety of fish and wildlife species at stable, healthy levels and to protect and enhance the many habitats on which they depend. The division runs many education programs to alert residents to the values inherent in our fish and wildlife and tries to foster positive human/wildlife coexistence. It also studies and maximizes the recreational and commercial use of fish and wildlife resources for future generations.

Another group at NJDEP, the Water Monitoring and Standards Program, is responsible an even more subtle task. It are tasked with monitoring the state's fresh, marine, and groundwaters for biological integrity, which includes collecting and categorizing a diverse group of aquatic organisms in streams, lakes, estuaries, and ocean waters. Collectively, these organisms are used as sentinels, as a canary in a coal mine, to measure upstream land use impacts by measuring subtle shifts in community structure for aquatic insects, freshwater fish, and even plant matter (algae). The records of these changes are used by regulators as report cards on each stream or waterway to assess changing water quality conditions and to seek upstream sources that might have caused impairment. In my research I have worked closely with the Water Monitoring and Standards Program to develop novel ways to sample streams and have spent many an hour seining or collecting specimens with kick-nets. We also electro-fish, a strange but efficient way to canvas a large stream reach in the shortest time possible.

I remember once we were electro-fishing a fast-flowing headwater stream high on a steep ridge above the Delaware Water Gap in Sussex County. Electro-fishing involves standing in a stream wearing rubber insulating waders with an electric battery strapped to your back attached to a long immersible rod held underwater. A small AC current runs through it for stunning nearby fish. The "shocker" is usually accompanied by a "netter," who scoops up the fish as they float past, placing the stunned animals in a bucket for species identification and a quick health check for fin rot or tumors. Typically, 98 percent of the fish caught this way are released unharmed, which allows the stream to maintain its biotic and ecological integrity. Like physicians, we field biologists and ecologists adhere to the Latin axiom of *Primum non nocere*, or "First, do no harm." I was the netter that day and had fallen into a mesmerizing routine as I repetitively scanned the water, swept the net down to pull out a stunned fish, quickly checked for tumors and dropped it into a bucket before returning my gaze to another sweep.

But as I reached for a fish beneath the exposed root of a willow tree in an eroded bank, I noticed that the stiffened root was actually a snake. A poisonous copperhead to be precise, *Agkistrodon contortrix mokasen*, with half its body out of the water and frozen in a statuelike rictus from the electrical current flowing through its torso. Its mouth was spread wide as if screaming with fangs bared, yet no sound pervaded the quiet of that glade except the soft gurgling of the water against my boots and the lithesome murmuring of the wind in the trees arching above. I looked about at the clear water, the brown stream bank, grey roots, and two bared fangs just centimeters from my extended fingertips. And I found in that incongruous moment a great joy go through me, untoward and immensely beautiful, even as tractor trailers hummed from somewhere beyond the trees on the highway. I admired the distinctive hourglass crisscrossing of red and brown scales that pulsed along the snake's body, its head copper-colored with the pit viper's heat-sensing holes, nostrils dilated and elliptical pupils slantwise and glaring helplessly. In that moment a resolve built within me, something like a religious fervor to protect that stream, to protect the snake and the entire watershed from the hands of a developer who might want to make a buck by erasing the legacy of the reptilian delight before me.

Then my coworker suddenly lifted her rod to free the copperhead from the current. It collapsed back into the water and swam slowly away, leaving in its wake an S-shaped trail on the water's surface. As I pondered its dragonlike beauty as it swam, I also knew that commercial development in New Jersey has become a highly visible and lucrative endeavor. Conservation today involves an unequal joust between two very different sets of laws and government entities—the municipalities that seek local economic expansion and state regulators entrusted with protecting the natural resources that are shared by all. Towns and counties derive their authority from the New Jersey Municipal Land Use Law, which gives them broad powers to regulate land use, with few requirements to consider neighboring or downstream impacts.[13]

Yet unbridled development in competing municipalities can lead to an out-come predicted in the classic ecological paradigm called the "tragedy of the com-mons," where individuals or towns sharing the same limited resource, such as sheep grazing on a common meadow, may doom the entire community to star-vation if the resource is overexploited and collapses.[14] For example, the grass can be overgrazed, the sheep die, and then the people starve. To circumvent these types of conflicts, state legislators have given state agencies the laws and regula-tions needed to arbitrate competing interests. These laws require to some extent that NJDEP take an eco-biased and conservative strategy in resource manage-ment, where decisions can be slightly weighted in favor of natural resources. In effect, NJDEP votes by proxy for fish, forests, and even insects. And the most powerful of these regulations is the New Jersey Surface Water Quality Standards, which the state is empowered to enforce through the federal Clean Water Act.[15]

The 1977 Clean Water Act directed USEPA and the states to restore and main-tain the "biological integrity" of the nation's surface waters. Biological integrity is defined as a balanced community of organisms comparable to the natural habitat of a region.[16] This integrity is a sign that a river or stream is in good health, as measured by various in-stream indicators, much as a human would get a health check up via by blood work or an X-ray. Unfortunately, the integrity of a water-way can be negatively impacted by chemicals that kill off sensitive species, agricul-tural erosion of sediments that smother bottom organisms, or an influx of nonnative species of plants and animals that out-compete native residents.

Initially, the health of aquatic systems was monitored through sampling for deleterious chemicals in the water such as phosphorus, heavy metals like arsenic, or pesticides. Chemical monitoring, however, provides only a snapshot of conditions at any one time and may fail to detect acute pollution events such as chemical spills or nonchemical pollution from upstream habitat alteration. In order to address these shortcomings, NJDEP supplemented its testing with biological monitoring of a suite of organisms such as aquatic insects, fresh-water fish, and microscopic plants (algae) suspended in the water. The power of biological monitoring is that these communities integrate and reflect long-term conditions in the environment and more accurately mirror the health of the entire upstream ecosystem.

Since 1994, and based on research performed by Jim Kurtenbach of USEPA, NJDEP has established a statewide network of more than eight hundred stations to monitor aquatic macroinvertebrate insects, one hundred stations to monitor fish, and eighty stations to monitor algae.[17] These procedures, built on an ecosys-tem concept pioneered by James Karr of the University of Washington, dovetails habitat features such as physical structure and flow regime with water quality parameters like pH or pollutant levels and biological measures such as the presence of pollution-tolerant or -sensitive fish and insects. It then compares the results with reference conditions collected elsewhere in the state at either a more pristine setting or at least a less impaired site.[18] A numerical score for biotic integrity is calculated based on biological attributes of a species, which respond predictably to a disturbance gradient of pollution. These species metrics are then combined into a single score called the index of biotic integrity (IBI).[19] Because the IBI method focuses on living organisms whose very existence represents an integration of conditions around them, biological evaluations expressed as an IBI score can grade chemical, physical, and/or biological impacts, as well as their cumulative effects on "beneficial uses." Beneficial uses are a legal concept and are defined under the Clean Water Act not only as biotic integrity but also as recreation (fishing and swimming), potability (drinking water supplies), and aesthetics (the beauty of a natural, clean, flowing waterway).

For the fish index of biotic integrity we electroshock and catch fish, then total up key attributes of the resident fish assemblage for classifying the streams as poor, fair, good, or excellent. Among other key metrics, we measure the total number of species present in the stream reach, the number of fish that eat aquatic insects, the number of trout and sunfish species, and the number of species intolerant to pollution. We also look for individuals with disease or physical malformations. The streams ranked as poor or fair are added to a list for follow-up investigations, and upstream sources of impairment are sought through reviews of aerial photographs, stream-bank surveys for outfall pipes and agricultural runoff, or in some cases increased sedimentation from storm drains or poor tillage practices at farms. Detailed annual results of these surveys can be found at the NJDEP Web site.[20]

Natural Capital

The rapid bioassessment protocols used by NJDEP and the scientifically defensible methods that underpin the various IBI indices of biotic integrity give the state a means to draw a line in the sand for developers. We can say: "No farther than here!" A similar logic was employed in the Pinelands Commission's settlement over preserving parts of the Sanctuary for timber rattlesnake habitat. IBI and similar biological indices give NJDEP the tools necessary to vote for fish and fowl, and the means to induce landholders to follow the guidelines of sustainable development.

For at this point in New Jersey's history, suburban sprawl had become like the "Blob" in that old Steve McQueen horror movie, an amorphous, unstoppable, creeping being that dissolves land and natural resources like an amoebic monster. However, unlike the "Blob" in the movie, which arrived on

Earth inexplicably, suburban sprawl is driven by Keynesian economics, property values, and their associated natural resources, especially water-view property. And developable land is often seen by municipalities only as a commodity, because of the higher monetary yield it will create if developed compared with the lesser apparent value of leaving the land alone. Yet this argument is fallacious if one further investigates the hidden worth of undeveloped land. For example, Bill Mates, an economist within Science and Research, recently performed a research project to calculate the worth of "natural capital" in New Jersey.

Mates and his coauthor defined natural capital as "the components of the natural environment that provide long-term benefits to society."[21] Many of the benefits provided by natural capital come from ecosystems. These include a dynamic complex of plant, animal, and microorganism communities and their nonliving environment, all interacting as a functional unit. Forests, wetlands, and lakes are examples of natural capital ecosystems. Mates's study found that New Jersey's state parks and forests provided total annual gross benefits estimated at between $953 million and $1.4 billion. In a follow-up study, Mates's team also estimated the dollar value of the "services and goods" produced by New Jersey's natural capital. Taking the estimated values of goods and services together, the total value of New Jersey's natural capital appears to be about $20 billion per year. Freshwater wetlands and marine ecosystems have the highest eco-service values.[22] The annual value of the goods provided by New Jersey's natural capital was estimated at between $2.8 billion and $9.7 billion, with farmland, marine waters, and quarries providing the highest values of goods. In addition to goods and services provided by our state's natural capital "wildlife-related tourism" was estimated to generate about $3 billion of gross economic activity in New Jersey annually. This represents about $1 billion of wage and salary income annually, or about thirty-seven thousand jobs. Overall, the study concluded that wildlife-related tourism plays a significant role in New Jersey's economy.

THE PRECAUTIONARY PRINCIPLE

The philosophical approach that natural resource managers, policymakers, and politicians bring to the conundrum of weighing human land-use desires against what is sustainable by biological populations seems almost intuitive and unscientific. It's almost a commonsense approach dictated by the axiom "Do no harm!" Yet the concept of how to deal with the lack of data or uncertainty in the face of making an environmentally sensitive decision has been debated for years. The concept has a name: the "precautionary principle." The precautionary principle is a moral and political philosophy that postulates "if an action or policy might cause severe or irreversible harm to the public, in the absence of a scientific consensus that harm would not ensue, the burden of proof falls on those who would advocate taking the action."[23] The European Union's European Environment Agency notes that "the precautionary principle applies where scientific evidence is insufficient, inconclusive or uncertain and preliminary scientific evaluation indicates that that there are reasonable grounds for concern, that the potentially dangerous effects on the environment, human, animal or plant health may be inconsistent with the high level of protection chosen by the EU."[24]

In essence, the precautionary principle as it applies to environmental policy states: "For practices such as the release of radiation or toxins, or massive deforestation, or the loss of biodiversity or extinction of species, the burden of proof lies with the advocates." The salient point is "that in the face of uncertainty to do the more conservative action may be better in the long run than doing nothing at all."[25] It is better to act than to wait until the negative effects of a "no decision," or a poor decision have been allowed to run their course and possibly inflict irreversible harm on the environment.

Some individuals might think that the actions described in this chapter to protect wildlife may be irresponsible and precipitous in the face of the scientific uncertainties. Some might argue that the state is being overprotective and unnecessarily aggressive in the face of what we regulate. For example, there may be conflicting views from scientists at the Virginia Tech Crab Research Center and the U.S Fish and Wildlife Service over whether horseshoe crab populations in Delaware Bay are increasing or decreasing. Both of these organizations are represented by renowned and respected members of the scientific community. But at NJDEP, as stewards of the environment, we regulators face a potentially greater risk in doing nothing when faced with scientific uncertainty, especially when a species is threatened with extinction. Allowing commerce alone to dictate what can be done with a parcel of land, or a beach, or the harvest of a natural resource is inimical to good environmental stewardship and the protection of the beasts and plants of New Jersey. The resulting decision by the New Jersey Legislature to protect the apparent decline of Red Knots through a horseshoe crab harvest moratorium was based on the philosophy of the precautionary principle. And following these precepts, Governor Corzine made a decision to sign the crab harvesting moratorium bill. He trusted in the experience of his staff at the Endangered and Nongame Species Program. His action was predicated on the unacceptable result of the no-action alternative, the possible extinction of the Red Knot. The unavoidable conclusion in such a conundrum was that precautionary measures were needed.

The value of that decision can only be weighed over time, but recent investigations are encouraging. The most recent survey of the Red Knot holds cautious hope for recovery. In the spring of 2009, Larry Niles, now retired from NJDEP but a consultant for the nonprofit Conserve Wildlife Foundation of New Jersey, joined an international gathering of ornithologists on Delaware Bay to patiently catch, weigh, and band flocks of the birds. An Australian shorebird expert, Clive Minton, called it an exciting year: "We think we're really seeing the beginning of a possible turn-round in the fortunes of the crabs and the shorebirds," he said.[26] Based on the birds the biologists netted, they estimated that 60 percent had reached their optimum weight before heading north. The previous year, only about 15 percent had done so. Amanda Dey, the state biologist who replaced Niles as the resident Red Knot expert, felt that calm waters and warm temperatures in 2009 had caused thousands of horseshoe crabs to swarm ashore and deposit their eggs.

It is still unclear whether the horseshoe crabs or the birds have shown a comeback, and biologists fear the Red Knots could plummet into extinction with an event as simple as a summer snowstorm in the arctic, or an oil spill in South America. Yet New Jersey cannot be faulted for putting the birds at risk, since acting locally we lessened the impacts globally. This concept of managing global ecology as one great organism has gathered momentum lately especially, because of the documented worldwide impacts of climate change. These global warming effects are documented in the Intergovernmental Panel on Climate Change's exhaustive report.[27] This document lists multiple ecological impacts under way on a global scale, including earlier spring seasons. This may interfere with the genetically precise timing of millions of migrating species. Birds may arrive late onto their nesting grounds only to find the abundance of insects or seeds they need for survival and reproduction dissipated. And as the misused resources that drive this process are at our command to limit, such as carbon emissions, the tale cautions us to the lessons inherent in the tragedy of the commons. We need to manage the globe for the betterment of all.

In the next chapter I will again focus on New Jersey as a laboratory for this concept of integrated environmental management. I will examine a recently developed policy tool called the "watershed initiative," which is used to look synergistically at natural resource management. Building on the old adage that everyone lives upstream of someone else, this concept was used to empower stakeholder groups within watershed-based technical and policy committees to advise and work proactively with regulators on a wide range of issues. This integrative process fused the concerns of disparate stakeholders such as industry representatives, conservationists, and regulators to challenge the often self-centered political interests of the 566 competing municipalities and twenty-one counties in New Jersey.

CHAPTER 11

Headwaters and Watersheds

The Appalachian Mountains in winter creak like an old man and growl with thunder as if there were tigers above the clouds mourning summer's end. The cold cracks the bones, eats the sinews, and calls out with a mysterious indifference that no one can mistake for compassion. There is honesty in the November mountains that refuses complacency. This makes the weather small and insignificant compared with the truth of the mountains' geological certainty and the frozen woods that hide their sleeping creatures. My wife, Bernadette, and I had gone to the woods in winter on a whim many years ago. We didn't know what it meant to sleep in a wood-heated cabin in the early days of winter. We went to the isolated Spring Cabin in Stokes Forest filled with all the green happiness of our summer visit a few months before. Yet as we pulled up outside the door, we sensed in the quietude of the mountainside that nothing was as it appeared. The burbling spring in front of the cabin—which gave it its name—was limed with frost, as the tall, leafless oaks swayed in the wind along the ridges like hairs on the back of a great beast sleeping below the earth, bristling with an awareness of the setting sun.

The key was a huge bronze thing that clicked the tumblers in a series of loud snicks and then opened the door to a large common room. The cabin was built by the Civilian Conservation Corps during the Great Depression in the 1930s, many of them indigent workers recruited from breadlines in Jersey City and Newark, where the factories sat silent. Bernadette quickly went to work and swept the kitchen of mouse droppings as I carried logs in from the woodshed to feed the fieldstone fireplace of the great room. The men who had built the walls of rough-hewn logs, cut the saplings to make the bunk beds in the back room, and carried the fieldstones down from the hills to make the fireplace were not deep woodsmen but rather city slicks. They probably hung around Journal Square, as I did at their age, trying to make the young girls laugh, or else caught a movie at one of the many cinemas. Most likely they were fearless in a city canyon or a crowded street but terrified of the sullen quiet and harsh cold of the winter forest.

Suddenly Bernadette and I were on the side of a mountain with nowhere to turn, but to our love for each other and the land. We hiked up the Appalachian Trail with the chill wearing off as we moved across Sunrise Mountain past groves of mountain laurel, pitch pine, and leafless scrub oak. On steep slopes we walked single file, Bernadette's red coat a flag beckoning me onward like a matador's cape. Eventually the trail narrowed and pulled us higher into a fog—at least I thought it was a fog, but we were actually climbing into a cloud bank. For suddenly heavy flakes filled the air around us, not so much falling as floating about in a swirl of wind and creaking tree trunks. The trailhead edged in closer as the white-out surrounded us, a solitary pair in a silent world of falling crystals, our only path a dim outline of protruding rocks on the white blanket covering the forest floor.

Higher and higher we climbed, until Bernadette suddenly stopped and looked down. There was a hunter's blind laid across the path, a nearly invisible lean-to of white canvas. It was empty except for a backpack and some gear, the owner not at home but somewhere out in the blizzard around us. We looked at each other and silently nodded. The hunter was out and possibly too focused on discovering deer in the valley below to notice our footfall in the deep snow. And because we might stumble into his sights, we silently backed away and down the trial, leaving the deer hunter to his part of the mountain. We retraced our steps out of the clouds and back into the brown leaf-strew plateau below, where the Spring Cabin awaited us with its promise of warm food and a glowing fire. We passed the spring and our footfalls released tiny bubbles from its sandy bottom, probably water seeping through cracks and fissures that ran up and above us through the mountain's spine to end near the hunter's toes.

And as we shook off the snow from our coats and sat huddled for warmth in our cozy cabin, I thought about the falling snow outside and the liquid hiding in the rocks. Each drop of water was blood from the mountain's heart and as precious to the watershed below as my love for Bernadette in our mountain solitude. And it is a small miracle, I remember saying to her, that hillsides shed their groundwater into pools that freeze and then run again in the spring. For then the water will flow downhill faster, the sun rising ever higher in the sky as winter recedes, the sea eventually tasting the snowfall that Bernadette and I walked upon. And perhaps we would meet those headwaters again someday, I said, possibly mixed with salt in the ocean while playing with our children not yet born on that November's day.

HEADWATER PROTECTION

The idea of a headwater stream is intuitively apparent; you climb as high as you can up a slope until the streambed disappears onto bare slopes and the rainfall moves downhill in what hydrologists call sheet-flow. Not until gravity pulls this water into a declivity do a channel and a real stream form. The mighty Hudson River, the Delaware, even the mighty Mississippi at some point dwindle upstream to rivulets so small you can step across them with ease. Yet scientifically we need a better way to quantify and separate streams for measurement and characterization as they move from headwater to stream to river and ocean. For streams of different sizes have different fluvial features and different plants and animals that can exist in them. Headwaters are usually cold, shallow, and fast-flowing waters that few large fish can navigate, whereas deep downstream streams and rivers are warmer and more placid.

In 1952, Arthur Newell Strahler, a geosciences professor at Columbia University, devised a stream ordering hierarchy that facilitated quantitative geomorphologic assessment, which for the first time allowed scientists to classify streams in a categorical fashion.[1] The "Strahler stream ordering system" is a simple hydrology formula for categorizing rivers from their smallest flows in the mountains to their widest main stem as they slow down and approach the counterforce of tidal currents near the sea. The ordering system defines stream size based on a hierarchy of tributaries to a main stem that look like the branching pattern of a tree to its trunk. For example, the tiny stream fed by the spring at the cabin in Stokes Forest would be given the lowest number (1), as a first-order stream. When two of these first-order streams come together, they form a second-order stream. When two second-order streams join, they form a third-order stream, and so on. According to these strictures, most large rivers are, at most, fourth- or fifth-order streams.

Conservative estimates indicate that headwater streams account for more than 70 percent of stream-channel length in the United States.[2] Yet in spite of this, almost all federal and state water quality regulations are focused on fourth- or fifth-order streams in the lower river basins. The reasons for this lapse include poor quality maps that do not show the small streams, limited financial resources in manpower and equipment to monitor them, and the fact that up until quite recently most development took place downstream. However, this has changed recently owing to the rapid build-out of the landscape in lower river valleys. As a result, headwaters have now become the target of developers and the latest recipient of all the negative aspects of suburban sprawl. Unfortunately, most states cannot protect these headwaters because a lack of scientifically defensible standards and monitoring tools.

For example, the existing fish index of biotic integrity (IBI) used in New Jersey (see chapter 10) was developed by Jim Kurtenbach from USEPA for larger streams; those with drainage area greater than five square miles.[3] Unlike downstream waters, however, there are only a few aquatic families and species in these fast shallow waters to create an index of biotic integrity. Typically, you need at least five to six species of fish or aquatic insects to create an IBI decision model. However, smaller streams are often of management interest because of their intrinsic ecological functions and potential effects on the integrity of downstream reaches. As well as providing unique habitats for aquatic biota, headwater streams are the most active sites for physical and biological processing of inputs of organic matter from the watershed, such as falling leaves. The unique insect shredder-based communities in these ecosystems convert this detritus into coarse and then finer particulate material, which are important food resources for aquatic communities downstream. Headwater streams are also sites of the most active uptake and retention of nutrients from litter fall, such as phosphorus and nitrogen, which reduces their downstream transport and uptake by aquatic plants that might choke streambeds.

Despite their biological importance, headwater streams are among the most threatened aquatic environments in the United States. Immediate threats to headwater streams by development include channelization, piping, and even complete elimination through agricultural irrigation, urbanization, groundwater withdrawal, and mining practices. Alteration of headwater streams can result in increased water temperature and sedimentation in downstream reaches, increased nutrient transport, and changes in food-web structure. To address this evolving need, I devised a strategy to develop biological indicators for headwater streams and contacted Richard Horwitz, head of the Fisheries Department at the Patrick Center for Environmental Research in the Philadelphia Academy of Natural Sciences. What drew me to Rich for the headwater study was his iconic research from the 1970s on temporal stream variability patterns and the distribution patterns of stream fishes.[4] This paper showed that the diversity of fishes increased rapidly from upstream to downstream sections and that headwater fish diversity was lowest in rivers with the most variable headwaters. Other studies showed changes in fish reproductive and development strategies too, as well as temporal variations in community structure. Upstream species had shorter life-spans, smaller body sizes, and earlier sexual maturity than downstream species.[5] Unfortunately, these finding made it difficult to develop a fish-based index of biotic integrity in headwaters because it would be difficult to distinguish between changes in communities based on natural variability versus human disturbances.

Horwitz therefore decided to take a multifaunal approach, adding other aquatic families to the list of indicator species, including crayfish and salamanders. Crayfish are freshwater crustaceans resembling small lobsters that typically live only in fast-flowing, cool, rocky streams. They breathe through featherlike gills and are found in bodies of water that do not freeze to the bottom and are mostly found in brooks where there is fresh running water and rocks that shelter them against predators. There are six species of crayfish in New Jersey waters and three are believed to be invasive. The most common is the Appalachian brook crayfish (*Cambarus bartonii*). Most crayfish cannot tolerate polluted water, although some species, such as the invasive red swamp crayfish (*Procambarus clarkii*), are hardier.[6]

Salamanders are from the Class Amphibia, which include frogs, toads, and newts. Amphibians are all tetrapods, having four feet and/or fins, and are ectothermic, or cold-blooded, animals that metamorphose from a juvenile water-breathing form to an adult air-breathing form. Unlike other land animals, amphibians lay their eggs in water. Amphibians are regarded by many scientists as uniquely evolved to be indicators of a region's health, as they are the first organisms to respond to harmful environmental changes such as pollutants and higher temperatures. Basically, if we find problems in the amphibian community, it's just a matter of time before larger organisms such as fish, birds, and wildlife will be affected as well. Amphibian populations are declining worldwide as a result of a number of factors, including water pollution, increased pesticide use, and instream habitat and riparian corridor loss. Riparian corridors are the floodplains that border streams and may be the most significant factor of all, because most amphibians depend on both terrestrial and aquatic habitats throughout their life cycles.[7] Thus, the loss of a forest or the filling-in of a nearby wetland can lead to changes in the terrestrial habitat that dooms an amphibian as much as increased temperature of the water resulting from loss of the overhead canopy. Fragmentation of habitat can also play a critical role in the demise of an amphibian population, as they need to travel from terrestrial to aquatic habitats at different parts of their life cycle. Amphibians also become easy prey targets in open human spaces such as lawns, driveways, and roads. They can also succumb to desiccation at barriers such as curbs and fences, which are often impossible to cross.

In our headwater study we sampled a number of test sites selected to span a range of headwater conditions, from pristine to highly urbanized. We electroshocked for fish, collected crayfish using kick-nets, and salamanders were collected from the surrounding floodplain by turning over rocks and logs. After two years of specimen collections, we developed sampling protocols for all three species that showed differences between reference and impaired sites. This included changing gradients in fish species from cold water to warm water downstream and for salamanders a change in species richness (number of different species present). Not surprisingly, aquatic salamanders decreased quickly with deforestation, and the Appalachian brook crayfish was a good indicator for baseline reference conditions.[8] Presence of the brook trout, *Salvelinus fontinalis*, was also an indicator of high water quality.

This work continues today, as it may take five years of data collection to develop a scientifically defensible index of biotic integrity that can be used to develop enforceable regulations. Other factors being studied include specimens in areas with specific stressors such as low-gradient headwater streams in the coastal Pine Barrens, streams affected by agriculture, and sites with upstream ponds whose warming effects might skew results. Once refined, these protocols will be added to the bioassessment tools of fish, insects, and algae used in the deeper waters downstream, where flows increase and higher stream orders predominate. These combined tools will then be integrated into a complete watershed matrix of indicators that protect not only the coveted headwaters but all the land in the basin as water moves downstream.

THE WATERSHED INITIATIVE

I love to stand beside a river and drift into reverie. Whether it's on the banks of the Hudson River watching ocean liners cruise from New York Harbor or else straddling a headwater stream high on the Kittatinny Ridge as water comes bubbling from an underground spring a thousand years old. There is a satisfying sense of impermanence and yet solidity to a river. For a river is more than the water flowing before your eyes. The sense of a river needs to be encapsulated in a greater vision—one that flows from the tiny headwater stream down through the ridge and valley past Highland farms and Piedmont villages until all the flows are gathered into a spider web of streams. Only then does it become wild and unstoppable, pushing on into the salt-saturated bays and the abyssal depths of the ocean. This idea of a descending, dendritic (branching) river is called a "watershed" or "river basin," which includes every small streamlet from source to harbor mouth.

Unfortunately, for many years the waterways in the United States were monitored and assessed for water quality based only on the near-field view of a particular stream segment. Essentially what was managed lay just upstream and downstream of any given community, agricultural plot, or industrial point source. This piecemeal approach resulted in a patchwork form of environmental protection and regulation, with separate rules for permitted dischargers, dredging, filling in of wetlands, and forest and farm management. Point sources, such as sewage treatment plants with fixed pipes discharging into waterways, and non-point sources, such as diffuse municipal storm drains, were both traditionally permitted under the old paradigm at levels protective only of nearby receptors. Yet this approach overlooked the cumulative impacts of river water on ecological and human communities that were dozens, perhaps hundreds, of miles downstream.

For example, perennial flooding on the Passaic River in New Jersey is the cumulative result of numerous yet separate land-use decisions by municipalities that allow housing and commercial developments to be sited on their local flood-plains, where wetlands are nature's only means to dissipate and swallow flood-waters. Naturally porous areas are paved over and become impervious. Similarly, unimpeded population growth across a watershed will result in increased demand for sewage treatment, since the burgeoning number of households will overwhelm the localized capacity of rivers to dilute and degrade contaminants from outfalls. Often this will result in negative cumulative impacts many miles downriver, such as sulfurous-smelling algal blooms, low dissolved oxygen, and fish kills. New Jersey finally recognized this basinwide connectivity—that water, soil, sediments, and associated contaminants all flow downstream—when it established a watershed management program within NJDEP.

In 1997, Governor Christine Whitman by executive order created the Division of Watershed Management within NJDEP and tasked it with administering waterways on a watershed- rather than a site-specific basis. Governor Whitman claimed watershed management was a component of her new governance philo-sophy, what she called "sustainable management." By this she meant to simulta-neously conserve environmental quality, account for economic costs, and prevent social inequities. The sustainable management program called for a lot of public participation, including comprehensive planning where citizens, businesses, scientists, local governments and other stakeholders could have a voice. This approach encompassed in one paradigm the tiniest headwater stream in the mountains to the widest deep-water river flowing into the sea.

NJDEP's mission was to identify long-range goals and then to establish environmental indicators, or measurable markers, for tracking progress toward these goals, supported by sound scientific data. Concurrent with Whitman's executive order, NJDEP's Office of Environmental Planning developed a planning document summarizing the approach, titled "The Draft Statewide Watershed Management Framework Document for the State of New Jersey." This white paper defined a watershed as "the land area that drains water to a particular stream, river, or lake. It is a land feature that can be identified by tracing a line along the highest elevations between two areas on a map, often a ridge. Large watersheds, like the Mississippi River basin contain thousands of smaller watersheds."[9] The Framework Document noted that watersheds are "nature's boundaries" and that watershed management is the process of man-aging all of the water resources within the entire area of a watershed, rather than on a site-specific basis. To manage within this new paradigm, NJDEP divided the state into twenty watershed management areas and five water regions for the implementation of watershed regulatory activities on a targeted, cyclical basis. These activities included water quality monitoring and assessment, discharge permitting, stormwater management, potable withdrawals, and all other water-related elements to integrate future statewide planning. It was postulated that these plans would potentially reduce flooding, prevent pollution, and produce cost efficiencies through the development of regional/watershed-based solutions in lieu of site-specific requirements.

Leslie McGeorge, the director of Science and Research at the time, was asked to play a pivotal role in this new process through the development and testing of measurable indicators of environmental degradation. To facilitate this process, McGeorge supplied a grant to the New Jersey Agricultural Experiment Station at Rutgers University to establish a Center for Environmental Indicators. This center was tasked with developing a comprehensive set of measurements and enforcement triggers to inform decision makers, so that management decisions could be based on sound science. Some of these projects were extremely innovative and supplied NJDEP with data, models, and monitoring networks that are still being used today. Watershed projects that came out of the center included the establishment of the New Jersey atmospheric deposition network,[10] the comparative risk project,[11] the development of indicators linking respiratory health and air pollution, and the creation of a GIS-based vegetation map of plant biodiversity in the state.

McGeorge also established a watershed assessment team to act as liaison with other programs at NJDEP for scientific support in addressing technical needs and research at a more basic level. The team was asked to compile all extant air, water, soil, hazardous materials, and ecological data into reports for all twenty watershed management areas as a preliminary means to characterize and assess each basin.[12] I was recruited to the watershed assessment team, which initially focused on numerous public presentations to educate the citizenry on what the new framework called for. As a result, I spent a lot of time in late-night meetings in town halls all over New Jersey. These meetings made for some strange bedfellows. It was interesting to see the two faces of environmentalism in one room, where "mom and pop" local conservation organizers sat side-by-side with petrochemical company lawyers and engineers. The going was rough at times, but accommodations were made as corporations brought in their consulting engineers to explain the technical basis of a decision to expand a plant, or municipalities defended the need to take land by eminent domain for public parks or highway expansions. In contrast, environmental advocates like the Nature Conservancy and the New Jersey Public Interest Research Group riposted with requests for green-space land donations, odor controls at a sewerage plant, and curtailment of potential negative impacts from an upstream municipality's land-use decision.

A more technical portion of the team's time, however, was spent determining where more data or assessment tools were needed to support a regulatory decision by an operating division, such as land use, water quality, or hazardous site remediation. Governor Whitman, as part of this new approach, made research funds available to support watershed initiatives. Part of my job was to consult with NJDEP staff in the operating divisions, find out what new technical information they needed, and frame their questions into formal requests for proposals from academics and other researchers for funding. These projects that our team funded were often more applied than the indicator research projects and addressed more expansive watershed issues. For example, one project performed by Colleen Hatfield at Rutgers University developed wetlands biological assessment methods for New Jersey.[13] Mary Downes Gastrich, within Science and Research, developed a "brown tide assessment" project to evaluate the underlying environmental causes of these insidious harmful algal blooms that perennially smother shell beds and kill off acres of sea grass in the state's back bays.[14]

I personally developed a research agenda for an issue that has plagued the state's waterways for generations: cultural eutrophication. Eutrophication is an increase in chemical nutrients like phosphorus and nitrogen in a lake, river, or embayment. It can be a natural process, as in shallow lakes that slowly fill in with sediment and are overgrown, or human-induced, which we call cultural eutrophication. USEPA has identified elevated levels of nutrients as the leading cause of water quality impairment in the United States. In New Jersey alone, almost one-third of all freshwater streams monitored do not attain their designated uses of biotic integrity, owing to excessive phosphorus loads. Significant adverse ecological impacts from cultural eutrophication are harmful algal blooms, loss of aquatic habitats, fish kills, natural flora and fauna replacement, and hypoxic dead zones in waterways or the near-shore ocean. As a consequence, one of New Jersey's top priorities has been protecting and restoring its waters from the effects of nutrient pollution.

New Jersey manages nutrient loads to waterways through officially promulgated water quality criteria and standards. The ambient water criterion for total phosphorus was set in 1973 to "not exceed 50 micrograms per liter (μg/L) in any reservoir, lake, and pond or in a tributary at the point where it enters such bodies of water." However, with experience NJDEP learned that a one-size-fits-all phosphorus criterion did not work well in application. For example, a level greater than 100 μg/L could result in nutrient-related problems in one water body but not in another. In some waters the phosphorus level varied by season and could be quite high in the spring and then negligible in the summer. However, by August the stream was choked with vegetation and anoxic because the phosphorus had been converted to oxygen-consuming biomass. Ironically, if the water was sampled in August, the chemical criteria alone would indicate no violation. Therefore, in 1984 the standards were modified to incorporate nutrient policies and narrative criteria that specified "nutrients shall not be allowed in concentrations that cause objectionable algal densities, nuisance aquatic vegetation or otherwise render the water unsuitable for the designated uses."[15] The problem with this amendment, however, was that no one had specified what an objectionable or nuisance level of algae or aquatic plants really was. At the time it was nonquantifiable and purely subjective.

Stepping into this debate in 2003, USEPA published guidance on deriving nutrient criteria on an ecoregional basis that the states had to adhere to.[16] There are fourteen distinct ecoregions in the continental United States, which are mapped based on an overlay of geologic and ecological features. EPA recommended ecoregional criteria because a nutrient load in New Jersey may have a different impact on local water quality than the same load in Nebraska, owing to site-specific land forms and biological features. In New Jersey there are five ecoregions: the Northeast Highlands, the Middle Atlantic Coastal Plain, the Northern Piedmont, the Ridge and Valley, and the Atlantic Coastal Pine Barrens. The upshot of this directive by USEPA meant that New Jersey might need five new sets of criteria for phosphorus and nitrogen. But USEPA also recognized the ambiguities cited above in establishing purely chemical criteria without taking into consideration ecological responses such as nuisance algal blooms.

USEPA's ecoregional approach therefore required criteria for both "causal parameters," such as total phosphorus and total nitrogen, as well as "response variables," such as the level of the plant pigment chlorophyll a and some measurement of water clarity or turbidity. However, the agency did give the states latitude to develop other parameters, such as algal community structure, as long as they reflected the stressor-response model approach. The key questions became "What is a nuisance algal bloom?" and "What is a measurable level or unacceptable biological response to nutrient loadings in a waterway?" In essence, how do we define cultural eutrophication at an ecoregional scale? To answer these questions, I decided to return to where I had been trained as a limnologist, or freshwater biologist—to the Academy of Natural Sciences in Philadelphia.

THE TROPHIC DIATOM INDEX

When I attended the University of Pennsylvania, most of the advanced field ecology courses were taught at the 160-year-old Academy of Natural Sciences. The lecture and labs were taught in improvised classrooms behind the dinosaur museum, where you could share you seating space with a stuffed antelope or a huge fossilized head of a triceratops. Field exercises were done at the Stroud Water Research Center in Chester County, where White Clay Creek was siphoned off in places to run through an atmospherically controlled space inside the building to create an indoor macrocosm. In this unique space we were trained to perform controlled experiments on water chemistry and the responses of aquatic insects, fish, and algae to stressors such as pesticides, increased water temperatures, and urban runoff.

One of my limnology teachers at the academy was Ruth Patrick. In November 2007, this pioneering stream ecologist was one hundred years old. She had began studying pollution's effect on streams in the 1930s, long before the public knew it was an issue.[17] This was years before environmentalist Rachel Carson's unprecedented book *Silent Spring* made concerns about pollution commonplace in America. In 1947, Patrick founded the Limnology Department at the Academy of Natural Sciences and implemented a new approach to studying water pollution based on environmental principles.[18] Environmental research of any kind was a novelty during the 1950s and 1960s, but Patrick's limnology department was even more unusual. It was a pioneer in "multidisciplinary research." Instead of specializing in one discipline, the department possessed expertise in all the major groups of aquatic organisms as well as in the analysis of a stream's chemical and physical characteristics. The department was also notable for its technical innovations. The most famous of these was the "diatometer," a device invented by Patrick in 1954 to systematically sample and analyze pollution-sensitive communities of microscopic algae called "diatoms."[19] Eventually the limnology department was renamed the "Patrick Center of Environmental Research" in her honor.

One of the powerful approaches pioneered by Patrick and other freshwater limnologists was that in a small drop of water you could find hundreds of microscopic species of animals, plants, and fungi that could tell you volumes about the health of that particular body of water. Specifically, the base of the food web in a stream is represented by both large-rooted plants and tiny single-cell plants called algae. These algae can float in the water as "phytoplankton" or else are attached to rocks on the bottom and called "periphyton." Diatoms are a major group of algae, Class Bacillariophyceae, with the unique characteristic of having cell walls made of silica, or bioengineered glass. These cell walls, or "frustules," show a wide diversity of distinct shapes that allow morphological identification under a microscope.[20] And since these frustules are resistant to biodegradation, they also leave a sedimentary signature of their presence, showing how these algal communities may have changed over time. For example, in lakes we can take cores of the bottom mud and go deep enough to find samples of diatoms that lived before the Industrial Revolution took place in North America. This allows us to see what communities of diatoms existed before humans increased the nutrient and toxic loads through agriculture and sewerage effluents and to estimate what the natural condition might have been in order to target a stream or lake for restoration activities. That is, as regulators instituted upstream restrictions on phosphorus sources we could monitor the shift in the diatom community to measure how quickly or completely the system returns to a more natural and unpolluted state. As a result of this predictive ability, diatom communities are a preferred tool for environmental monitoring. In New Jersey we made use of this class of algae in establishing an approach for managing the levels of both phosphorus and nitrogen released to our waters.

By the time I approached the Phycology Department at the Patrick Center to develop a means to assess cultural eutrophication in New Jersey streams, Ruth Patrick had retired, although she still went to work every day in her lab as a scientist emeritus. Her replacement, I found, was an equally formidable natural scientist named Donald Charles. Don and I, along with his research assistant, Karin Ponader, strategized an approach to New Jersey's cultural eutrophication problem using algal diatom communities as indicators. Over a period of five years, we meticulous sampled a hundred streambeds in the state, scraping rocks for diatoms, which were identified by species under microscope and categorized according to their tolerance or sensitivity to high concentrations of phosphorus and nitrogen in the passing water. We matched these specimens to chemical analyses and habitat data to create a stressor-response model that unambiguously linked nutrient levels to diatom community structure.

Our studies successfully developed two new regulatory tools for NJDEP that we called the northern and southern New Jersey Trophic Diatom Index (TDI).[21] Separate TDI models were needed for the southern and northern parts of the state in order to reflect differences in bottom substrate and flow; the upland streams were fast and rocky, whereas the Coastal Plain rivers were predominantly sand and silt. To determine what constituted a nuisance level, we placed our differing diatom communities on a linear scale broken up into four categories of impairment. These groupings were based on a literature search of studies associating nutrients and periphyton algae with deleterious effects on "designated uses" in the state's water quality standards such as swimmability, fishability, and aesthetics. That is, were there too many slimy algae on the rocks to be aesthetically pleasing, not enough for fish to hide in, or did they make it dangerously slippery for swimmers to access open water?

Overall, the two TDI studies we developed showed that diatom inference models could be used as a new reliable tool to assess river nutrient conditions in New Jersey both on a local and at a watershed scale. The stations could also be linked into hydrological models to predict the cumulative loadings of nutrient sources across an entire basin and predict how the algae would collectively respond downstream. Reciprocally, we could use other diatom algal indices (pH tolerant, motile diatoms as indicators of upstream erosion) from the same assemblages to identify sources of pollution throughout the watershed and apply restrictions on releases of nutrients and, it is hoped, track improvements downstream.

FRESHWATER WETLANDS AND VERNAL POOLS

Yet there are other physical features to a watershed besides the rivers and lakes that play an important role in regulating the ecological and human values we place on their protection. The shoulders of a waterway are its floodplain, the surrounding land that receives floodwater and acts as a buffer to many of the riverine and headland processes that interact and affect a watershed's functionality. This "riparian zone" alongside the river plays important ecological and public safety roles by filtering waterborne contaminants such as phosphorus and toxic chemicals, supplying habitat for wildlife, and lessening the impacts of flooding by allowing rivers to overtop their banks locally. Unfortunately, these natural areas nearby streams have been disappearing for years, owing to the aesthetically pleasing vistas so desirable to developers. And the areas most impacted by this degradation in the riparian zone are the freshwater wetlands and salt marshes. These sensitive ecosystems act as filtering kidneys to a waterway, as shelter for the numerous wildfowl and game that live along the fertile edge, and as nursery areas for the thousands of species of fish, salamanders, and aquatic insects that spawn in their secluded pools and rivulets.

Yet despite the benefits provided by wetlands, the United States loses approximately sixty thousand acres of wetlands every year.[22] USEPA defines wetlands subject to regulation as "areas that are inundated or saturated by surface or ground water at a frequency and duration sufficient to support, and that under normal circumstances do support, a prevalence of vegetation typically adapted for life in saturated soil conditions."[23] In more common language, wetlands are where a frequent and prolonged presence of water at or near the soil surface drives the natural system. This includes the kind of soils that form, the species of plants that grow, and the fish and/or wildlife communities that use the habitat. Freshwater wetlands in the United States fall into four general categories—marshes, swamps, bogs, and fens. Marshes are dominated by soft-stemmed vegetation, while swamps have mostly woody plants. Bogs are freshwater wetlands often formed in old glacial lakes and characterized by evergreen trees and shrubs and a floor covered by a thick carpet of sphagnum moss. Fens are freshwater peat-forming wetlands covered mostly by grasses, sedges, reeds, and wildflowers.

As a result of this wetland diversity, there was much confusion when the federal government sought to expand its role into regulating wetlands. Developers needed to know where to stop grading an upland area near a boggy site before they were in violation of the law. As a result and to clarify the physical demarcation as to where uplands ended, in 1987 the USEPA and the Army Corps of Engineers developed the *Wetlands Delineation Manual*, which organized the environmental characteristics of a potential wetland into three categories: soils, vegetation, and hydrology. This manual and the subsequent federal interagency version set definitional criteria for each of the three categories.[24] With this approach, an area that met all three criteria was considered a wetland and could not be built on unless it met certain specifications and allowed for mitigation.

On March 2, 1994, NJDEP assumed responsibility from USEPA for regulating wetlands in the New Jersey under our own Freshwater Wetlands Protection Act.[25] New Jersey is one of only two states with the delegated authority from the federal government to regulate wetlands. One of the more progressive and prescient actions made by NJDEP after delegation was passed include a state provision to protect "vernal pools." Vernal pools are defined by regulation as "wetlands or waters that occur in a confined basin depression without a permanent flowing outlet and with evidence of breeding by one or more species of fauna adapted to reproduce in ephemeral aquatic conditions. The habitat must also maintain ponded water for at least two continuous months of the year between March and September and be free of fish throughout the year."[26] More succinctly, vernal pools are confined wetland depressions "devoid of breeding fish populations." Yet in spite of this absence of fish, they are unique ecosystems providing habitat to many species of amphibians, insects, reptiles, plants, and other wildlife.

Vernal pools vary in size and can range from ten square feet to several acres. They have high biodiversity and provide foraging habitat for wading birds, turtles, snakes, and mammals, as well as habitat for some rare plants and invertebrates. The smallest vernal pool can be a puddle, an isolated depression within an upland forest that fills with salamanders in the spring rain and then quickly disappears. But no matter what their structure, all vernal pools should draw down to very shallow levels unsuitable for sustaining fish. Fish are highly predatory on amphibian eggs and larvae. Over the course of evolution, several species of salamanders and frogs exploited these fishless water bodies. Today, these species exhibit "hard-wired" genetic instincts and behaviors that are geared exclusively toward fish-free vernal habitats. Amphibians that are dependent on

Figure 12. New Jersey Pine Barrens tree frog. (Source: John F. Bunnell, New Jersey Pinelands Commission.)

vernal pools are known as "obligate vernal pool breeders." In New Jersey there are seven such species—two frogs and five salamanders—that fit this category. Another fourteen of New Jersey's amphibians also use vernal pools for breeding, but unlike the obligate species, these species can successfully reproduce in habitats that contain fish. Vernal pool amphibians include four species listed as endangered by NJDEP—the eastern tiger salamander, the blue-spotted salamander, the Pine Barrens tree frog, and the southern gray tree frog.

Amphibians are a unique group of vertebrates containing more than 6,300 known species. A recent assessment of the entire group by the International Union for Conservation of Nature found that nearly one-third of the world's amphibian species are threatened, representing 1,856 species.[27] Amphibians have existed on earth for more than 300 million years, yet in just the past two decades there have been an alarming number of extinctions. Nearly 168 species are believed to have gone extinct and at least 2,469 (39 percent) have populations that are declining. This indicates that the number of extinct and threatened species will probably continue to rise.

In New Jersey, as a means to protect the wetland habitats necessary for obligate vernal pool amphibians to survive, NJDEP developed a protocol for assessing vernal pools and maps of expert-certified vernal habitats using digital GIS overlays showing each location.[28] Therefore, when an application for a freshwater wetlands permit is submitted to NJDEP (land developers that impact wetlands must apply for a permit that NJDEP approves), permit writers look at the maps to determine if the site contains vernal habitat. And if it does, the applicant needs to apply a transition area or buffer around the proposed development to protect these species, as was done with the timber rattlesnake in the Pine Barrens. To facilitate the identification of these often ephemeral pools, NJDEP initiated a Vernal Pool Survey Project carried out by Richard Lathrop from Rutgers University's Center for Remote Sensing and Spatial Analysis (CRSSA). Lathrop was asked by NJDEP's Endangered and Nongame Species Program to develop a method for mapping potential vernal pools throughout New Jersey using GIS. The survey method consisted of mapping likely areas using remote-sensing techniques (aerial and satellite photographs), then ground-truthing and site visits, species surveys at verified vernal pools, and data integration of species lists and latitude and longitude coordinates into a publicly accessible vernal pool database. CRSSA identified more than thirteen thousand potential pools throughout the state and through field verification confirmed 88 percent of these as accurate. CRSSA also developed an interactive Internet mapping site to assist NJDEP and its citizen volunteer corps in locating and navigating to their survey areas and to facilitate the online submittal of survey observations.[29]

Yet in spite of all these efforts to protect vernal pools and the rare and endangered species that use them, recent federal litigation concerning wetlands calls into question whether the state or the federal government has the right to regulate certain wetlands that are not adjacent to navigable waters as specified in the Clean Water Act. On June 16, 2006, the U.S. Supreme Court ruled on certain aspects of the act that split the Court by a narrow margin (5–4) and affected the government's regulatory authority to protect wetlands.[30] In the so-called *Rapanos* decision, Justice Scalia, writing for the majority, ruled that the law only authorizes regulation of "permanent, standing, and continuously flowing bodies of water"—in effect, rivers, lakes, oceans, and streams. This makes it difficult to protect and regulate a wetland where rain and runoff water are filtered through vernal pools or other ephemeral waterways where there are no obvious streams and yet where the wetland plays an important functional role in regulating flooding, retaining groundwater, and supplying riparian habitat for fish and birds.

The *Rapanos* decision resulted in five separate written opinions, with no single justice's opinion commanding a majority of the court. A plurality of the court held that "wetlands adjacent to non-navigable tributaries are 'waters of the United States' under the Clean Water Act *only* if the tributary to which the wetland is adjacent is a relatively permanent waterbody and the wetland has a continuous surface connection with the tributary." Justice Kennedy concurred with the plurality that the cases should be remanded, but disagreed with the plurality's analysis. He argued that the government's jurisdiction over a wetlands depends on whether a "significant nexus" exists between the wetlands and navigable waters, and that a significant nexus between wetlands and traditional navigable waters exists "if the wetlands, either alone or in combination with similarly situated lands in the region, significantly affect the chemical, physical, and biological integrity" of traditional navigable waters.

There was that concept of "biological integrity" again, which formed the basis for the numerous bioassessment indices developed for macroinvertebrate insects, fish, and algae through my research in New Jersey. Yet here the missing element was how to define and measure biological integrity for wetlands. The federal manual on delineating wetlands did not help, since it was primarily concerned with proving where specific wetlands began and ended—not how they functioned for biological integrity. Subsequently, USEPA issued guidance on how to seek and manage wetlands protection using this "significant nexus." The guidance document stated that regulatory agencies have jurisdiction over traditional navigable waters, wetlands adjacent to traditional navigable waters, nonnavigable tributaries of traditional navigable waters that are relatively permanent (i.e., the tributaries typically flow year-round or have continuous flow at least seasonally), and wetlands that directly abut such tributaries. However, for less explicit wetlands (e.g., vernal pools) the guidance suggests that agencies decide jurisdiction over the waters based on a "fact-specific analysis" to determine whether they have a significant nexus with traditional navigable water.[31]

By fact-specific analysis, USEPA was empowering state regulators in all fifty states to use their best professional judgment in deciding on a case-by-case basis as to whether a wetlands permit was needed for each nontraditional wetlands. This is a dangerous and haphazard way to do business. The wetlands provisions of the Clean Water Act have preserved open space for many years, guaranteeing clean drinking water via filtration, supplying animal refugia, and adding aesthetic quality to shoreline vistas through scenic rivers and park-lined waterways. Unfortunately, the Supreme Court's spilt decision on *Rapanos* may muddy the regulatory waters and make it that much harder for states to act, or to act effectively and in coordination for watersheds shared between them, such as the Delaware or the Hudson rivers. As a result of the *Rapanos* decision there may be an accelerated loss of wetlands in the United States.

And it remains to be seen whether Congress will pick up this gauntlet and redefine what is meant by "navigable waters," or take it out of the Clean Water

Act. Fortunately for New Jersey, we continue to protect vernal pools and other atypical wetlands. As one of the states to which USEPA delegated authority to regulate wetlands, our Freshwater Wetlands Protection Act gives us the right to establish rules and regulate wetlands "as we see fit." Therefore the *Rapanos* decision does not prevent NJDEP from providing special protection to wetlands that are vernal habitats and the endangered amphibians they shelter.

In fact, as I have learned, some of these vernal pools and even more developed wetlands can pop up in the most unlikely places. Years after Bernadette and I spent our cold winter weekend in the Spring Cabin, we decided to bring our children there for vacations, albeit in the more halcyon days of summer. And on those heights below the Appalachian Trail we saw the spring in front of the cabin evolve into a mountain pond and then a draining wetland, all brought about by the claws and gnawing teeth of a hungry family of beavers. The first year we watched as the sleek animals arrived and built their dam to drown the hardwoods just below our small, bubbling spring. And over the years we watched from our secluded cabin as the drowned woodland became more denuded of trees by the cold spring water and the bark-devouring habits of the beavers. Slowly the depression below our cabin turned into an open pond filled with grasslands and hummocks, mountain laurel, passerine songbirds, and a million fireflies that filled the night sky like stars.

But then the beaver dam and pond were determined a nuisance by the Stokes Forest park rangers, as the pond flooded a fire road during a distinctly deadly fire season. So they blew the dam with dynamite and allowed the water to run free from the pond and the land to revert to its former dryness, slowly becoming a grassy wetland filled with grasses, sedges, reeds, and wildflowers. The stream from the spring has now slipped back to its former self, no more than a rivulet filled with bullfrogs and tiny crayfish. Since then the beavers have moved away, and the park rangers continue to maintain the fire road as the terrain slowly lapses through its successional phases, pond becoming wetland and meadow in some places. And I wonder if it will all eventually convert back to forest, and whether other people will come along someday in another thirty years to visit our Spring Cabin and be surprised by the conditions underfoot. Will they walk onto the incongruous spongy ground beneath an oak stand that still holds an atavistic memory of when the land was wetter, the soft springy footpath through the towering trees only a distant memory of swamp and meadow that old-timers will relate, shaking their heads and saying wistfully, "I remember when there was a swamp atop that ridge and a swimming hole, the waters filled with fish and bullfrogs and Kingfishers swooping from the trees. All gone now"—a testament to a beaver pond returned to oblivion's door or else to the spirit-land that the Leni Lenape Indians dreamed in, to aboriginals who lived here a thousand years before us and hunted these woods and watched it change around them as well, wondering about the mountain's moods as the land changed across their own lifetimes, intersecting their geographies with beaver logic and firefly wisdom.

And one day I hope my grandchildren are brought to the Spring Cabin and told fantastic stories by their parents about when they walked the land dazed with wonder; standing amidst a shaded forest and telling them of what happened when the natural cycle of plant and sun was displaced by a beaver's tooth and his broad tail; pointing at a copse of trees and describing a beaver hutch seemingly afloat in the center of a pond that's filled with sunshine and cold spring water held a millennia below ground, life a mysterious conjunction between unpredictable nature and indescribable beauty.

CHAPTER 12

Coastal New Jersey and Rising Waters

THE NEW JERSEY BARRIER ISLANDS

The lower two-thirds of New Jersey's 130-mile long coast is composed of sandy barrier islands that separate a series of shallow lagoonal back bays from the wave-driven force of the Atlantic Ocean. This system of coastal barriers minimizes the impacts of coastal storms and wind. Yet the dune scrub/shrub and woodland communities of the barrier islands, with the exception of the eight miles of Island Beach State Park, have been substantially altered and in many cases destroyed.[1] Coastal barrier islands are not meant to stay still but often erode along the shore and move back and forth with the seasons. In fact, the islands are the last in a set of submerged offshore sandbars that are pushed onshore by wave action. These sandbars are never static but can disappear after a large nor'easter storm sweeps them away. So, too, the barrier islands can be breached by a coastal storm that produces a sufficiently high tidal surge. So when people moved onto the islands and constructed multimillion-dollar beachfront homes, the government worked hard at developing fixes to arrest this erosion with engineering structures such as the jetties at the inlets, groins, and bullheads along the beach. Sand nourishment is also used to replenish lost beaches. Sometimes this works in the short term, but at others nature takes its course, and devastation follows when the ocean flows over the islands. This occurred with devastating results recently in Louisiana when Hurricane Katrina overtopped the barrier islands and drowned the city of New Orleans and other communities all along the Gulf Coast. In that catastrophic occurrence, the seas overwhelmed humans' puny attempt to hold back the flood tides, and the water ultimately went where it could.

NJDEP has an entire division tasked with managing coastal-engineered structures and beach replenishment. These efforts are typically subsidized by both state and federal funds since we share common interests to keep beaches

Figure 13. Barnegat Inlet, which separates two barrier islands on the New Jersey coast, with armored jetties facing the ocean (*left*) and undeveloped dunes, coastal forest, and salt marshes on protected Island Beach State Park to the north on the near-side of the inlet in the photo. (Source: Thomas Belton.)

available for recreation and shipping channels open. The Bureau of Coastal Engineering is responsible for administering beach nourishment, shore protection and coastal dredging projects in cooperation with the U.S. Army Corps of Engineers. Beach nourishment entails the placement of sand along a beach that has eroded. The sources of this sand can be neighboring beaches or sandbars, dredged material from nearby inlets, and offshore borrow pits.

In 1986, following severe oceanfront damage caused by nor'easter storms and Hurricane Gloria, the bureau commissioned the Richard J. Stockton College of New Jersey's Coastal Research Center and the Stevens Institute of Technology's Davidson Laboratory of Marine Hydrodynamics and Coastal Engineering to perform research in support of beach nourishment initiatives. The Coastal Research Center subsequently established a long-term shoreline monitoring and assessment program for the state called the New Jersey Beach Profile Network. This network involves more than one hundred sites along the oceanfront that are surveyed biannually in order to record dune, beach, and near-shore topography, as well as to monitor seasonal and annual coastal and shoreline changes.[2] Surprisingly, the network has also supplied us with information on the long-term evolution of the shoreline.

Stewart Farrell, professor of marine geology at Stockton and director of the Coastal Research Center, notes: "The rise in global sea level has been transpiring for the past 20,000 years at a variable rate following the melting of the last great ice sheet covering North America. The local change has been in the range of three hundred and fifty feet to four hundred feet vertically, which has produced a long-term westward migration of the shoreline."[3] Twenty thousand years ago, he points out, the eastward border of New Jersey lay at the edge of the continental shelf, some eighty to ninety miles east of its present location. As the Laurentide ice sheet retreated into Canada after the most recent ice age, the ocean filled with the meltwater and marched across the relatively flat continental shelf, constantly changing the position and configuration of this ancient coast.

In support of this conclusion on a more human scale, Farrell reviewed property records from the seventeenth century for Monmouth County, New Jersey. He concluded that up to two thousand feet of shoreline had retreated (or was submerged) since 1650. Lands mentioned in seventeenth-century documents are now ocean, having vanished as the sea continued its march westward in direction and upward in elevation. This long-submerged part of the eastern Atlantic coast now makes up what oceanographers call the "continental shelf." It is a relatively shallow sea fringing the continent, but beyond it lie the great abyssal depths. There the shelf drops off precipitously to twelve thousand feet of cold, dark water. There roam the creatures that New Jersey commercial and recreational fishermen seek from our many seaports—the northern lobster, the swift tuna, and the voracious sharks.

THE ABYSSAL DEPTHS

When I was in grammar school, my dad, an avid *Reader's Digest* fan, was offered a free gift for renewing his subscription to that celebrated periodical of expurgated novels. He ordered a bright blue globe of the world, the likes of which I'd never seen before. When he pulled it out of the big cardboard box, it seemed rough to the touch and damaged. But Dad, oblivious to my concerns, just spun it on its axis, whirring like a blue and brown top, until he quickly placed a forefinger alongside and brought it to a screeching halt. An embossed ridge like the seam of a baseball rolled through all the oceans of the world, down through the Atlantic and around the bottom near Antarctica and then up again like a plowed furrow across both sides of the Pacific. "It's a relief map," Dad said proudly, spinning it on its axis again. "The brochure says it shows the world in relief with mountains and hills raised up, valleys and plains flatter. See here," he added, "here are the Appalachian Mountains in New Jersey."

"But, but . . ." I remember stammering, "What about those mountains at the bottom of the Atlantic Ocean? Are they for real?"

"I don't know," Dad replied, but let's find out," as he made off to look it up in the *Encyclopedia Britannica*, which dominated my simple library, cum vestibule, cum bedroom in our housing project apartment, which I shared with my brothers.

But we found no mention of the submerged mountain ring around the earth in the encyclopedia or in the other geography books that I researched the next day. It was not until the librarian at my local library directed me to the science section at Saint Peter's College that I discovered what I was looking for. And it still wasn't easy! A reference in a book led me to the theory of continental drift by Alfred Wegener,[4] another to Admiral Harry Hess and his theory of plate tectonics and seafloor spreading.[5] This was an incredible discovery for my young mind and changed the way I looked at the ocean forever.

I often wondered what it was like to work in the deep sea but had little appreciation for it until I was about to finish graduate school at City College in New York City. I applied for a job at Columbia University's Lamont Dougherty Geologic Center up on the Palisades cliffs across from Harlem. The job was to analyze deep-sea bottom photographs taken by a sled pulled behind a research vessel in the middle of the Atlantic Ocean. The camera snapped shot after shot of bare sediment until once in a blurry moment a shark or a crab or some other unidentifiable and mysterious creature slipped into view. The project's goal was to count the creatures and try to estimate the relative density of deep-sea fauna based entirely on a subsample of gridded cells taken randomly and at various depths across the Atlantic. I never took the job, as it was too far away from my life in Philadelphia, but the researcher I might have worked with described her trips down in the *Alvin*, one of the first bathyscaphes used in twentieth-century deep-sea exploration. The *Alvin*, which is owned and operated by Woods Hole Oceanographic Institution, was the first deep-sea submersible vehicle capable of carrying passengers in untethered dives to depths of nearly fifteen thousand feet. Designed to withstand the crushing pressure of the deep ocean, it is capable of maneuvering around rugged sea mounts on the bottom of the sea or hovering in water to perform scientific experiments.

I later had the good fortune to work with two scientists here in New Jersey who went down in the *Alvin* and made one of the most startling and spectacular discoveries in marine science. J. Frederick Grassle, founder and former director of Rutgers University's Institute of Coastal and Marine Sciences, was the leader of the expedition. Richard Lutz, who became the head of the Rutgers

Shellfish Laboratory in Bivalve, New Jersey, accompanied him. In 1979, they descended in the *Alvin* and were among the first scientists to witness deep-sea "hydrothermal vents."[6] These vents are found along the mid-ocean ridge system, a forty thousand–mile long underwater mountain range that stretches around the planet like the stitching on a baseball. This underwater chain of mountains is formed by geologic processes associated with seafloor spreading and plate tectonics, which were the basis for the undersea mountains my dad and I puzzled over so many years before.

The mid-Atlantic oceanic ridge is where the tectonic plates separating the American continents from Europe and Africa are slowly spreading apart and increasing the size of the ocean, as predicted by plate tectonics. Grassle and his team spent a lot of time maneuvering the *Alvin* to stay out of the superheated water coming off these vents, when they discovered something even more extraordinary. Some of the vents looked like giant chimneys with smoke pouring out of them. These so-called smokers were filled with sulfur that mixed with the seawater, causing chemical reactions that precipitated sulfide minerals. These precipitates formed chimneylike structures that projected dozens of feet into the surrounding ocean. Yet the most amazing discovery was still to come, for as they maneuvered to get a better photograph of these smokers, they saw life within the ebony sandstorm.

It was an entire new ecosystem never before witnessed by humans. Moving among these sulfur clouds were tubeworms, mussels, crabs, squat lobsters, limpets, alvinella worms, scale worms, eelpouts, and octopus. Grassle and his team of scientists took as many samples of water, sediment, and organisms as they could stuff into the *Alvin*'s carry-all cage. And when they came back to the surface, they were equally amazed to discover that the black suspended matter coming out of the chimneys was bacteria, sulfur bacteria comprising a wholly unexplored ecosystem. Because of the absence of sunlight, no plants were found. Instead, microbes of primitive "archaeabacteria" served as the base of a food chain. These microscopic organisms were "chemotropic," using energy from hydrogen sulfide in the vent fluid and oxygen and carbon dioxide from the seawater to create simple sugars. The black plume was filled with volcanic sulfur and immense colonies of these psycrophilic, or heat-loving, sulfur bacteria—a species capable of feeding on pure elemental sulfur. This is the equivalent of you or I eating rocks and gravel for sustenance.

Some of the microbes lived symbiotically with other organisms such as tubeworms and mussels. Others lived on surfaces, including rocks, tubeworm tubes, and other animals. The larger animals lived off these microscopic organisms, the filter-feeding tubeworms and bivalves gaining sustenance from the deep, dark cloud of matter flowing downward. It was one of the first ecosystems discovered by humans that was not dependent on sunlight to drive cellular processes. The bacterial base of this fragile food web supplied the filter-feeders, which were consumed by worms and shrimps, who in turn were devoured by crabs and deep-sea bottom fish that hovered around the fuming seamounts as if they were lighthouses in the wilderness of the abyss.

Richard Lutz is now considered one of the foremost authorities on the ecology of deep-sea hydrothermal vents and their associated communities. His ongoing studies in this unique natural deep-sea laboratory have dramatically altered our views of the biological and geological processes that interact to create ecosystems at the extreme limits of darkness and pressure found at the bottom of the sea. When I met Rich Lutz in 1984, he was the chairman of the Department of Oyster Culture at the Rutgers University Agricultural Experiment Station and director of the Haskin Shellfish Research Laboratory. At that time, Bruce Ruppel and I approached him to investigate whether clam shell growth rings could be used to assess water quality. This would be similar to the way that foresters use tree rings to infer age and past environmental impacts from growth patterns. Lutz hypothesized that environmental stresses for particular years might be read in a clam's shell structure, such as decreased growth rates resulting from hurricanes, salinity fluctuations, temperature changes, and even pollution events such as oil spills.

He and Lowell Fritz, also from the lab, collected four species of shellfish from seven sites along the coast of New Jersey and analyzed them for shell growth patterns. These included different species of bivalves across a range of salinities from fresh to marine waters, including two commercial infaunal, or buried, species, *Mercenaria mercenaria* (hard clam) and *Mya arenaria* (soft clam), as well as two epibenthic species (attached to rocks or marshes) *Geukensia demissa* (ribbed mussel) and *Mytilis edulis* (blue mussel). The results showed that bivalves could indeed document and record both human-made and natural environmental fluctuations in shell growth and could be used as indicators of environmental stress for possible use in a routine monitoring program for New Jersey's coastal bays.[7]

COASTAL BACK BAYS

I remember once being on the water with evening coming on in a nineteen-foot open power boat. Keith Lockwood was driving the boat as we ran fast and slightly north of Barnegat Inlet, where we wanted to arrive on the coast, quartering a swell so as to keep the spray out of our faces. The sun was setting on the horizon and burnishing the wave-tops in long, receding wires of bright, copper-colored light that ran before us, seeming to race us ashore. My friends and I were bone-tired from a day at sea trolling for bluefish and tuna to test for contaminants, our three bodies in a line behind the console and set against the rocking motion of the flying boat. We had set our forearms and legs, braced to bend with each swell as we passed over it, as if we rode a great stallion in a stee-plechase, following its long, loping strides across hedges and creeks to shore.

Looking up, I noticed the sunset was a strange reddish-green color, the dim coastline a brown smudge on the horizon. And a weird feeling came over me in my lethargy; a sense that I was hovering high above and looking down at the water's surface, which had turned to a scrim of crystal glass and the fathoms beneath turned transparent with all the billions of creatures moving about unaware and unconcerned with our passage. And as I dreamed our boat was flying over this translucent sea, I envisioned the thousands of shark and tuna chasing millions of tiny prey fish, which fled in huddled schools, maneuvering to avoid the serrated teeth, and current-borne jellyfish ballooning out in bulging pockets of water to eat phytoplankton, the tiny algae sunning them-selves and growing larger with each packet of sunshine that fell into the nurturing water. And all along the bottom, worms slithered and crabs scuttled about, cuttlefish rocketing across the vast sandy spaces, tiny wavelet dunes on the bottom mimicking those ashore, the silent sucking of the planetary cur-rents pulling finless cells into the mouths of the filter-feeding sponges and coelenterate anemones who needed them most.

But I was pulled from this reverie as we entered Barnegat Inlet and drove into the bay beyond, noticing that the green and red shroud moving off the land to swallow the sunset was actually photochemical smog—a pea-green soup of particulates, ozone, nitric and sulfuric acid—all the air pollutants refracting the setting sun into its extraordinary color. And this frightened me. Knowing that smog was an airborne killer, a soup of chemicals soon to be deposited on the bay and ocean, absorbed by all the creatures swimming beneath our feet, I was frightened for them, frightened for the people ashore who would eat these poisoned fish, and frightened for the future of the seas as waves of pollutants washed off the continent, mimicking in reverse the ocean waves pushing us ashore.

To help protect these sensitive, shallow, back bay regions of the nation, Congress authorized USEPA to create the National Estuary Program in 1987 for improving the water quality in estuaries of national importance.[8] Recognizing that estuaries are often shared by different states, USEPA developed a proce-dure for merging both governmental and private interests to create manage-ment committees (water quality, fisheries, restoration) made up of diverse stakeholders' groups. These groups could then apply for recognition as a national estuary program, with joint local, state, and federal authority to develop management plans in order to balance competing economic and environmental interests. The overarching goal was to protect water quality in estuaries, promoting a balanced, indigenous population of shellfish, finfish, and wildlife. It also allowed the management committees to seek and control sources of pollution.

Since its inception, USEPA has concluded that nationally designated estuaries have a better record of long-term environmental successes because they focus on an upstream watershed approach and use science to inform decision making. They also emphasize collaborative problem solving and involve the public so that regulatory decisions are vetted prior to implementation. New Jersey has three national estuaries: the Delaware Estuary Program (New Jersey, Pennsylvania, and Delaware), the New York–New Jersey Harbor National Estuary, and the Barnegat Bay National Estuary. The Barnegat Bay program is the only one that lies completely within the territorial jurisdiction of New Jersey.

Each of the twenty-eight national estuary programs must develop and implement a Comprehensive Conservation and Management Plan (CCMP), which establishes priorities for activities, research, and funding for the estuary. The Barnegat Bay CCMP was developed over a period of years through cooperative committees established by USEPA, NJDEP, municipalities, academics, and various community stakeholders living on and around the bay.[9] The CCMP serves as a policy blueprint to guide decisions and actions by numerous and often diametrically opposed stakeholders to address a wide range of environmental issues. The CCMP typically begins with a scientific characterization of the estuary, including both biological and hydrological resources, as well as a review of the human sources impacting the waters.

For example, the Barnegat Bay CCMP opens with the observation that the estuary encompasses thirty-seven municipalities and is filled with great aesthetic, economic, and recreational value, although the back bay is now affected by many human impacts that potentially threaten its ecological integrity. The watershed lies in one of the most rapidly growing counties in the northeastern United States. Since 1950, Ocean County's population has increased by more than 775 percent, with municipalities on the barrier islands experiencing a tenfold increase in population during the summer. More than 70 percent of the Barnegat Bay estuarine shoreline buffer zone is developed or altered, leaving only 29 percent in natural land covers. Approximately 45 percent of the estuarine shoreline is bulk-headed.

In the seventeenth century, the bay was settled by Europeans, who displaced the indigenous Native Americans and immediately altered the natural environment through multiple changes in land use. These included lumbering and sawmills, bog iron mining, and charcoal manufacturing. But as the natural resources supporting these activities were depleted (e.g., most of the white cedar forests were cut down for roofing shingles and siding), the industries died out, and the residents who stayed behind turned to farming, hunting, fishing, and berry harvesting in a few small colonial settlements. By the late nineteenth and early twentieth centuries, major railroads and highways were constructed, bringing enormous growth in residential properties, as the recreation and tourism industries expanded into the region. Today, tens of thousands of permanent and summer transient residents rely on Barnegat Bay and its resources for their livelihoods. This includes commercial and recreational fishing, tourism, and water-dependent recreation such as boating, swimming, and surfing.

Barnegat Bay is actually composed of three shallow microtidal bays—Barnegat Bay, Manahawkin Bay, and Little Egg Harbor, with a nearly continuous barrier island complex running along its eastern edge, separating it from the Atlantic Ocean. Seawater enters Barnegat Bay from three narrow points—through the Point Pleasant Canal in the north, Barnegat Inlet at mid-bay, and Little Egg Harbor to the south. This restricted flow and the enclosed physical nature of the bay makes it vulnerable to degradation. Because the bay is shallow, with relatively small amounts of freshwater coming in from tributaries and a limited connection with the sea, pollutants remain there for a long time, affecting submerged vegetation and aquatic life. One of the major factors causing impairment in Barnegat Bay, as determined in the early characterization phase of the CCMP, was nutrient loading and its negative secondary impacts.

Excessive levels of these nutrients stimulate the growth of algae, and as the algae grow, they block sunlight needed by the submerged aquatic vegetation of the bay. Then when the algae die and decay, they reduce the level of oxygen in the water, which can result in large fish kills. The inputs of these nutrients come from many sources, such as street runoff, leaking or failed septic systems, animal wastes, and fertilizer used in landscaping and agriculture. Today, most of the surplus nutrients in Barnegat Bay come from non-point sources such as lawn fertilizers, mainly through stream and river discharges and groundwater influx, although atmospheric deposition is also a major source, making up 39 percent of the nitrogen load dropping into the bay.[10]

More than 70 percent of the total submerged aquatic vegetation (SAV) acreage in New Jersey is located in Barnegat Bay, generally composed of wigeon grass, *Ruppia maritima*, and eelgrass, *Zostera marina*. SAV serves major ecological functions in the estuary, including oxygenating the bay waters and providing grazing and critical habitat for numerous aquatic animals. Studies funded by Science and Research and others have shown significant loss of SAV

since the 1990s.[11] It is unclear, however, whether this is the result of eutrophication, which causes increased turbidity from algal blooms, which in turn shades
out the plants, or if it instead is related to physical disturbances such as
increased boat traffic, wave runner usage, and bulk-heading of the shoreline.
During the late spring and summer, the southern estuary has been the site
of intense, harmful algal blooms. For example, large blooms of *Aureococcus
anophagefferens*, a species of brown algae, were documented during the 1990s.
Because such blooms can drop dissolved oxygen concentrations to levels that
threaten shellfish, Science and Research developed a detailed study of this alga
under the supervision of Mary Gastrich.[12]

Yet is spite of this intense development, a functioning and dynamic ecosystem still thrives in Barnegat Bay and the other shallow coastal embayments in
New Jersey. Microscopic organisms such as phytoplankton and zooplankton
form the basis of the estuarine food chain. In addition, large and diverse populations of aquatic life that depend on the phytoplankton and submerged
aquatic vegetation flourish in the shallow salt marshes of the estuary. These
include more than 200 species of benthic invertebrates (crabs, worms, and
clams) and about 110 species of fish, including recreationally and commercially
important flounder, bluefish, and striped bass. Yet until recently, there was no
comprehensive biological assessment as to the status and trends of the water
quality in the bays to make good regulatory decisions. This changed in 2000,
when USEPA, in cooperation with coastal states, initiated the National Coastal
Assessment program.

THE NATIONAL COASTAL ASSESSMENT

When I hear the term "breadbasket of America," I think of John Deere
Harvesters riding in winged echelons across the amber waves of grain in some
midwestern state, reaping the brushy-headed seeds of the Great Plains grasses
into mobile hoppers. Recently I found myself looking out on another field of
grain with a crew from the New Jersey Sea Grant Program, cruising down Great
Bay at the mouth of the Mullica River in an open workboat. Cord grass (*Spartina
alterniflora*), the grass of New Jersey's salt marshes, is much shorter and tougher
than its midwestern plains cousins, for it has been molded in the forge of sun and
sea, and evolution-crafted by harsh salt and roaring hurricanes. And although
I did not see John Deere Harvesters mowing the long, flowing heads off those
beautiful salt marshes, the importance of the grasslands community could be
understood by simply turning around and looking out on the bay, where clam-
mers planted and tended their shell beds like farmers and red-top floats from the
crab traps stretched in one long, converging line toward the horizon.

Our goal was to sample the waters as part of the National Coastal Assessment, a collaborative effort between the coastal states and USEPA. Our approach was to measure the health of the nation's estuaries, using five indicators of ecological condition: a water quality index (including dissolved oxygen, chlorophyll *a*, nitrogen, phosphorus, and water clarity); a sediment quality index (including sediment toxicity, sediment contaminants, and sediment total organic carbon); a benthic index; a coastal habitat index; and a fish tissue contaminants index. We were one boat out of hundreds throughout the nation simultaneously sampling the coastal waters by dredging mud from the bottom and sorting out the resident worms, clams, and crustaceans. We would then have the sediments analyzed for industrial pollutants. Later we dropped a bottom trawl, its long green net billowing out behind us as we slowly plowed the river bottom for flounder and blue crab. Pulling the net from the brown, silty water, we then separated our catch into the abacus of nature: how many animals live here, how many species, how big, how healthy—all metrics as important as any human census, for without these resources to feed tomorrow's children, we would be in dire straits.

The National Coastal Assessment started in the year 2000, with reports released every two years summarizing data that showed whether the waters were improving or worsening over time. In the 2006 version of the Coastal Condition Report, USEPA decided to focus on the waters in the national estuary programs. The overall condition of Barnegat Bay National Estuary was rated as "fair."[13] The more critical environmental concerns in Barnegat Bay were non-point source pollution and water quality degradation, loss of habitat, and its alteration caused by human activities. The apparent decline in submerged aquatic vegetation beds was also a cause for concern and warranted further investigation. The report noted that some causes of habitat loss and fragmentation and the decline of fish and wildlife species in Barnegat Bay were not well understood. Similarly, although there was a clear indication that human development had caused declining water quality, quantifying this impact was more difficult. USEPA recommended that more research was needed to understand the relationship between habitat loss and alteration in the estuary watershed and to apportion its impacts to the appropriate source (e.g., eutrophication, boating, bulk-heading).

In response, on June 1, 2008, Lisa Jackson, then commissioner of NJDEP and now head of USEPA, announced an important initiative that the department would undertake with the estuary program and its partners, "based on an assessment by the department that, without question, there was evidence of ecological decline in Barnegat Bay."[14] She listed the concerns, including evidence of increased loads of nitrogen in the bay, decline of historic sea grass beds, reduction in the numbers of shellfish, and the more frequent occurrences of stinging sea nettles, which indicated that all was not well in Barnegat Bay. In order to learn why we were seeing these declines and to understand the sources of the problems and how best to correct them, she proposed immediate and measurable steps that the state would take to determine the nature and extent of the degradation so that protective measures could be implemented to ensure the ecological integrity of Barnegat Bay. She said NJDEP would fund more research and fieldwork to track down the sources of pollution so that cause and effect could be better understood for restoration projects and so that responsible parties could be forced to clean up and correct the problems.

And although Jackson left the department a short time thereafter, her comments set into motion a series of research projects that have become the focus of work I am currently involved with to this day. These include the development of nutrient criteria for New Jersey's estuaries, a salt marsh wetlands assessment project, and the development of more state-specific biological indicators of biotic integrity than those used in the national coastal assessment. Ironically, the one issue that she failed to mention was the one most pressing for any forward-looking marine scientist: climate change and global warming that could accelerate sea level rise.

CLIMATE CHANGE AND SEA LEVEL RISE

The debate over climate change has flowed back and forth over the past few decades, as politicians and diplomats have argued about its very existence and the costs of controlling greenhouse gases, the source of the phenomenon. Let us hope that the reality of this runaway global threat has been unambiguously confirmed by the 2007 release of the Fourth Assessment Report by the Intergovernmental Panel on Climate Change. The report was a remarkable collaborative achievement, considering that it involved more than five hundred lead authors and two thousand expert reviewers, building on the work of a wide scientific community and submitted to the scrutiny of delegates from more than one hundred participating nations. The report's major conclusion was that "warming of the climate system is unequivocal, as is now evident from observations of increases in global average air and ocean temperatures, widespread melting of snow and ice and rising global average sea level."[15]

Recently the Union of Concerned Scientists published a report summarizing potential climate change impacts on New Jersey. It noted that "spring is arriving earlier, summers are growing hotter, and winters are becoming warmer and less snowy."[16] Average temperatures across the northeastern United States have risen more than 1.5°F since 1970, with a 20 to 30 percent rease in winter precipitation. The frequency and severity of heavy rainfall :nts are expected to escalate, as are the occurrences of short-term droughts. These changes could increase stress on both natural and managed ecosystems, requiring a reassessment of the many wildlife and forest management strategies I have described previously. The report notes that global warming causes ocean water to expand, and it melts land-based ice. Without a change in the current high emissions of greenhouse gases, it projects that global sea level will rise between ten inches and two feet by the end of this century. Under these projections, New Jersey's densely populated coast faces substantial increases in the extent and frequency of coastal flooding, erosion, and property damage.

On a more exacting scale, regionalized studies have raised a clarion call about the vulnerabilities of New Jersey's low-lying coastal communities to rising seas. A study developed by Mike Aucott of Science and Research used deep sediment cores and the analysis of sediment types and the shells of amoeboid "foraminifera" species to show a relatively constant rise of sea level in New Jersey from approximately five thousand years ago to the present day, at a rate of 2 millimeters per year.[17] Surprisingly, only about half of this increase is the result of rising seas. It seems that the New Jersey coast is sinking. Apparently, this has been going on for a while, owing to coastal plain subsidence after the retreat of the Laurentide ice sheet from the most recent ice age, twenty thousand years ago. This ice sheet covered most of North America and was so heavy it caused the ground underneath to subside while the land in front was uplifted like a standing wave. Once the ice sheet melted, however, and moved north, this process reversed and the subsided areas began to lift as New Jersey's shoreline began to sink. Unfortunately, this sinking of the land is yoked to the accelerated process of sea level rise attributable to global warming such that the overall effect is attenuated to twice what is found in New England. It is even worse at some state locations, where overall sea level rise was projected to exceed 4 millimeters per year. These sites are primarily on barrier island locations such as Atlantic City, where the numerous casinos and hotels have caused sediment compaction of the underlying land, which is then exacerbated by groundwater withdrawals that cause even higher rates of localized subsidence.

In 2005, a Princeton University study assessed the extent of New Jersey coastal areas projected to be permanently inundated and subject to expanded one hundred–year flooding, given medium and high-end projections of present rates of sea level rise.[18] It estimated that 1 to 3 percent of New Jersey's land area will be affected by inundation and up to 9 percent by episodic coastal flooding over the next century. The researchers also made the controversial suggestion that, where possible, a gradual withdrawal of development on some areas of New Jersey's coast may be the "optimum management strategy" for protecting natural ecosystems. This is good ecological advice under the scenarios they present for inundation; however, it may run afoul of the barrier island municipalities who seek only to grow their footprints with houses and marinas. And the municipal land-use law in New Jersey gives them the power to enact these changes with little input from the state. Unfortunately, these towns may not see the long-term picture of inexorable change resulting from sea level rise as of paramount importance.

The American Littoral Society and the Center for Remote Sensing and Spatial Analysis (CRSSA) at Rutgers University also analyzed where adequate wetlands existed behind the barrier islands for their retreat under the onslaught of rising seas and where such land may be impeded by physical infrastructure such as roads and buildings.[19] They concluded that New Jersey's coastal zone is already heavily impacted by development, with a high degree of developed land uses in close proximity to the tidal waters and thereby vulnerable to future sea level rise. The majority of this near-shore coastal zone (less than 1,600 feet from tidal water) is in some form of human-dominated land use. Therefore they argued for a new management paradigm in the face of these impediments to natural shoreward migration for barrier islands, many now fixed in place by engineered sea walls and groins. They concluded that to ensure the vitality of our coastal habitats for the long term we need to plan for and design flexible adaptation strategies that recognize the dynamic nature of our coastlines rather than just build more sea walls and levees.

To date, sea level rise and associated problems of shoreline erosion and storm surges have been primarily addressed through "hard" structural approaches to protect existing developed infrastructure (groins, jetties, and sea walls). The CRSSA researchers suggested that future adaptation to sea level rise should *not* be viewed as an engineering problem but rather a *land-use issue*. To that end, they recommended that any new development should be minimized in beach, dune, and coastal wetland retreat zones. This will provide room for future shoreline retreat and minimize the need for investment in structural protection. These buffer zones should to be "rolling" to reflect changes as sea levels rise and the water/wetland boundary retreats landward. In application, this means that where existing beach or bay front development is threatened by shoreline erosion, "soft" approaches, such as dune protection/stabilization and salt marsh restoration, should be used rather than shoreline armoring.[20] And it is this exploration of salt marsh ecology as refugia from sea level rise that my most recent research interests have taken me.

I am currently involved in a series of projects within Barnegat Bay addressing sea level rise. One study involves David Velinsky and Donald Charles, from the Philadelphia Academy of Natural Sciences, and Christopher Sommerfield,

from the University of Delaware. Specifically, we are developing ecological
indices of ecosystem health in New Jersey's shallow coastal bays so as to prioritize salt marshes for potential protection, restoration, and/or acquisition. To
that end we collected 3-meter-deep salt marsh cores on transects from the top
of the Barnegat Bay to the bottom near the inlet and analyzed the peat soils.
These cores will be sectioned to determine sedimentation rates in the marshes,
which will allow us to estimate any increased loads of pollutants and their
effects on salt marsh growth. Upon completion of the project, we will have
much-needed information on the pollution histories of the bay in support of
nutrient criteria development and any future restoration efforts. In addition,
specific analyses will be targeted to understand how ecological conditions may
or may not have changed over the past eighty to one hundred or more years.
Importantly, this study will help provide a timeline for ecological changes that
could be used as a baseline for water quality modeling and adaptive management methods for both short-term human impacts (decreasing discharge of
lawn fertilizer) and long-term impacts (trends assessment for sea level rise).

Another study involves Ocean County College and the Barnegat Bay
National Estuary Program, which have received a grant from USEPA to

Figure 14. Members of the Patrick Center for Environmental Research and the
University of Delaware coring in the Barnegat Bay salt marsh to estimate the rate of
sea level rise in New Jersey. (Source: Patrick Center for Environmental Research.)

develop a tidal wetlands assessment methodology for ascertaining the ecological condition of these wetlands. This rapid bioassessment protocol could then be used as a routine monitoring tool by NJDEP and the local municipalities to prioritize and manage development around these sensitive ecosystems. Fixed monitoring stations will be established at priority locations and used to assess any changes over time associated with major stressors (e.g., sea level rise, sediment budgets, temperature) and shifts in ecological function in the estuary. This may prove a critical yardstick for future attempts to protect these ecologically important salt marshes. It will give us the information we need to predict change and, it is hoped, to forestall such catastrophic losses as we have already experienced with submerged aquatic vegetation in the bay. And we should not be too short-sighted on the value of these studies, for sometimes things change so imperceptibly that we grow inured to the threat.

For example, the deep-coring project that Science and Research funded in the coastal bays that I mentioned above may add perspective to this complacency. Data from these deep-sediment cores suggested that stable barrier islands with shallow lagoons and salt marshes behind them evolved in New Jersey only four thousand years before the present.[21] Prior to that, the ocean swept in unhindered to crash against the continental margin. Native Americans arriving on the eastern coast of North America about ten thousand years ago may have witnessed the slow rise of these shoals into islands, their greening by windblown seeds, and eventual colonization by diverse animal species during winter freezing of the bays. Eventually this gave rise to the unique forested ecosystem that Europeans found in the sixteenth century and that still persists in protected areas today.

The tragedy is that in this current era our children may have the reciprocal experience of watching helplessly as the islands are reclaimed by the sea, owing to human negligence. The waves pushed ashore will be aided by our unseen hand, the greenhouse gases of our Industrial Revolution undoing in a century what it took a millennia for storm surge and wind to create. So from my perspective, sea level rise research projects are more critical and convey a greater sense of urgency than any that have gone before. Because of the greater risk at stake, it is important that we study, plan, and act now before it's too late. The coastal landscape in New Jersey will most likely be different to my grandchildren's eyes, as it was to mine and my father's in his day. And seeing this change they may wonder what we did, or did not do, to protect that most valuable natural resource. I would like to think I could answer that I helped to preserve a beach or a forest—even a beaver pond restored to forest along a mountain ridge on the Appalachian Trail. And when they saw it, they might say, "Yes, that's beautiful."

WHERE SEA MEETS SKY

As a marine biologist, I have always looked forward to the end of winter and those sunny trips to the Jersey shore, but it's the classicist in me that relishes the memory of walks with my daughter, Laura, as a child and the ancient stories I told her about the things we found at the water's edge. Usually we would splash along, ignoring the tourists who leapt past us into the surf shrieking. We would keep our heads down and steadily search for nature's jewelry—those resplendent seashells that lay upon the sand. But to my daughter's dismay, I often ignored the pretty ones for the fractured, their peculiar mottled markings speaking to me of life-and-death struggles. I would show her signs on the shells that told of monstrous battles writ large from the tiny puncture holes where predatory snails rasped their way slowly, methodically, against the barricaded clam until finally the protective fortress was breached and the animal within devoured.

Then I usually rewarded her indulgence of my biologist's eye with a story from the Greek myths. The moon snail, *Polynices*, was named after a son of Oedipus, that ill-fated Greek king left to die as a child on a mountaintop because of a prophecy that he would kill his father and marry his mother. Miraculously, Oedipus was saved, grew to manhood, and unknowingly fulfilled the prophecy. When he learned the truth, he blinded himself and left his kingdom to his sons—including Polynices—who waged a bloody civil war that left his entire family dead or cursed. Perhaps the biologist who named the voracious, predatory moon snail saw something of Polynices in it, a reminder that humans and their baser desires—like ambition and pride—are not so far removed from the animal kingdom and its laws of tooth and claw. Heady stuff, you might think, for an afternoon walk at the beach, but the greatest stories ever told.

I remember one day Laura pointing along the sand at a row of tiny brown creatures that looked like shiny marbles tumbling up the beach face before a crashing wave. As it dissipated, the marbles amazingly sprouted tiny pointed legs, which scrabbled and dug, burying the strange creatures before a flock of screaming gulls could sweep down and snap them up like after-dinner mints. They were a host of *Emerita*, or mole crabs, and once safely buried, they adroitly lifted their feathery antennae like a tiny forest into the backwash of the next breaker to sieve for microscopic food. Then, losing their precarious grip on the bottom to the next passing wave, they were pulled from their burrows and on into the swift bubbling heart of water, where they rolled and swallowed their food until finally digging themselves in again for cover. And that's how they live their lives, as nature's beautiful barrel-dancers.

Pointing at the water, I told her to imagine *Emerita*'s tiny food—whip-tailed swimming plants called dinoflagellates and pork-bellied rotarians flitting by like spinning screws, both chased by tiny crablike animals called zooplankton. I told her to close her eyes and imagine mountains beneath the sea as tall as the Rockies, the sea's abyss a deep bathtub getting darker and darker as she descended until the mountain slopes finally flattened before a broad abyssal plain where the sunlight was swallowed in perpetual darkness, and the bottom slowly filled with falling silt and dying animals enslaved to gravity as they dropped into the abyss.

And there I told her she would see the most bizarre creatures of all—anglerfish with long protuberant noses that glowed phosphorescently and acted as fish lures in the dark, and strange "tripod fish" with long, stilted fins that looked like legs, which they used to walk past glowing volcanic gardens and sulphurous chimney vents, all surrounded by millions of writhing shrimp seeking the lava for heat and light at the extremes of existence.

And as I remember, she opened her bright green eyes and blinked them in the sunshine. I can still see her smiling face transformed in pure joy like Proteus, the sea nymph and demigod to Neptune, the lord of the seas. Proteus had the power to change into any creature or shape at will: the red-bearded jellyfish, the armored horseshoe crab, or the glorious dolphin that leaps into the sky above the waves like a bird. Smiling, I would grab her hand and begin walking again, the two of us oblivious to the dunes and the sunbathers. Then looking up she would say, "Tell me another story, Daddy."

And as I looked out over the aquamarine waters of the Atlantic Ocean, I suddenly remembered my father's face on another day as he strained against twin oars and rowed me across the mighty Hudson River. He sang a tune popular with the GIs during World War II as I asked him questions about life. Why he became a policeman? How do you swim against an outgoing tide? Did we each have a guardian angel sitting on our shoulders, as the nuns in grammar school taught us? Then Dad, he'd pause a second with a wizened look on his face, gaze off over the skyscrapers of New York City as the river carried us along for a bit, and then he would commence to row again, telling me stories about how it all got that way.

Afterword

I've found that research science is important to public policy, especially decisions that affect human health and vital natural resources such as plentiful and clean drinking water. It is even more vital that these environmental studies be vetted in nonpolitical forums such as professional conferences and scientific symposia. It is only then that scientifically defensible laws and regulations can be enacted that preclude partisan political tinkering. With good science, our lawmakers and administrators can move forward without blinders to initiate protective legislation that avoids environmental impairment with sometimes catastrophic consequences. Think of Hurricane Katrina in 2005 and the fate of New Orleans in the absence of adequate planning. Two avoidable things were indirectly responsible for the storm surge that came ashore along the entire Gulf Coast and killed thousands. Both involved a lack of technical foresight with resultant environmental and human health impacts.

First, the local and state planning boards in Louisiana, Mississippi, and Texas allowed the deforestation of salt marshes and barrier islands along the Gulf Coast to facilitate human habitation. This occurred in spite of the fact that the naturally erodable and moveable islands were nature's way of buffering the coastline against hurricane storm surges. Second, and even more politically sinister, was the corrupt relinquishment of the levee system in New Orleans to the control of local political bosses ensconced in "levee committees" that had the power to write separate construction contracts whose design specifications were overviewed by engineers from each parish. Subsequent evaluation by independent engineers found inadequate anchoring of the levies in poor-quality concrete and footings, unstable soil, and haphazard maintenance, all of which resulted in the eventual failure, releasing tons of water into New Orleans, effectively killing it as a functioning American city.

And as is often the case where municipal law supersedes the state and federal laws, or where disrespect for scientific oversight of public policy occurs, the adage of Benjamin Franklin holds true:

For the want of a nail, the shoe was lost;
for the want of a shoe the horse was lost;
and for the want of a horse the rider was lost,
being overtaken and slain by the enemy,
all for the want of care about a horseshoe nail.

(Benjamin Franklin, *Poor Richard's Almanac*)

Political stars may rise and fall every few years based on vagrant exigencies such as the economy, wars, or which politician is stupid enough to take the wrong money or seek sexual favors from an intern or aide. Yet in spite of this cult of personality, which we euphemistically call politics in America, government by the people still persists. Why? As every civil servant knows, a large part of governmental constancy rests on the backs of the bureaucracy hired to support it—clerical workers who continue to keep the records when politicians fail at the polls; inspectors who keep looking for code violations; and scientists who seek answers to epidemics like HIV/AIDS, develop new weather predictions to save foundering boats from hurricanes, or else chest their way into the corporate boardrooms to cow the recalcitrant profiteers from dumping hazardous wastes down sewers and into our nation's waterways.

When we were young environmental professionals, just out of school, we were energized with facts and raw emotion. We often refer to our zeal as "enviro-religion." Being green is a crusader's quest, matching Don Quixote's desire for tilting at windmills in pursuit of the impossible, idealistic dream. We want America safe from the dragons of industry that inundate our lives with plastic poisons, cancer, and toxic waste dumps. We spend a decade pummeling the societal forces with our righteousness. But then, inevitably, after a period of time, something changes. It's not that we grow tired of the chase, it's that we have developed a more worldly perspective, a realization that modern society and its benefits, which include many useful things made from plastics, such as computers, medicines, and power facilities, are not inherently bad. They are useful for humankind but only if used in a sustainable way, allowing us to thoughtfully manage the negative impacts and to seek balance with the environment.

In our professional lives we interact with model corporate citizens, filled with a respect for the world we live in, but also with recalcitrant polluters, who are willing to save money at the expense of their neighbors' health. These polluters spend millions on advertising rather than cleanup or prevention, attempting to woo the citizenry with false and absurd claims of good neighborliness. But we environmental professionals have not gone away. Nor have we stopped thinking about reducing the risks of exposure to toxic chemicals for our children and ourselves. We are still here trying to address the situation by catching and analyzing fish in the rivers in order to issue consumption advisories and by developing new technologies for immobilizing or purging contaminated sediments.

But we have also learned how to work cooperatively with good corporate citizens who want to develop green manufacturing practices, pollution prevention policies, and management solutions that preclude cleanups. We have also learned how to create scientifically defensible cases for litigation to challenge those corporations that will pay any price to meet their profit margins rather that admit to their environmental responsibilities.

So those of us in the environmental field, at least those who have been around a while, lose some our evangelicalism and become pragmatic, more realistic, and cajoling. We don't throw away our enforcement stick but now try the carrot first. We both litigate and use friendly persuasion to bring corporate America to some understanding that we have not gone away, that no matter who is in office, we will still need to enforce forty years of good environmental laws and regulations. For it is good business to be green, as even Fortune 500 CEOs have learned, since their grandchildren will also suffer the effects of global warming and sea level rise, and will be exposed to cancer-causing chemicals in the air they breath and the water they drink.

So we stay and we work. We are trained for this job and enthusiastic about our work. We love it! And maybe we still have that unique enviro-religion pulsing in our veins. We are pragmatists, yet we will not let a false sense of economic need and a desire for increasing profits dictate what can be done in America. We still believe that America is a generous nation and that we can absorb the added costs of a safe environment for our children's sakes.

Notes

CHAPTER 1 — THE WAR ON CANCER

1. Richard Nixon, Annual Message to the Congress on the State of the Union, January 22, 1971, http://www.presidency.ucsb.edu/ws/index.php?pid=3110.

2. T. Mason and F. W. McKay, *US Cancer Mortality by County: 1950–1969*, U.S. Dept. of Health, Education, and Welfare, pub. no. NIH-74-615 (Washington, D.C., 1973).

3. T. Mason et al., *Atlas of Cancer Mortality for US Counties: 1950–1969*, U.S. Dept. of Health, Education, and Welfare, pub. no. NIH-75-780 (Washington, D.C. 1975).

4. M. Greenberg, *Highlights of the Spatial Distribution of Cancer Mortality and of Factors Associated with Increased and Reduced Risk of Cancer Mortality in the New Jersey–New York–Philadelphia Metropolitan Region, 1950–1969 and 1968–1972*, report to the Toxics Substances Program, New Jersey Department of Environmental Protection (Trenton, 1980).

5. M. Greenberg, "Cancer Atlases: Uses and Limitations," *Environmentalist* 5, no. 3 (1985): 187–191.

6. *Cancer and the Environment: What You Need to Know; What You Can Do*, U.S. Department of Health and Human Services, National Institutes of Health, National Cancer Institute, National Institute of Environmental Health Sciences, NIH pub. no. 03-2039 (Washington, D.C., 2003).

7. "Creation of Cabinet Committee on Cancer Control," Executive Order no. 40, *New Jersey Register*, May 26, 1976, http://www.lexisnexis.com/njoal.

8. Ralph Stuart, "Command and Control Regulation," in *Encyclopedia of Earth*, ed. Cutler J. Cleveland (Washington, D.C.: Environmental Information Coalition, National Council for Science and the Environment, 2007); Vito De Lucia, "Polluter Pays Principle," in *Encyclopedia of Earth*, ed. Cutler J. Cleveland (Washington, D.C.: Environmental Information Coalition, National Council for Science and the Environment, 2008), both at http://www.eoearth.org.

9. *New Jersey Statutes Annotated* (hereafter NJSA); these acts are, respectively, NJSA 58:10-23.11, NJSA 13:1E-49 through 91, NJSA 34:5A-1 et seq. (specifically, 34:5A-30), NJSA 13:1K-6 et seq., and NJSA 13:1K-19 et seq., http:www.njleg.state.nj.us.

10. M. Greenberg et al., "High Cancer Mortality Rates from Childhood Leukemia and Young Adult Hodgkin's Disease and Lymphoma in the New Jersey/New York/Philadelphia Metropolitan Corridor, 1950–1969," *Cancer Research* 40 (1980): 439–443.

11. National Toxicology Program, *Report on Carcinogens, Eleventh Edition*, U.S. Department of Health and Human Services, Public Health Service, National Toxicology Program (Washington, D.C., 2005), http://ntp.niehs.nih.gov/ntp/roc/toc11 .html.

12. M. Greenberg et al., "Approaches and Initial Findings of a State-Sponsored Research Programme on Population Exposure to Toxic Substances," *Environmentalist* 1, no. 1 (1981): 53–63.

13. E. Stevenson et al., *The New Jersey Industrial Survey Project (1979–1982): Final Report*, Office of Science and Research, New Jersey Department of Environmental Protection (Trenton, 1986).

14. "Fact Sheet: Cancer Clusters," National Cancer Institute, U.S. National Institutes of Health (Washington, D.C., 2005), http://www.cancer.gov/cancertopics/factsheet/Risk/ clusters.

15. T. A. Burke et al., "An Environmental Investigation of Clusters of Leukemia and Hodgkin's Disease in Rutherford, New Jersey," *Journal of the Medical Society of New Jersey* 77 (1980): 259–264.

16. *Childhood Cancer Incidence Health Consultation: A Review and Analysis of Cancer Registry Data, 1979–1995 for Dover Township (Ocean County), New Jersey*, New Jersey Department of Health and Senior Services (Trenton, 1997).

17. *Reich Farm, New Jersey, Superfund Site (EPA ID#: NJD980529713)*, USEPA Region 2, National Priorities List (NPL) Listing History, proposed: December 1, 1982, final: September 1, 1983; *Ciba-Geigy Corp. New Jersey Superfund Site (EPA ID#: NJD001502517)*, USEPA Region 2, NPL Listing History, proposed: December 1, 1982, final: September 1, 1983, http://www.epa.gov/superfund/sites/npl.

18. Linda Gillick, "Toxic Environment Affects Children's Health (T.E.A.C.H.)," http://www.tr-teach.org/cause/outrage.html.

19. *Dover Township Childhood Cancer Investigation: Public Health Response Plan*, prepared by the New Jersey Department of Health and the Agency for Toxic Substances and Disease Registry in coordination with the Citizens Action Committee on Childhood Cancer Cluster and the Ocean County Health Department, June 24, 1996, http:// www.state.nj.us/health/eoh/hhazweb/phrdover.pdf.

20. *Case-Control Study of Childhood Cancers in Dover Township (Ocean County), New Jersey Volume I: Summary of the Final Technical Report*, Division of Epidemiology, Environmental and Occupational Health, New Jersey Department of Health and Senior Services, in cooperation with Agency for Toxic Substances and Disease Registry, U.S. Department of Health and Human Services, January 2003, http://www.state.nj.us/ health/eoh/hhazweb/case-control_pdf/Volume_I/vol_i.pdf.

21. "Environment and Health; Toms River Settlement," *New York Times*, January 27, 2002.

22. C. W. Trumbo, "Public Requests for Cancer Cluster Investigations: A Survey of State Health Departments," *American Journal of Public Health* 90, no. 8 (2000): 102–130.

23. Atul Gawande, "The Cancer Cluster Myth," *New Yorker*, February 8, 1999.

24. Richard Clapp, "Atul Gawande: Great Surgeon, Not So Great on Cancer Clusters," The Pump Handle, November 20, 2006, http://thepumphandle.wordpress.com/2006/ 11/20/atul-gawande-great-surgeon-not-so-great-on-cancer-clusters.

25. D. Kennedy, "*The New Yorker* Ignores Leukemia in Woburn" *Boston Phoenix*, February 8, 1999.

26. *Light after Life: Experiments and Ideas on After-Death Changes of Kirlian Pictures* (New York: Backbone Publishing, 1998).

27. David K. Espey et al., "Annual Report to the Nation on the Status of Cancer, 1975–2004," *Cancer* 110, no. 10 (2002): 2,119–2,152.

CHAPTER 2 — POISONED FISH

1. "Ambient Water Quality Criteria for Polychlorinated Biphenyls. EPA-440/5–80–068," Office of Water Regulations and Standards, U.S. Environmental Protection Agency (Washington, D.C., 1980).

2. "Anniston PCB Site Update—2007 (USEPA ID: ALD000400123)," http://www .epa.gov/region4/waste/npl/nplal/annpcbal.htm.

3. Michael Grunwald, "Monsanto Held Liable ror PCB Dumping," *Washington Post,* February 23, 2002.

4. Soren Jensen, "Report of a New Chemical Hazard," *New Scientist* 32 (1966): 612.

5. *Polychlorinated Biphenyls,* technical report to the National Academy of Sciences, Environmental Studies Board, Commission on Natural Resources, National Research Council (Washington, D.C.: National Academy of Sciences, 1979); *Polychlorinated Biphenyls and Polybrominated Biphenyls,* International Agency for Research on Cancer, Monographs on the Evaluation of the Carcinogenic Risks to Humans, vol. 18 (Lyon: IARC, 1978).

6. *Statute, Regulations & Enforcement of Toxic Substances Control Act (TSCA),* U.S. Environmental Protection Agency, October 11, 1976, http://www.epa.gov/compliance/ civil/tsca/tscaenfstatreq. html.

7. *Hudson River PCBs Superfund Site, New York (EPA ID#: NYD980763841),* U.S. Environmental Protection Agency Region 2, NPL Listing History, proposed: September 8, 1983, final: September 21, 1984, http://epa.gov/region02/superfund/npl/ 0202229c.pdf.

8. Dan Weissman, "Cancer Tides: DEP Studying Depth of Plastic Peril in Waterways," *Star-Ledger* (Newark, N.J.), February 19, 1975.

9. F. Cordle et al., "Risk Assessment in a Federal Regulatory Agency: An Assessment of Risk Associated with the Human Consumption of Some Species of Fish Contaminated with PCBs," *Environmental Health Perspectives* 45 (1982): 171–182.

10. T. J. Belton et al., "Polychlorinated Biphenyls in Fish Tissues throughout the State of New Jersey USA: A Comprehensive Survey," *Bulletin of the New Jersey Academy of Science* 27, no. 1 (1982): 39.

11. Thomas Kean, *The Politics of Inclusion* (New York: Free Press, 1988).

12. "Fisheries Closures and Advisories for Striped Bass, American Eel, Bluefish, White Perch and White Catfish Taken from the Northeast Region of the State," New Jersey Department of Environmental Protection, adopted emergency new rule and concurrent proposal, *New Jersey Administrative Code,* 7:25-18A, December 15, 1982.

13. "NJDEP Report on PCB Fish Levels," press release, New Jersey Department of Environmental Protection, December 13, 1982.

14. Bob Duffy, "Blues' PCB Alert Nets Response," *Star-Ledger* (Newark, N.J.), December 22, 1982.

15. Bob Duffy, "Virginia Downplaying NJ Bluefish Warning," *Star-Ledger,* November 9, 1983.

16. Bob DeSanto, "Government Won't Finance Fish Study as NJ Requested," *Asbury Park [N.J.] Press,* September 30, 1983; "US Agencies Decline to Lead Coastal Fish Contaminant Study," *Boston Globe,* October 1, 1983.

17. Bruce D. Stutz, "Outdoors: Fishermen Seek Clearer PCB Rules," *New York Times,* October 23, 1983.

18. "Report on 1984–1986 Federal Survey of PCBs in Atlantic Coast Bluefish, Data Report," report to Congress by the National Oceanic and Atmospheric Administration, Food and Drug Administration, and Environmental Protection Agency, April 1986, available from the National Technical Information Service: PB86-218070/XAB; "Report on 1984–1986 Federal Survey of PCBs in Atlantic Coast Bluefish, Interpretive Report," report

to Congress by the National Oceanic and Atmospheric Administration, Food and Drug Administration, and Environmental Protection Agency, March 1987, available from the National Technical Information Service: PB87-214672/XAB.

19. J. M. O'Conner and R. J. Huggett, "Aquatic Pollution Problems, North Atlantic Coast, Including Chesapeake Bay," *Aquatic Toxicology* 11 (1988): 163–190.

20. P. J. Eldridge, "Potential Impact of PCB's on Bluefish, *Pomatomus saltatrix*, Management—Polychlorinated Biphenyls," *Marine Fisheries Review* (Fall 1992): 19–23.

21. *Bluefish Fisheries Management Plan*, amendments 1 and 2 (Dover, Del.: Mid-Atlantic Fishery Management Council, 1990); *2007 Review of the Fishery Management Plan for Bluefish (Pomatomus saltatrix)*, prepared by Erika Robbins, Najih Lazar, and Wilson Laney (Washington, D.C.: Atlantic States Marine Fisheries Commission, 2007).

22. "Persistent Bioaccumulative and Toxic (PBT) Chemical Program," U.S. Environmental Protection Agency, 2009, http://www.epa.gov/pbt.

23. Jeffrey Ashley and Richard J. Horwitz, *Assessment of PCBs, Select Organic Pesticides and Mercury in Fishes from New Jersey: 1998–1999 Monitoring Program, Report No. 00–20D* (Philadelphia: Patrick Center for Environmental Research, Academy of Natural Sciences, 2000).

24. "The Fish Story," *Hudson Dispatch* (Union City, N.J.), December 19, 1982.

CHAPTER 3 — THE QUALITY OF WATER

1. "Suction Holds a Diver at Base of Great Dam; Horses Fail to Drag Man from Grip of Rushing Water," *New York Times*, April 13, 1904.

2. J. DeLu, *Sedimentology of the Rockaway River and Boonton Reservoir, New Jersey*, final report to New Jersey Department of Environmental Protection from Rutgers University, Dept. of Geological Sciences, 1982, http://geology.rutgers.edu/thesis.shtml.

3. I. W. Suffet et al., "Trace Organic Analysis of Suspended Sediments Collected with an In-Stream Composite Sampler: The Need for a Standard Method," 184–203, in *Chemical and Biological Characterization of Sludges, Sediments, Dredge Spoils, and Drilling Muds*, ed. J. J. Lictenberg, J. A. Winter, C. I. Weber and L. Fradkin (New York: American Society for Testing and Materials, 1988).

4. *Ambient Aquatic Life Water Quality Criteria for Nonylphenol—Draft*, United States Environmental Protection Agency, Office of Water, 4304T (EPA 822-R-03-0290), (Washington, D.C., 2003).

5. B. Hileman, "California Bans Phthalates in Toys for Children," *Chemical and Engineering News*, October 22, 2007; *Directive 2005/84/EC Amending for the 22nd Time Council Directive 76/769/EEC*, European Union of the European Parliament and Science Council, December 14, 2005, http://europa.eu/legislation_summaries/consumers/consumer_safety/l32033_en.htm.

6. *NTP-CERHR Expert Panel Report on DI n Butyl Phthalate*, National Toxicology Program, National Institute of Environmental Health Sciences, Center for the Evaluation of Risks to Human Reproduction, NTP-CERHR-DBP-00 (Washington, D.C., 2000).

7. R. K. Tucker, *Groundwater Quality in New Jersey: An Investigation of Toxic Contaminants* (Trenton: New Jersey Department of Environmental Protection, Office of Toxic Substances Research, 1981).

8. *Maximum Contaminant Level Recommendations for Hazardous Contaminants in Drinking Water*, report by the New Jersey Water Quality Institute, submitted to the New Jersey Department of Environmental Protection, March 26, 1987, http://www.nj.gov/dep/watersupply/njdwqinstitute.htm.

9. *National Primary Drinking Water Regulations: Volatile Synthetic Organics*, U.S. Environmental Protection Agency, *Federal Register* 49, no. 114 (1984): 24,330–24,355.

10. HDR Engineering, Inc., *Handbook of Public Water Systems*, 2nd ed. (New York: John Wiley, 2001).

11. *A Giant Step for Public Health: Chlorination in Chicago and Jersey City* (Arlington, Va.: American Chemistry Council, 2008).

12. *Stage 1 Disinfectants and Disinfection Byproducts Rule*, U.S. Environmental Protection Agency, EPA 815-F-98–010, December 1998, http://www.epa.gov/OGWDW/mdbp/dbp1.html; *National Primary Drinking Water Regulations: Disinfectants and Disinfection Byproducts, Federal Register* 63, no. 241 (1998): 69,389–69,476.

13. *Microbial and Disinfection Byproduct Rules Simultaneous Compliance Guidance Manual*, USEPA-815-R-99-015 (Washington, D.C., 1999); *Alternative Disinfectants and Oxidants Guidance Manual*, USEPA 815-R-99-014 (Washington, D.C., 1999).

14. K. R. Fox and D. A. Lytle, "Milwaukee's Crypto Outbreak: Investigation and Recommendations," *Journal of the American Water Works Association* 88, no. 9 (September 1996): 87–94.

15. *The Interim Enhanced Surface Water Treatment Rule: What Does It Mean to You?* EPA 816-R-01-014, U.S. Environmental Protection Agency, United States Office of Water (Washington, D.C., 2001).

16. "Basic Information: Perfluorooctanoic Acid (PFOA) and Fluorinated Telomers," U.S. Environmental Protection Agency, 2009, http://www.epa.gov/oppt/pfoa/pubs/pfoainfo.html.

17. "Provisional Health Advisories (PHA) for PFOA and PFOS," U.S. Environmental Protection Agency, 2009, http://www.epa.gov/waterscience/criteria/drinking.

18. Gloria B. Post et al., "Occurrence and Potential Significance of Perfluorooctanoic Acid (PFOA) Detected in New Jersey Public Drinking Water Systems," *Environmental Science and Technology* 43, no. 12 (2009): 4,547–4,554.

19. Robert D. Morris, *The Blue Death: Disease, Disaster and the Water We Drink* (New York: HarperCollins, 2007).

20. P. E. Stackelberg and R. L. Lippincott, *Occurrence, Distribution, and Concentration of Pharmaceuticals and Other Organic Wastewater-Related Compounds in New Jersey's Surface-Water Supplies*, research project summary, New Jersey Department of Environmental Protection, Division of Science, Research, and Technology (Trenton, 2003).

21. Sherline H. Lee et al., "Surveillance for Waterborne-Disease Outbreaks—United States, 1999–2000," U.S. Centers for Disease Control, Morbidity and Mortality Weekly Reports (MMWR) Surveillance Summary, 51(SS08) (November 22, 2002): 1–28, http://cdc.gov/mmwr/preview/mmwrhtml/ss5108a1.htm.

22. *Final Long Term 1 Enhanced Surface Water Treatment Rule*, 67 FR 1812 (January 14, 2002); *Final Long Term 1 Enhanced Surface Water Treatment Rule*, USEPA 815-F-02-001 (January 2002), http://www.epa.gov/safewater/mdbp/lt1eswtr_fact.html.

23. *Water Treatment: WSO Series* (Denver: American Water Works Association, 2003).

CHAPTER 4 — RADIATION PROTECTION

1. "Fact Sheet on the Three Mile Island Accident," United States Nuclear Regulatory Commission, 2009, http://www.nrc.gov/reading-rm/doc-collections/fact-sheets/3mile-isle.html.

2. "Fact Sheet: How Big Is a Picocurie?" U.S. Army Corps of Engineers, Formerly Utilized Sites Remedial Action Program, http://www.lrb.usace.army.mil/fusrap/docs/fusrap-fs-picocurie.pdf.

3. "Radiation Exposure from Iodine 131: Standards and Regulations," Agency for Toxic Substances and Disease Registry, http://www.atsdr.cdc.gov/csem/iodine/standards_regulations.html.

4. Ralph E. Lapp, "Thoughts on Nuclear Plumbing," *New York Times*, December 12, 1971.

5. "Mountain of Trouble: Mr. Obama Defunds the Nuclear Repository at Yucca Mountain. Now What?" *Washington Post*, March 8, 2009.

6. *15 Years after Chernobyl Disaster*, Committee on the Problems of the Consequences of the Catastrophe at the Chernobyl (Minsk, 2001), 5–6; *Mail Table of Official Data on the Reactor Accident* (Kiev: Chernobyl Interinform Agency, 2007).

7. Claudia Clark, *Radium Girls: Women and Industrial Health Reform, 1910–1935* (Chapel Hill: University of North Carolina Press, 1997).

8. R. Mullner, *Deadly Glow: The Radium Dial Worker Tragedy* (Washington, D.C.: American Public Health Association, 1999).

9. *Health Consultation: U.S. Radium Corporation, Orange, Essex County, New Jersey*, CERCLIS no. NJD980654172, prepared by the New Jersey Department of Health and Senior Services, Consumer and Environmental Health Services, under Cooperative Agreement with the Agency for Toxic Substances and Disease Registry, June 2, 1997, http://state.nj.us/health/eoh/hhazweb/radpt1.pdf.

10. Richard Rhodes, *The Making of the Atomic Bomb* (New York: Simon and Schuster, 1986).

11. "Former Military Sites of New Jersey," U.S. Army Corps of Engineers, http://aesop.rutgers.edu/~humeco/morren/NJ_FORMER_MIL_FAC.DOC.

12. *Public Health Assessment: Boeing Michigan Aeronautical Research Center/McGuire Missile, New Egypt, Ocean County, New Jersey (EPA Facility Id: NJ2570026268)* September 23, 2002, prepared by the Agency for Toxic Substances and Disease Registry, Division of Health Assessment and Consultation, Federal Facilities Assessment Branch (Washington, D.C., 2002).

13. See note 9, above.

14. *EPA Superfund Record of Decision: Montclair/West Orange Radium Site, EPA ID: NJD980785653, OU 03, Montclair/West Orange, NJ 06/01/1990*, USEPA/ROD/R02–90/126, http://epa.gov/superfund/sites/rods.

15. Leonard A. Cole, *Elements of Risk: The Politics of Radon* (Washington, D.C.: American Association for the Advancement of Science Press, 1993).

16. Commissioner Richard Dewling, *The Record* (Hackensack, N.J.), June 14, 1987.

17. Thomas M. Gerusky, *The Pennsylvania Radon Story*, Pennsylvania Department of Environmental Resources, Bureau of Radiation Protection, Radon Division, http://www.dep.state.pa.us/brp/Radon_Division/PA_Radon_Story1.htm.

18. Jamie Murphy, "The Colorless Odorless Killer," *Time*, April 12, 2005.

19. *New Jersey Radon Laws*, N.J. Pub. L. 1985, chap. 408, January 10, 1986; and N.J. Pub. L. 1986, chap. 83, August 14, 1986 (NJSA 26:20 et seq. and NJAC 7:28).

20. Donald A. Deieso, "An Overview of the Radon Issue in New Jersey," in *Radon and the Environment*, ed. William Makofske and Michael Edelstein (Mahwah, N.J.: Institute for Environmental Studies, Ramapo College of New Jersey, 1987).

21. Susan H. Roberts, "National Radon Meeting Highlights: Radon Leaders Saving Lives," *Alabama Quarterly Report and Newsletter* 10, no. 4 (2007), http://www.aces.edu/department/family/radon/publications/newsletters/NEWS_Q4_2007.pdf.

CHAPTER 5 — ENVIRONMENTAL CRIME

1. D. D. McKean, *The Boss: The Hague Machine in Action* (New York: Russell and Russell, 1967).

2. *Resource Conservation and Recovery Act (RCRA)*, U.S. Code 42 (1976), §§6901–6992k; *USEPA Waste Management Regulations* are codified at *Code of Federal Regulations*, title 40, pts. 239–282.

3. Alex Nussbaum and Tom Troncone, "Big Profits from Illegal Dumping; Now We're Paying," *The Record* (Hackensack, N.J.), October 5, 2005.

4. Alan A. Block and Frank R. Scarpitti, *Poisoning for Profit: The Mafia and Toxic Waste in America* (New York: Morrow, 1985).

5. Ralph Blumenthal, "Mob Funds Traced in Toxic Waste Plant's Takeover," *New York Times*, January 4, 1981.

6. Alan A. Block, "Environmental Crime and Pollution: Wasteful Reflections," *Social Justice* 29, nos. 1–2 (2002): 61–81.

7. Testimony of Maurice D. Hinchey, chairman, New York State Assembly Standing Committee on Environmental Conservation, *Criminal Infiltration of the Toxic and Solid Waste Disposal Industries in New York State* (Albany: September 13, 1984); Alan A. Block, ed., *The Business of Crime: A Documentary Study of Organized Crime in the American Economy* (Boulder, Colo.: Westview Press, 1991), 175–196.

8. New Jersey Department of Environmental Protection, "Hudson County Chromate Chemical Production Waste Sites," http://www.state.nj.us/dep/srp/siteinfo/chrome/bkgrnd.htm.

9. T. Burke et al., "Chromite Ore Processing Residue in Hudson County, New Jersey," *Environmental Health Perspectives* 92 (May 1991): 131–137.

10. "Death Blamed on Chromium," *Jersey City Reporter*, November 6, 1988.

11. *Chromium, Environmental Health Criteria* (Geneva: World Health Organization, 1988), 61; S. Langard, "One Hundred Years of Chromium and Cancer, A Review of Epidemiologic Evidence and Selected Case Reports," *American Journal of Industrial Medicine* 17, no. 2 (1990): 189–215.

12. Maria Newman, "Court Orders Honeywell to Clean Up 34-Acre Site," *New York Times*, May 17, 2003.

13. Ken Thorbourne, "Paydirt! Chromium Cleanup Begins after 11-Year Legal Fight," *Jersey Journal* (Hudson County), April 4, 2006; "Allied-Signal Agrees to Clean Up Chromium Site," *New York Times*, November 26, 1992.

14. Peter J. Sampson, "Class Action Chromium Lawsuit: Judge Approves Class-Action Suit, Ball Field in Jersey City Contained Toxic Waste," Wilentz, Goldman and Spitzer, P.A., http://www.wilentzpersonalinjurylawyers.com/press/articles/article_chromium_contamination_lawsuit.html.

15. Anthony DePalma, "Finding the Bottom of a Polluted Field," *New York Times*, February 5, 2006.

16. New Jersey Department of Environmental Protection, *New Jersey Chromium Workgroup Report*, 2005, http://www.state.nj.us/dep/dsr/chromium/report.htm.

17. "DEP to Begin Cleanup at Three Jersey City Chrome Sites: Attorney General Files Suit Naming Honeywell, Occidental Petroleum, and PPG Industries Liable for 106 Sites in Hudson, Essex Counties," New Jersey Department of Environmental Protection press release, May 3, 2005.

18. P. J. Lioy et al., "Micro Environmental Analysis of Residential Exposure to Chromium-Laden Wastes in and around New Jersey Homes," *Risk Analysis* 12, no. 2 (1992): 287–299; N. C. Freeman et al., "Exposure to Chromium Dust from Homes in a Chromium Surveillance Project," *Archives of Environmental and Occupational Health* 52, no. 3 (1997): 213–219.

19. Paul J. Lioy et al., *Chromium Exposure and Health Effects in Hudson County: Phase I*," report to New Jersey Department of Environmental Protection, submitted by UMDNJ-Robert Wood Johnson Medical School and Environmental and Occupational Health Sciences Institute, November 24, 2008; *Analysis of Lung Cancer Incidence near Chromium-Contaminated Sites in Jersey City: A Citizen's Guide, Jersey City, Hudson County, NJ,* report to New Jersey Department of Environmental Protection, submitted by UMDNJ-Robert

Wood Johnson Medical School and Environmental and Occupational Health Sciences Institute, October 2008, http://www.state.nj.us/dep/dsr/chromium/cit%20guide.pdf.

20. *Citizens Guide to Chromium Exposure and Health Effects Dust Study*, New Jersey Department of Environmental Protection, Division of Science, Research, and Technology (2008), http://www.state.nj.us/dep/dsr/chromium/chromium_dust_citizen_guide.pdf.

21. *Health Consultation: Analysis of Lung Cancer Incidence near Chromium-Contaminated Sites in New Jersey (a/k/a Hudson County Chromium Sites) Jersey City, Hudson County, New Jersey*, U.S. Department of Health and Human Services, Public Health Service Agency for Toxic Substances and Disease Registry, Division of Health Assessment and Consultation, (Washington, D.C., 2008).

22. *Technical Fact Sheet for Chromium Hazards and Alternatives*, U.S. Environmental Protection Agency, Region 5, USEPA 905-F-00-027 (Washington, D.C., 2000).

23. "Toxic Chromium Clean-Up Battle in Jersey City Heads to Federal Court, Lawsuit against PPG Follows Successful $400 Million Case against Honeywell," Natural Resources Defense Council, Newark, N.J., press release, February 3, 2009.

24. Wright quoted in Amy Sara, "File Chromium Suit; Accord 'Near,'" *Jersey Journal* (Hudson County), February 4, 2009.

25. "Attorney General, DEP Announce Settlement with PPG; Agreement Means Clean-Up of Chromium Sites in Hudson County," New Jersey Department of Environmental Protection, press release, February 19, 2009.

26. Ted Sherman, "As the Rivers Suffered, Firms Changed Hands," *Star-Ledger*, June 24, 2008.

CHAPTER 6 — ENVIRONMENTAL WARFARE

1. Thomas H. Kean, *The Politics of Inclusion* (New York: Free Press, 1988). All of the following quotes about the dioxin emergency are from this source.

2. *Technical Requirements for Site Remediation—Last Amended September 2, 2008* New Jersey Department of Environmental Protection, 2009, *New Jersey Administrative Code*, title 7, subchap. 26E, http://www.nj.gov/dep/srp/regs/techrule/techr1oo.pdf.

3. A. Poland and A. Kende, "2,3,7,8-Tetrachlorodibenzo-p-Dioxin: Environmental Contaminant and Molecular Probe," *Federal Proceedings* 35, no. 2 (1976): 2,404–2,411; R. D. Kimbrough et al., "Health Implications of 2,3,7,8-Tetrachlorodibenzodioxin (TCDD) Contamination of Residential Soil," *Journal of Toxicology and Environmental Health* 14, no. 1 (1984): 47–93; *Toxicological Profile for Chlorinated Dibenzo-p-Dioxins*, U.S. Department of Health and Human Services, Agency for Toxic Substances and Disease Registry (Washington, D.C., 1998).

4. *Veterans and Agent Orange; Update 2004*, National Academy of Sciences, Institute of Medicine (Washington, D.C., 2004).

5. T. J. Belton et al., *A Study of Dioxin (2,3,7,8-TCDD) Contamination in Select Finfish, Crustaceans and Sediments of New Jersey Waterways*, (New Jersey Department of Environmental Protection, technical report (Trenton, 1985).

6. Michael A. Kamrin et al., "Taking the Risk out of Reporting Risk Assessment," in *Reporting on Risk: A Journalist's Handbook on Environmental Risk Assessment* (Ann Arbor, Mich.: Foundation for American Communications and the National Sea Grant College Program, 1995).

7. C. Rappe et al., "Levels and Patterns of PCDD and PCDF Contamination in Fish, Crabs and Lobsters from Newark Bay and the New York Bight," *Chemosphere* 22 (1991): 239–266.

8. T. J. Belton et al., *2,3,7,8-Tetrachlorodibenzo-p-Dioxin (TCDD) and 2,3,7,8-Tetrachlorodibenzo-p-Furan (TCDF) In Blue Crabs and American Lobsters from the New York Bight*, New Jersey Department of Environmental Protection, Division of Science and

Research (Trenton, 1988); P. Hague et al., "Dioxin (2,3,7,8-TCDD) and Furans (2,3,7,8-TCDF) in Blue Crabs and American Lobsters from the Hudson Raritan Estuary and the New York Bight," *Bulletin of Environmental Contamination and Toxicology* 52 (1994): 734–741.

9. R. F. Bopp et al., "A Major Incident of Dioxin Contamination: Sediments of New Jersey Estuaries," *Environmental Science and Technology* 25 (1991): 951–956; D. A. Chaky, *Polychlorinated Biphenyls, Polychlorinated Dibenzo-p-Dioxins and Furans in the New York Metropolitan Area: Interpreting Atmospheric Deposition and Sediment Chronologies* (Ph.D. diss., Rensselaer Polytechnic Institute, 2003).

10. *Ocean Dumping Ban Act of 1988, U.S. Code*, title 33, chap. 27; *United States Public Vessel Medical Waste Anti-Dumping Act of 1988, U.S. Code*, title 33, chap. 38.

11. "Record of Decision for Diamond Shamrock Superfund Site, Essex County, New Jersey," U.S. Environmental Protection Agency (Washington, D.C., 1987); NPL Fact Sheet for Diamond Alkali Co., U.S. Environmental Protection Agency, 2006, http://www.epa.gov/Region2/superfund/npl/0200613c.pdf.

12. Alexander Lanes, "A Long Poisonous Wait: As Dioxin Spreads through State Waterways, the DEP Accuses Two Firms of Intentionally Avoiding a Long-Mandated Cleanup," *Star-Ledger* (Newark, N.J.), August 6, 2006.

13. Timothy J. Iannuzzi et al., eds., *A Common Tragedy: History of an Urban River* (Amherst, Mass.: Amherst Scientific Publishers, 2002).

14. *The Lower Passaic River Restoration Project*, U.S. Environmental Protection Agency, 2008, http://www.epa.gov/region2/superfund/npl/diamondalkali; Brian T. Murray, "Cleanup to Begin on a River Befouled: A Stretch of Passaic Being Dredged in 2010," *Star–Ledger* (Newark, N.J.), January 12, 2009.

15. "Lower Passaic River Restoration Project—Fact Sheet," U.S. Environmental Protection Agency, 2008, http://www.nan.usace.army.mil/project/newjers/factsh/pdf/lowerpass.pdf.

16. *An Inventory of Sources and Environmental Releases of Dioxin-Like Compounds in the United States for the Years 1987, 1995 and 2000*, USEPA/600/P-03/002F, U.S. Environmental Protection Agency (Washington, D.C., 2006).

CHAPTER 7 — THE LURE OF BROWNFIELDS

1. Buckminster Fuller, *Operating Manual for Spaceship Earth* (New York: E. P. Dutton, 1963).

2. *Comprehensive Environmental Response, Compensation, and Liability Act (CERCLA)* (December 11, 1980), *U.S. Code* title 42, chap. 103, subchap. I.

3. *New Jersey Environmental Cleanup Responsibility Act of 1983*, NJSA 13:1K-6 to 13.

4. *New Jersey Industrial Site Recovery Act of 1993*, NJSA 13:1K and NJAC 7:26B.

5. James, Lloyd, and Hughes quoted in Charles Strum, "New Jersey Moves to Standardize the Cleanup of Toxic Waste," *New York Times*, December 8, 1991.

6. Florio quoted in *HazNews*, August 1, 1993.

7. United States *"Brownfields and Land Revitalization,"* EPA 560-F-04-258, U.S. Environmental Protection Agency (Washington, D.C., 2008).

8. *Small Business Liability Relief and Brownfields Revitalization Act*, NJSA 58:10B-1 et seq.

9. *New Jersey Brownfield and Contaminated Site Remediation Act (BCSRA) of 1998*, NJSA 58:10B-1.1 et seq.

10. "Known Contaminated Sites in Jersey Reports," New Jersey Department of Environmental Protection, http://www.nj.gov/dep/srp/kcs-nj.

11. Edward F. McTiernan, "The Role of Institutional Controls in Brownfield Redevelopment," paper presented at Brownfields 2000 Research and Regionalism: Revitalizing the American Community, October 11–13, 2000.

12. H. Gillette Jr., *Camden after the Fall* (Philadelphia: University of Pennsylvania Press, 2005).

13. Camden Church Studio—The Recording Studio of Victor Talking Machine Company, http://www.stokowski.org/Camden%20Church%20Studio%20Recording%20Location.htm.

14. Michael R. Greenberg, "Reversing Urban Decay: Brownfield Redevelopment and Environmental Health," *Environmental Health Perspectives* 111, no. 2 (February 2003): 111.

15. M. Greenberg, "Brownfield Redevelopment and Affordable Housing: A Case Study of New Jersey," *Housing Policy Debate* 12, no. 3 (2001): 515–540.

CHAPTER 8 — ENVIRONMENTAL JUSTICE

1. George Prowell, *The History of Camden County* (Philadelphia: R. L. Richards, 1986), http://www.keltaskavern.com/camden/cramerhill.html.

2. *Camden Strategic Revitalization Plan*, Economic Recovery Board for Camden, July 2003, http://www.camdenerb.com/srp_final/CamdenSRP_July03.pdf.

3. McGreevey quoted in Jack Lyne, "$1.1B Redevelopment Targets Camden, N.J., One of Nation's Poorest Cities," The Site Selection, January 5, 2004, http://www.siteselection.com/ssinsider/snapshot/sf040105.htm. See also Office of the Governor, press release, June 13, 2002, "McGreevey Announces Backing of Plan to Revitalize Camden: Camden Plan Stresses Economic Development, Public Safety, Fiscal Accountability and Infrastructure Improvements."

4. The Cramer Hill Study Area Redevelopment Plan was approved by the Camden City Planning Board on May 18, 2004. The Camden City Council approved the plan twice in 2004. However, because of questions about which City Council members could vote on the plan, an additional vote was required. In July 2005, Council approved the plan, 4–2. The plan was subsequently voided by a State Superior Court judge on a technicality.

5. The Municipal Rehabilitation and Economic Recovery Act (MRERA) restructured Camden, New Jersey's governance and created a five-year recovery period in which the city would be run by a chief operating officer. The initial legislation was enacted in July 2002. Following several lawsuits, MRERA was amended in December 2002. MRERA also included $175 million in funds for capital projects to be administered by the State Economic Recovery Board. On June 21, 2007, the state legislature approved legislation (Bill A4129) that extended state oversight and the term of the chief operating officer, but did not provide additional funding for projects in Camden. However, the city would continue to receive special state aid to balance its operating budget.

6. "Camden Officials Withdraw Cramer Hill Redevelopment Plan," South Jersey Legal Services press release, May 25, 2006, http://www.lsc.gov/press/updates_2006_detail_T160_R13.php.

7. *Cramer Hill Community Benefits Survey*, report prepared by CAMConnect, April 2006, http://www.cramerhillcdc.org/CHCDC_survey.pdf.

8. "Environmental Justice Policy," New Jersey Executive Order no. 96, February 19, 2004, http://www.nj.gov/dep/ej/ejeo.pdf.

9. Eileen McGurty, *Transforming Environmentalism* (New Brunswick, N.J.: Rutgers University Press, 2009).

10. *Siting of Hazardous Waste Landfills and Their Correlation with Racial and Economic Status of Surrounding Communities* (GAO/RCED-83–168), General Accounting Office (Washington, D.C., 1983).

11. Charles Lee, *Proceedings: The First National People of Color Environmental Leadership Summit* (Cleveland, Ohio: United Church of Christ Commission for Racial Justice, 1992).

12. "Federal Actions to Address Environmental Justice in Minority Populations and Low-Income Populations," Executive Order no. 12898, February 11, 1994, http:// www.epa.gov/oswer/ej/html-doc/execordr.htm.

13. Laura Mansnerus, "A Governor Resigns: Overview; McGreevey Steps Down after Disclosing a Gay Affair," *New York Times*, August 13, 2004.

14. Environmental Justice Web site, New Jersey Department of Environmental Protection, http://www.nj.gov/dep/ej.

15. "Camden Enforcement Initiative," New Jersey Department of Environmental Protection, http://www.state.nj.us/dep/enforcement/camden.pdf.

16. *Camden Waterfront South Report (Jan. 2002–Dec. 2005) and Action Plan*, Environmental Justice Task Force, January 12, 2006, http://www.nj.gov/dep/ej/docs/ camden_report20060223.pdf.

17. A. Haynes and B. D. Smedley, *The Unequal Burden of Cancer* (Washington D.C.: National Academy Press, 1999).

18. *Asthma in New Jersey*, New Jersey Department of Health and Senior Services (Trenton, 2003).

19. "Camden Waterfront South Air Toxics Pilot Project," New Jersey Department of Environmental Protection and Environmental Justice Task Force, 2006, http://www .nj.gov/dep/ej/camden/index.html.

20. *South Camden Citizens in Action et al. v. NJ Department of Environmental Protection*, U.S. District Court, District of New Jersey, Docket no. 01-CV-702, 14–15, 27.

21. Phyllis Holmes, "South Camden Warriors Battle Environmental Racism: An Interview with Phyllis Holmes," interview by Robert D. Bullard, Camden, N.J., June 19, 2001, for the Environmental Justice Resource Center, Clark Atlanta University, http:// www.ejrc.cau.edu/camdeninterview.html).

22. *Alexander v. Sandoval*, 121 S. Ct. 1511 (2001).

23. K. Newman, "A History of the Places We Don't Know: Putting Camden on the Map," book review of *Camden after the Fall*, by H. Gillette Jr., in *New Jersey History Book Reviews*, April 2006.

24. H. Gillette Jr., *Camden after the Fall* (Philadelphia: University of Pennsylvania Press, 2005).

25. Robert Caro, *The Power Broker: Robert Moses and the Fall of New York*, (New York: Knopf, 1974).

26. Joel Rast, "Environmental Justice and the New Regionalism," *Journal of Planning Education and Research* 25, no. 3 (2006): 249–263.

27. Howard Gillette Jr., "The Wages of Disinvestment," in *Beyond the Ruins: The Meanings of Deindustrialization*, ed. Jefferson R. Cowie and Joseph Heathcott, 140–158 (Ithaca, N.Y.: ILR Press, 2003).

28. Foster Church, "Can Nevada Keep America's Sizzling Nuclear Waste out of Its Backyard?" *Governing* (April 1990): 21–24.

29. D. R. Faber and E. J. Kreig, "Unequal Exposure to Ecological Hazards: Environmental Injustices in the Commonwealth of Massachusetts," *Environmental Health Perspectives* 110, suppl. 2 (2002): 277–288.

30. *Brownfields Title VI: Case Studies, Environmental Protection Agency*, USEPA 500-R-99–003 (Washington, D.C., 1999), http://www.epa.gov/brownfields.

31. National Environmental Justice Advisory Council, *Unintended Impacts of Redevelopment and Revitalization Efforts in Five Environmental Justice Communities* (Washington, D.C., 2006).

32. J. S. Litt, N. L. Tyan, and T. Burke, "Examining Urban Brownfields through the Public Health Macroscope," *Environmental Health Perspectives* 110, suppl. 2, (2002): 183–193.

CHAPTER 9 — THE WOODLANDS

1. Richard H. Widmann, *Forests of the Garden State*, U.S. Department of Agriculture, Forest Service, Northeastern Research Station, resource bulletin NE-163 (Washington, D.C., 2005).

2. *Pinelands Protection Act*, NJSA 13:18A-1 et seq., June 28, 1979. *NJ Pinelands National Reserve*, Public Law 95-625, *U.S. Statutes at Large* 92 (1978): 3467 and codified in scattered sections of *U.S. Code* 16.

3. "International Biosphere Reserve Designation," United Nations Educational, Scientific and Cultural Organization, 1983, http://www.unesco.org/mabdb/br/brdir/directory/biores.asp?mode=all&code=USA+4.

4. *Pinelands Comprehensive Management Plan*, NJSA 13:18A-1 et seq. R.1981 d.13, effective January 14, 1981, updated October 2006, http://www.state.nj.us/pinelands/cmp.

5. Cartica quoted in Anthony DePalma, "New Jersey Acts to Save a Pygmy Forest of Pine and Oak," *New York Times*, December 8, 1989.

6. *Prescribed Burning in NJ Forests*," New Jersey Department of Environmental Protection, N.J. Forest Fire Service, NJSA title 13, and as specified in the N.J. Air Pollution Control Code, title 7, subchap. 27.

7. *A Guide for Prescribed Fire in the Southern Forests*, National Wildfire Coordinating Group and U.S. Forest Service (Washington, D.C., 1989).

8. Richard G. Jones and Nate Schweber, "Fire Spotlights Concerns of Living near Fighter Jets," *New York Times*, May 17, 2007.

9. J. Dighton and R. A. Skeffington, "Effects of Artificial Acid Precipitation on the Mycorrhizas of Scots Pine Seedlings," *New Phytologist* 107 (1987): 191–202.

10. A. E. Jansen and J. Dighton, "Effects of Air Pollutants on Ectomycorrhizas," Secretariat of the Commission of Environmental Cooperation (CEC) Air Pollution Research Report 30 (Montreal, 1990).

11. A. R. Tuininga et al., "Burn, Moisture, and Litter Quality Effects on N, P, and K Uptake by Pitch Pine (*Pinus rigida*) Seedlings in a Greenhouse Study," *Soil Biology and Biochemistry* 34 (2002): 865–873; A. R. Tuininga and J. Dighton, "Changes in Ectomycorrhizal Communities and Nutrient Availability Following Prescribed Burning in Two Upland Pine-Oak Forests in the New Jersey Pine Barrens," *Canadian Journal of Forest Research* 43 (2004): 1,755–1,765.

12. *NOx: How Nitrogen Oxides Affect the Way We Live and Breathe*, U.S. Environmental Protection Agency, Office of Air Quality Planning and Standards, USEPA-456/F-98-005 (Washington, D.C., 1998).

13. *2002 Annual Summary*, National Atmospheric Deposition Program, NADP Program Office, Illinois State Water Survey, 2002, http://nadp.sws.uiuc.edu/lib/data/2002as.pdf.

14. J. Dighton et al., "Impacts of Atmospheric Deposition on New Jersey Pine Barrens Forest Soils and Communities of Ectomycorrhizae," *Forestry Ecology and Management* 201 (2004): 131–144.

CHAPTER 10 — THE BIOTIC MOSAIC

1. R. A. Zampella et al., *The Rancocas Creek Basin: A Report to the Pinelands Commission on the Status of Selected Aquatic and Wetland Resources* (New Lisbon: New Jersey Pinelands Commission, 2003); R. A. Zampella et al., *The Great Egg Harbor River Watershed Management Area: A Report to the Pinelands Commission on the Status of Selected Aquatic and Wetland Resources* (New Lisbon: New Jersey Pinelands Commission, 2005).

2. Jeremy Pearce, "Trouble in Paradise," *New York Times*, June 23, 2002.

3. Jackson-Gould and Montgomery quoted in Debra Galant, "Your Friend, the Endangered Timber Rattler," *New York Times*, January 6, 2002.

4. K. J. Laidig and D. M. Golden, *Assessing Timber Rattlesnake Movements near a Residential Development and Locating New Hibernacula in the New Jersey Pinelands* (New Lisbon: New Jersey Pinelands Commission, 2004).

5. "Commission Approves Ocean Acres Ordinance, Authorizes Sanctuary Agreement Measures Will Protect Endangered Pine Snakes at Two Pinelands Housing Developments," press release, New Jersey Pinelands Commission, November 12, 2004.

6. Rachel Carson, *Silent Spring* (Boston: Houghton Mifflin, 1962).

7. L. Niles et al., "Status of Bald Eagle Nesting in New Jersey," *Records of NJ Birds* 17, no. 1 (1991): 2–5.

8. L. Smith and K. Clark, *New Jersey Bald Eagle Project, 2008*, New Jersey Department of Environmental Protection, Division of Fish and Wildlife, Endangered and Nongame Species Program (Trenton, 2008).

9. L. J. Niles et al., *Status of the Red Knot* (Calidris canutus rufa) *in the Western Hemisphere*, prepared for the U.S. Fish and Wildlife Service, Ecological Services, Region 5, New Jersey Field Office, May 2007, http://www.fws.gov/northeast/redknot.

10. *Horseshoe Crab Technical Committee Report*, Virginia Tech Horseshoe Crab Research Center, updates to the Atlantic States Marine Fisheries Commission, January 17, 2008, http//:www.asmfc.org/speciesDocuments/horseshoeCrab/meetingsummaries/tc/hscTC ReportJan08.pdf.

11. Fisher and DiDomenico quoted in Robert Strauss, "In a Legal Tug of War, It's Bird vs. Crab Egg," *New York Times*, March 2, 2008.

12. "Governor Signs Moratorium on Harvesting Horseshoe Crabs: Preservation of Food Supply for Red Knots Will Prevent Extinction," State of New Jersey press release, March 25, 2008, http://www.state.nj.us/dep/newsrel.

13. *New Jersey—Municipal Land Use Law*, NJSA 40:55D-1 et seq.

14. G. Hardin, "The Tragedy of the Commons," *Science* 162 (1968): 1,243–1,248.

15. *Surface Water Quality Standards (SWQS), New Jersey Administrative Code*, 7:9B, http://www.nj.gov/dep/rules.

16. *Biological Criteria; National Program Guidance for Surface Waters*, U.S. Environmental Protection Agency, Office of Water and Regulatory Standards, Criteria and Standards Division (Washington, D.C., 1990).

17. J. Kurtenbach, "A Method for Rapid Bioassessment of Streams in New Jersey Using Benthic Macroinvertebrates," *Bulletin of the North American Benthological Society* 8, no. 1 (1990): 129.

18. M. T. Barbour et al., *Rapid Bioassessment Protocols for Use in Streams and Wadeable Rivers: Periphyton, Benthic Macroinvertebrates and Fish*, 2nd ed., USEPA 841-B-99–002, U.S. Environmental Protection Agency, Office of Water (Washington, D.C., 1999), http://www.epa.gov/OWOW/monitoring/techmon.html.

19. J. R. Karr and D. R. Dudley, "Ecological Perspective on Water Quality Goals," *Environmental Management* 5, no. 1 (1981): 55–68; J. R. Karr et al., *Assessing Biological Integrity in Running Waters: A Method and Its Rationale* (Chicago: Illinois Natural History Survey Special Publication 5, 1986).

20. New Jersey Department of Environmental Protection, Water Monitoring and Standards, Bureau of Freshwater and Biological Monitoring, "Publications," http://www.state.nj.us/dep/wmm/bfbm/publications.html.

21. W. J. Mates and J. L. Reyes, *The Economic Value of New Jersey State Parks and Forests*, New Jersey Department of Environmental Protection, Division of Science Research and Technology (Trenton, 2004, revised 2006).

22. *Valuing New Jersey's Natural Capital: An Assessment of the Economic Value of the State's Natural Resources*, New Jersey Department of Environmental Protection, Division of Science Research and Technology, April 2007, http://www.state.nj.us/dep/dsr/naturalcap.

23. C. Raffensberger and J. Tickner, eds., *Protecting Public Health and the Environment: Implementing the Precautionary Principle* (Washington, D.C.: Island Press, 1999).

24. Janna G. Koppe and Kane Keys, "PCBs and the Precautionary Principle," in *Late Lessons from Early Warnings: The Precautionary Principle 1896–2000*" (Copenhagen: European Environment Agency, 2001).

25. B. D. Goldstein and R. S. Carruth, "Implications of the Precautionary Principle: Is It a Threat?" *International Journal of Occupational Medicine and Environmental Health* 17, no. 1 (2004): 153–161.

26. Minton quoted in Sandy Bauers, "Biologists Hopeful Red Knots Have Turned a Corner," *Philadelphia Inquirer*, June 3, 2009.

27. R. K. Pachauri and A. Reisinger, eds., *Climate Change 2007: Synthesis Report*, contribution of Working Groups I, II, and III to the Fourth Assessment Report of the Intergovernmental Panel on Climate Change (Geneva: IPCC, 2007).

CHAPTER 11 — HEADWATERS AND WATERSHEDS

1. A. N. Strahler, "Hypsometric (Area Altitude) Analysis of Erosional Topology," *Geological Society of America Bulletin* 63 (1952): 1,117–1,142.

2. W. H. Lowe and G. E. Likens, "Moving Headwater Streams to the Head of the Class," *BioScience* 55, no. 3 (March 2005): 196–197.

3. J. P. Kurtenbach, *Index of Biotic Integrity Study of Northern New Jersey Drainages*, U.S. Environmental Protection Agency, Region 2, Division of Environmental Assessment (Edison, N.J., 1994).

4. R. J. Horwitz, "Temporal Variability Patterns and the Distributional Patterns of Stream Fishes," *Ecological Monographs* 48 (1978): 307–321.

5. Isaac J. Schlosser, "Environmental Variation, Life History Attributes, and Community Structure in Stream Fishes: Implications for Environmental Management and Assessment," *Environmental Management* 14, no. 5 (1990): 621–628.

6. David Holdich, ed., *The Biology of Freshwater Crayfish* (Ames, Iowa: Blackwell Scientific Press, 2002).

7. Jackie Gessner and Eric Stiles, *Field Guide to Reptiles and Amphibians of New Jersey*, New Jersey Department of Environmental Protection, Division of Fish and Wildlife, Endangered and Nongame Species Program, 2001, http://www.state.nj.us/dep/fgw/ensp/pdf/salmandr.pdf.

8. Richard J. Horwitz, *Development of an Integrated Biotic Index for Headwater Streams in New Jersey Based on Fish, Crayfish, and Salamanders: Phase II*, Patrick Center for Environmental Research, Academy of Natural Sciences of Philadelphia, prepared for New Jersey Department of Environmental Protection, Division of Science Research and Technology (Trenton, 2007).

9. *Draft: Statewide Watershed Management Framework Document for the State of New Jersey*, New Jersey Department of Environmental Protection, Office of Environmental Planning, January 1997, http://www.nj.gov/dep/watershedmgt/DOCS/pdfs/FRAME97fixed.pdf.

10. *Atmospheric Deposition Network*, New Jersey Department of Environmental Protection, http://www.state.nj.us/dep/dsr/njadn.

11. *Comparative Risk Project*, New Jersey Department of Environmental Protection, http://www.state.nj.us/dep/dsr/njcrp.

12. *Watershed Characterization and Assessment Reports*, New Jersey Department of Environmental Protection, http://www.nj.gov/dep/watershedmgt/publications.htm.

13. *Development of Wetland Quality and Function Assessment Tools and Demonstration*, New Jersey Department of Environmental Protection, http://www.state.nj.us/dep/dsr/wetlands2/report.pdf.

14. *Brown Tide Assessment*, New Jersey Department of Environmental Protection, http://www.state.nj.us/dep/dsr/browntide/bt.htm.

15. *Surface Water Quality Standards (SWQS), New Jersey Administrative Code*, 7:9B, http://www.nj.gov/dep/rules.

16. *Nutrient Criteria Development; Notice of Ecoregional Nutrient Criteria, Federal Register* 68, no. 3 (January 2003).

17. R. Patrick, "Some Diatoms of the Great Salt Lake as Indicators of Present and Geological Water Conditions," *Biological Bulletin*, 69, no. 2 (1935): 338.

18. R. Patrick, "Is Water Our Next Crisis?" *Proceedings of the American Philosophical Society* 138, no. 3 (1994): 371–376.

19. R. Patrick, "The Development of the Science of Aquatic Ecosystems," *Annual Review of Energy and the Environment* 22 (1997): 1–11.

20. E. F. Stoermer and John P. Smol, eds., *The Diatoms* (Cambridge: Cambridge University Press, 2001).

21. K. C. Ponader et al., "Diatom-Based TP and TN Inference Models and Indices for Monitoring Nutrient Enrichment of New Jersey Streams," *Ecological Indicators* 7 (2007): 79–93; K. C. Ponader et al., "Total Phosphorus Inference Models and Indices for Coastal Plain Streams Based on Benthic Diatom Assemblages from Artificial Substrates," *Hydrobiologia* 610, no. 1 (2008): 139–152.

22. *Wetlands Regulatory Authority*, U.S. Environmental Protection Agency, Office of Water, EPA 843-F-04-001 (Washington, D.C., 2004).

23. *Wetlands Overview*, U.S. Environmental Protection Agency, Office of Water, EPA 843-F-04-011a (Washington, D.C., 2004); "Section 404 of the Clean Water Act: How Wetlands Are Defined and Identified," U.S. Environmental Protection Agency, 2008, http://www.epa.gov/owow/wetlands/facts/fact11.html.

24. *Army Corps of Engineers Wetlands Delineation Manual, Technical Report Y-87–1*, Department of the Army, Waterways Experiment Station, Corps of Engineers (Washington, D.C., 1987); *Federal Manual for Identifying and Delineating Jurisdictional Wetlands*, interagency cooperative publication: U.S. Environmental Protection Agency, Fish and Wildlife Service and Department of the Army and Soil Conservation Service (Washington, D.C.,1989).

25. *New Jersey Freshwater Wetlands Protection Act*, NJSA 13:9B-2; *Guide to New Jersey's Freshwater Wetlands Permitting Program*, New Jersey Department of Environmental Protection, Land Use Regulation Program (Trenton, 1999).

26. *New Jersey Administrative Code—Section 7:7A, Appendix 1*, New Jersey Department of Environmental Protection, Land Use Regulation Program, 2002.

27. "Red List of Threatened Species—Amphibians," International Union for Conservation of Nature, http://www.globalamphibians.org; S. Stuart et al., "Status and Trends of Amphibian Declines and Extinctions Worldwide," *Science* 306 (2004): 1,783–1,786.

28. "Freshwater Wetlands Vernal Habitat Protocol (Updated 05/17/02)," New Jersey Department of Environmental Protection, 2002, http://www.state.nj.us/dep/landuse/forms/vernalpr.pdf.

29. Richard G. Lathrop et al., "Statewide Mapping and Assessment of Vernal Pools: A New Jersey Case Study," *Journal of Environmental Management* 76 (2005): 230–238. For the online maps, see CRSSA, "Mapping New Jersey's Vernal Pools," http://www.dbcrssa.rutgers.edu/ims/vernal.

30. *Rapanos v. United States*, 547 U.S. 715 (2006).

31. "Corps and EPA Responses to the *Rapanos* Decision: Key Questions for Guidance Release," U.S. Environmental Protection Agency, 2000, http://www.epa.gov/owow/wetlands/pdf/13RapanosQ&As.pdf.

CHAPTER 12 — COASTAL NEW JERSEY AND RISING WATERS

1. Norbert P. Psuty and Douglas D. Ofiara, *Coastal Hazard Management: Lessons and Future Directions from New Jersey* (New Brunswick, N.J.: Rutgers University Press, 2002).

2. S. C. Farrell et al., *New Jersey Beach Profile Network Annual Report on Shoreline Changes in New Jersey Coastal Reaches One through Fifteen, Raritan Bay to Delaware Bay Spring of 2003 to Fall of 2004*, Richard Stockton College, Coastal Research Center Report (Pomona, N.J., 2005).

3. S. C. Farrell et al., *New Jersey Beach Profile Network Report Covering Fifteen Years of Study on Shoreline Changes in New Jersey Coastal Reaches One through Fifteen, Raritan Bay to Delaware Bay Spring of 2003 to Fall of 2004*, Richard Stockton College, Coastal Research Center Report (Pomona, N.J., 2003).

4. Alfred Wegener, *The Origin of Continents and Oceans*, trans. from the 4th rev. German ed. by John Biram (New York: Dover, 1966).

5. H. H. Hess, "History of Ocean Basins," Scripps Institution of Oceanography Library, paper 23, November 1, 1962, http://repositories.cdlib.org/sio/lib/23.

6. J. F. Grassle et al., "Galapagos 79: Initial Findings of a Deep-Sea Biological Quest," *Oceanus* 22, no. 2 (1979): 2–10.

7. L. W. Fritz and R. A. Lutz, "Environmental Perturbations Reflected in Internal Shell Growth Patterns of *Corbicula fluminea* (Bivalvia)," *Veliger* 28 (1986): 401–417; L. W. Fritz, L. M. Wargo, and R. A. Lutz, "Utilization of Bivalve Shells for Assessment of Environmental Stress," Rutgers University Department of Oyster Culture, technical report for the New Jersey Department of Environmental Protection, Division of Science and Research (Trenton, 1989).

8. National Estuary Program, U.S. Environmental Protection Agency, http://www.epa.gov/nep.

9. *Comprehensive Conservation and Management Plan, Approved May 2002*, Barnegat Bay National Estuary Program, Ocean County College, Toms River, N.J., http://www.bbep.org.

10. Michael J. Kennish et al., "Barnegat Bay–Little Egg Harbor Estuary: Case Study of a Highly Eutrophic Coastal Bay System," *Ecological Applications* 17 (2007): S3–S16.

11. M. J. Kennish, S. M. Haag, and G. P. Sakowicz, *Demographic Investigation of SAV in the Barnegat Bay–Little Egg Harbor Estuary with Assessment of Potential Impacts of Benthic Macroalgae and Brown Tides*, technical report 107-15 (2007) Institute of Marine and Coastal Sciences, Rutgers University, New Brunswick, N.J., http:www.bbep.org/dwnloads/SAV.pdf.

12. *Brown Tide Assessment*, New Jersey Department of Environmental Protection, http://www.state.nj.us/dep/dsr/browntide/bt.htm.

13. *National Estuary Program Coastal Condition Report*, U.S. Environmental Protection Agency, Office of Water, EPA-842/B-06/001 (Washington, D.C., 2006).

14. "DEP Barnegat Bay Action Plan Announcement," by Commissioner Lisa P. Jackson at Guardians of the Barnegat Bay Ceremony at the Barnegat Bay Festival, June 1, 2008, Wanamaker Complex, Island Heights, N.J., http://www.nj.gov/dep/watershedmgt/bbep_dep_strategy.htm.

15. R. K. Pachauri and A. Reisinger, eds., *Climate Change 2007: Synthesis Report*, contribution of Working Groups I, II, and III to the Fourth Assessment Report of the Intergovernmental Panel on Climate Change (Geneva: IPCC, 2008).

16. *Confronting Climate Change in the U.S. Northeast—New Jersey*, Union of Concerned Scientists, 2008, http://www.climatechoices.org/assets/documents/climatechoices/new-jersey_necia.pdf.

17. Kenneth G. Miller et al., "Sea Level Rise in New Jersey over the Past 5,000 Years: Implications to Anthropogenic Changes," *Global and Planetary Change* 66, nos. 1–2 (2009): 10–18.

18. M. Cooper et al., *Future Sea Level Rise and the New Jersey Coast: Assessing Potential Impacts and Opportunities*, Science, Technology and Environmental Policy Program, Woodrow Wilson School of Public and International Affairs, Princeton University, 2005, http://www.princeton.edu/step/people/faculty/michael-oppenheimer/recent-publications/Future-Sea-Level-Rise-and-the-New-Jersey-Coast-Assessing-Potential-Impacts-and-Opportunities.pdf.

19. Richard G. Lathrop Jr. and Aaron Love, *Vulnerability of New Jersey's Coastal Habitats to Sea Level Rise*, Center for Remote Sensing and Spatial Analysis (CRSSA), Rutgers University (New Brunswick, N.J., 2007).

20. J. G. Titus, "Sea Level Rise and Wetland Loss: An Overview," in *Greenhouse Effect, Sea Level Rise, and Coastal Wetlands*, ed. J.G. Titus, EPA 230-05-86-013, U.S. Environmental Protection Agency (Washington, D.C., 1988), http://papers.risingsea.net/federal_reports/sea-level-rise-and-wetlands-toc.pdf.

21. Alissa Stanley et al., *Holocene Sea-Level Rise in New Jersey: An Interim Report*, Rutgers University, Center for Environmental Indicators, submitted to the New Jersey Department of Environmental Protection (Trenton, 2004).

Index

About the Author

Thomas Belton is a research scientist in the Office of Science within the New Jersey Department of Environmental Protection. He has a bachelor of arts degree in classical languages from St. Peter's College in Jersey City, New Jersey; attended the University of Pennsylvania for graduate work in ecology and biology; and has a master of science degree in marine biology from the City University of New York. He currently designs and performs applied environmental research projects for investigating human impacts on air, water, and wildlife, as well as studies into preserving the ecology of state forests, wetlands, and waterways.